THE NEW NATURALIST

A SURVEY OF BRITISH NATURAL HISTORY

THE FOLKLORE OF BIRDS

The aim of this series is to interest the general reader in the wild life of Britain by recapturing the inquiring spirit of the old naturalist. The Editors believe that the natural pride of the British public in the native fauna and flora, to which must be added concern for their conservation, is best fostered by maintaining a high standard of accuracy combined with clarity of exposition in presenting the results of modern scientific research.

THE DEATH OF THE BIRD-MAN

Rock painting at Lascaux. Beside the bird-headed man, whose lance has pierced the charging bison, is set what appears to be a cult object—a model of a bird on a pole. This may be a representation of the external soul. *Courtesy French Vogue*

THE NEW NATURALIST

THE FOLKLORE OF BIRDS

An Enquiry into the Origin & Distribution
of some Magico-Religious Traditions

by
EDWARD A. ARMSTRONG

WITH 55 PHOTOGRAPHS
85 ILLUSTRATIONS IN THE TEXT

COLLINS
ST JAMES'S PLACE, LONDON
1958

To
William Homan Thorpe

Other Works
by the same Author
*

BIRDS OF THE GREY WIND
(*3rd. edition 1946*)

SHAKESPEARE'S IMAGINATION
(*Revised edition 1946*)

BIRD DISPLAY AND BEHAVIOUR
(*2nd. edition 1947*)

THE WAY BIRDS LIVE
(*4th. Impression 1947*)

BIRD LIFE
(*1949*)

THE WREN
(*1955*)

© *Edward A. Armstrong, 1958*
Printed in Great Britain by
Willmer Brothers & Haram Ltd., Birkenhead
For Collins Clear-Type Press, London and Glasgow

CONTENTS

LIST OF PLATES

EDITORS' PREFACE

E. A. ARMSTRONG will be already known to the readers of the New Naturalist Series as the writer of one of the most important monographs on a single species of animal, his famous study, *The Wren*, published in 1955.

Wide scholarship and talents have fitted him uniquely for the authorship of *The Wren's* most unusual sequel. We use the word 'unusual' deliberately because his *The Folklore of Birds* is a most extra-ordinary book. It could only have been written by a scholar with a deep understanding, not only of ornithology, but of social anthropology, psychology and religion.

Armstrong has selected an assemblage of well-known birds upon which to base what he describes in his sub-title as "An enquiry into the origin and distribution of some magico-religious traditions." He has set himself the task of revealing the general principles that underlie the evolution and diffusion of beliefs and symbols. With the scientist's eye and the scientist's methods of analysis and investigation he has examined the development of myth and ritual with originality and ingenuity. It is hard for us to make a choice from the multitude of those odd and interesting facts which Armstrong cites in this book, to bring to the reader's attention. Customs such as "breaking the wish-bone" are explained with new and brilliant reasoning. Every kind of naturalist—and archaeologists, folklorists and ornithologists are all naturalists—will follow with interest his compelling studies of the origins of such beliefs as those concerning weather-prophet birds, and of such fables as that of the generation of the barnacle goose from barnacles.

We do not know of any previous attempt of such importance to trace beliefs concerning birds as far back as possible in time, and to identify the cultures in which they must have originated. Armstrong has examined groups of folk-lore beliefs, it seems to us, in just the same way as an archaeologist examines a series of artifacts; and we know of no other scholar who has given folk-lore just this sort of treatment, classifying beliefs and notions in a system based upon the eopchs in which they originated.

Armstrong has, indeed, combined the facts derived from archaeology with oral and literary traditions, to illustrate the origins and significance of much of the current folk-lore of birds. Some of the magico-religious myths and cults, of which these fragmentary traditions are the relics, prevailed in the past throughout most of northern Europe and Asia and in some areas of North America. Such beliefs were carried about the world in the streams of culture, and their travels are often illuminated by graphic motifs and imagery, much of which is reproduced in the pages of this book, and some of which— from the old Stone Age to modern times—can be held to be artistic masterpieces.

Promoting, as it does, our understanding, both of man and nature, this is a book that we are proud to sponsor.

THE EDITORS

AUTHOR'S PREFACE

THE collectors of British folklore who were active in Victorian times and into the beginning of this century were just in time to record much of interest which has now disappeared. A few enthusiasts, notably the members of the Folklore Society and contributors to its journal, keep alive an interest in the subject, yet the study of folklore is currently regarded more as a recreation for the dilettante than as a respectable occupation. This may be due, in part, to the authors of many English books on the subject being content with presenting a pot-pourri of Victorian gleanings. Elsewhere, notably in Eire, Finland and Sweden, and at some universities in the United States, folklore research is conducted by highly trained scholars whose work has been an inspiration to their countrymen and a valuable contribution to man's understanding of his past. Inspired by the ambition "to gather up the fragments that remain that nothing be lost" they have rescued much material from oblivion and, in some realms, especially the study of the folk-tale, laid solid foundations for further work. The increasingly rapid spread of industrialism and the standardisation of modes of thought due to modern means of communication are now eliminating ancient beliefs and practices over most of the world and consequently the geographical distribution of folk tradition is becoming obscured. The attrition of ancient folklore in this country has been particularly severe and its last strongholds, such as the Hebrides, are now under assault. It is but small consolation to hope that radio and television, which are doing so much to standardise thought, may eventually arouse interest in folklore as they have done in archaeology.

An essay on British bird folklore cannot be a review of recent field work, partly because of the decay of such folklore but also owing to the absence of intelligent public interest in collecting it, though high appreciation must be accorded the effective labours of workers in Ireland and North Britain. The opportunity for gleaning folklore is rapidly passing but this makes it all the more important to try to assess the significance of our traditions in the hope of stimulating a more just appraisal of what folklore may teach us concerning the mental and spiritual interests of our forefathers. Those who know something of the rock whence they were hewn will order their present affairs with greater wisdom. I am more optimistic than some archaeologists in their attitude to the thought-life of folk who lived long ago. Professor Gordon Childe, for example, has expressed the opinion that "the content of religious belief" of pre-literate peoples is "irretrievably lost." We are justified in believing that folklore, in alliance with other sciences, especially archaeology, anthropology and comparative religion, can give us some insight into the spiritual culture of pre-historic peoples as well as shed light on the beliefs and practices of communities, and the psychology of individuals, up to and including, our own times.

The conviction underlying this survey is that it is possible to analyse a group of beliefs current in a modern, highly mechanised society, in such a way as to identify particular traditions, with a considerable degree of probability, as originating during certain epochs and belonging to specific culture-complexes. I would not claim that the evidence marshalled in support of this belief is as complete and cogent as might be desired but I hope that the feasibility of such an approach has been demonstrated and that others, more adequately equipped, may apply similar methods to other realms of folklore. I have no doubt—and I trust that I can carry the reader with me in this—that most ancient beliefs which have come down to us and seem now not much more than flotsam and jetsam on the tide of modern man's thought were once closely integrated into the spiritual life of earlier communities. As kindred studies of this type proceed it should be possible to date more accurately the cultures to which certain ideas belong and so to establish a stratigraphy of the non-material aspects of man's past.

If items of folklore, such as beliefs that certain birds foretell bad weather, were only the drifting scraps of information, true or false, that they have often been taken to be, they would merit no more than the anecdotal treatment they have usually received. But this is a superficial view. They are rather to be compared with the floating leaves and blossoms of water lilies springing from plants rooted far below. As the biologist is able to understand more clearly the nature of an organism if he can ascertain its evolutionary tree, so the folklorist must view items of folklore in their evolutionary setting. The biologist and palaeontologist can reciprocally illuminate each others' studies; similarly the folklorist and anthropologist on the one hand, and the historian (or prehistorian) and archaeologist on the other, may cross-check their inferences.

Beliefs and rituals, like organisms, have participated in a process of progressive differentiation and specialisation. Pursuing our analogy, we may think of a basic human concern, such as the desire for fertility in man, beast and crop, as the root from which has sprung, during the course of millennia, stems, branches and fronds, represented by the divergent beliefs and customs which have sprouted into the ideas and practices of today. Such a postulate enables us to bring unity into apparent chaos, for by tracing folklore into the past we find apparently unrelated beliefs to be connected and are able to enquire how, why, and when divergence occurred. So strong is the conservatism of ancient and primitive communities that occasionally we may light upon items of folklore which have survived for an immense period and serve a similar function for the folklorist to that of "living fossils," such as the maiden-hair tree and the coelacanth fish, for the biologist. Inferences about the past can thus be compared with survivals from it. By such procedures biologist and folklorist avoid mistaking similarities due to convergence for evidence of relationship.

It would have given a false impression, alike of the nature of bird folklore and of the forces which have moulded it, to select for discussion a group of birds simply on the basis of their lore being apparently particularly ancient. I have therefore chosen to deal with practically all the wild birds on the British list important in our folklore, omitting, or making only brief allusion to, species which have insufficient claim to be included in this category. The latter include domestic birds, apart from the goose whose folklore is essentially that of the wild goose, birds, such as the magpie, which have acquired traditions derived from related species, foreign and mythological birds, including those mentioned in the Bestiaries and consequently often represented in the ornamentation of churches. A distinction has been made between oral and literary lore, though exceptions have been admitted, as for example by including the nightingale, mainly because of its importance in literary tradition, and the Barnacle Goose which provides too effective an illustration of literary plagiarism to be excluded.

Unfortunately, in the space allotted to me it has not been possible to discuss either the rôle of birds in Christian folklore or in the traditions of sacred and secular art. However, consideration of these themes does not properly belong here, as we are concerned primarily with oral lore. Contrary to general opinion oral traditions connecting birds with Christ or the saints are not common in this country. Legends such as those telling of the compassion of the robin, swallow and crossbill for our Lord on the Cross appear to have reached us from the continent and are not the product of English piety. Although Celtic legends speak of the compassion of the saints for birds these tales belong to literature rather than folklore. Scribes rather than simple folk have given us the stories of St. Columba's kindness to the heron, the nesting of the blackbird in St. Kevin's hand and the wren in St. Malo's cloak, the restoration to life of St. Kentigern's robin and St. Werburga's goose, and the friendship of St. Hugh with the whooper swans.

It will be found that tracing the folklore of the birds of our islands takes us far afield in time and space. Aspects of our discussion have a bearing on bird folklore throughout the world. Indeed, our theme is the origin and transmission of magico-religious beliefs, choosing beliefs about birds for special scrutiny and illustration. However, the region with which we are particularly concerned is Eurasia, though there are some references to North America and occasional allusions to other regions. This is the less to be regretted as, if the arguments set out are sound, there was in the past considerable cultural homogeneity throughout most of this area.

The controversy between the diffusionists, who maintained the direct derivation of most forms of ceremonial from Egypt, or at least the ancient centres of culture in the Middle East comprised in the valley of the Nile and the Fertile Crescent, has lost much of its acerbity, partly because, in a more or less modified form, the diffusionist view has commended itself to most anthropologists, but also because the rapid advance of archaeological discovery and anthropological techniques has compelled caution. The reader must form his own opinions on the basis of the data presented here. In those fields which I have studied in detail I have found much evidence for culture borrowing (with modifications of the loans) and little or no proof of repeated independent invention. To think in terms of development rather than independent creation is rewarding. Advance in biology was stultified so long as scientists thought of the path of creation being strewn with arbitrary interventions, and to postulate repeated human inventions of notions or crafts, unless compelled to do so by facts rather than ignorance, may sometimes be more a manifestation of timidity than of discretion. But those whose sympathies are with the proponents of diffusion need to be on their guard against assuming that similarities are proof of common origin. When culture-complexes composed of a number of elements in association appear together in separated communities then we have strong reason to suspect the existence of an earlier cultural continuum or the transference of beliefs and customs through personal contacts. Evidence for diffusion is most convincing when it is cumulative and conclusions drawn from different sets of data confirm each other. Thus, to add weight to arguments supporting the temporal and geographical continuity of oral traditions I have chosen as illustrations symbols and designs which are known to have been transmitted down the centuries from culture to culture. The survival of visual motifs for thousands of years indicates that there is a strong presumption that beliefs may be equally long-lived.

No community which loses its sense of continuity with the past can be socially and spiritually healthy, nor can institutions be intelligently reformed without a knowledge of their history. Tradition has sometimes become the dead hand of the past on the present but this is not our danger today. Many are so far from overvaluing the past as to be unaware that they belong to any ancient tradition. Technological advance and the new ways of thinking which accompany it menace the good life unless new knowledge is integrated with the old. Perhaps this study, by calling attention to the significance of a neglected aspect of our heritage, may encourage, not merely an academic interest in ancient things still present with us, but the personal identification with tradition which gives a community strength and has so often been the inspiration of saints, patriots, poets and musicians, as well as a solace and delight, accepted almost as unconsciously as the air they breathe, by simple folk.

For many of us in these sophisticated times this identification with the past is not attained without love and toil but those born outside tradition may yet find a spiritual home within it. Through the gate of sympathetic understanding they may still enter the strange, enthralling realm where the hopes and fears, loves and loathings of their forefathers people the shades. We may still stand like Aeneas on the banks of Lethe and seek acquaintance with those who dwell on the other side.

quae sint ea flumina porro,
quive viri tanto complerint agmina ripas.

Some, to whom in childhood the past was almost like a playmate, feel a duty laid upon them to hint to others what can scarcely be expressed in words. So the boy, reared where holy well and fairy thorn, cromlech and cairn were continual reminders of the ever-present past, whose mother spoke of the banshee wailing out there in the tempestuous night and whose father had stories of the fairies dancing around the clumps of ragwort may try to repay in different and, it may be, inferior coin, his debt to tradition. Study has confirmed what emotion prompted—the stones around him had witnessed strange things and the bushes indeed burned with fire.

In venturing into regions so wide and enchanted I cannot have escaped making errors both of omission and commission. My apology is that of Camden: "In the studies of Antiquity there is a food for the mind well befitting such as are of honest and noble disposition. If any there be that are desirous to be strangers in their owne soile and forrainers in their owne citie, they may so continue and therein flatter themselves. For such like I have not written these lines, nor taken these pains. There may be mistakings in regard to my own unskilfulness, for who is so skilful that struggling with Time in the foggie dark sea of Antiquity may not run upon the rockes? It may be that I have been mislead by the credit of authors and others whom I took to be most true and worthy of credit." We are all fallible, but each in his generation may strive to prevent beauty and truth out of the past from perishing, not merely unhonoured but unrecognised.

E. A. A.

Cambridge, 1956.

CHAPTER I

THE PREHISTORIC BACKGROUND
TO BIRD FOLKLORE

EARLY man in search of food robbed nests, like his pre-human ancestors, trapped birds and slew them with clubs and missiles. We may assume that when human population was much sparser than it is now many species were less afraid of man and that hunters had no scruples about seizing, bludgeoning or snaring the parent bird on the nest. The bird-protection enactment of Deuteronomy (xxii, 6-7), forbidding the taking of both parent and offspring dates from a very much later time than that with which we are concerned here. Eggs must have been relished by early primitive people for they have a high food value and can be eaten on the spot with no more preparation than cracking the shell. Fragments of ostrich eggs have been found at ancient human settlements in China and North Africa. Nesting colonies of marine species were raided. Bones discovered in Oronsay must be the remains of birds caught when breeding, and the presence of parts of the skeleton of the great auk in these and other prehistoric refuse heaps, as at Whitepark Bay in County Antrim, suggests that this species nested further south in post-glacial times than during the period of documented history. Bones of the young were discovered at a Mesolithic settlement in Denmark and a Neolithic site in Norway. Remains of great auks slaughtered by Neanderthal man occur as far south as Apulia and Gibraltar.

Fowlers of the Old Stone Age obtained birds for the pot outside the breeding season, sometimes with throwing-sticks or by adroit stone-throwing. The invention of the bow provided a more effective weapon. The pelvis of a willow grouse perforated by an arrow, discharged apparently from below, testifies to an archer's good marksmanship. He was one of the Schleswig-Holstein hunters who apparently performed sacrificial rites in which reindeer were involved—an early indication of magico-religious ceremonial in connexion with the chase. Innumerable relics from rock-shelters and middens show that birds of many kinds were exploited, but although willow grouse may have been systematically hunted and snared in winter, human communities relied for food mainly on slaughtering other game and on fishing, except when a near-by breeding colony provided supplies during some weeks in summer. Probably such folk, like many primitive peoples today, were not fastidious about the freshness of their food and ate with relish birds which had been stored. More recent communities, as far apart as the Maori of New Zealand and the St. Kilda islanders had devices for preserving the carcasses of sea-birds.

Fowlers' trophies sometimes served other than gastronomic uses. Bird bones were used as tools, as tubes to hold artist's ochre, and possibly as whistles. On a needle case contrived from a bird's bone a reindeer is engraved and a herd of these animals was delineated by a Palaeolithic artist on a bone of an eagle. Capsian peoples made ostrich eggshell bottles and potters of the Peterborough culture used avian bones to impress patterns on their utensils. Possibly white of egg was mixed as a binding ingredient with pulverised pigments by artists of the Spanish Levant.

Until the end of last century, when designs in caves were acknowledged to be at least as old as the artifacts found with them, it was believed that Palaeolithic man's relationship to the animals around him was merely that of a predator in danger of being preyed upon. Since then the decorated walls of cavern after cavern and the carved and engraved objects found at inhabited sites have shown that the people of Aurignacian, Perigordian and Magdalenian times were by no means the brutish creatures which popular imagination, and even scholarly works, once pictured them to be. When the early discoveries were made archaeologists found it difficult to reconcile such competent art with the primitive way of life indicated by the material culture. Even now it is not easy for us to do so. Almost every year sees further discoveries revealing the artistic ability of people who were yet so ignorant that they did not know how to shape or bake a pot. Moreover, their work indicates much more than good craftsmanship. It reveals that Stone Age man cherished magico-religious conceptions.

On entering one of these caverns the visitor is apt to experience a bewildering sensation, for the twentieth century mind finds itself disorientated in a prehistoric sorcerer's studio adorned with up-to-date

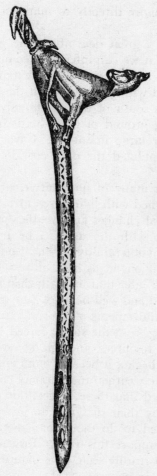

FIG. 1. Spearthrower carved in bone representing a young chamois with passerine birds perched on ludicrously exaggerated extruded faeces. Mas d'Azil. Cf. Garrod, D.A.E. 1955. *Proc. Prehist. Soc.* (After Maringer and Bandi, 1953).

decorations. A magazine illustrator might have designed the wild horses which trot around the walls of Lascaux. The file of deer swimming a river would make a lively tail-piece for a chapter in a modern monograph on the ungulates. In any exhibition of craftsmanship the propulsor from Mas d'Azil, carved to represent a chamois poised on a crag and looking back at the birds perched near its rump, would excite admiration (Fig. 1). So, too, would the blackcock (or related Tetraonid species) on another propulsor from the same site (Plate 1, p. 16).

Indeed, Palaeolithic art speaks more directly to many people today than ultra-modern art.

These representations tell us a great deal about the people who made them and there is much that we can infer with confidence concerning the significance of cave art. It is evident that men of this epoch were intensely preoccupied with animals. Well they might be, for the tundra and steppe lands south of the enormously expanded polar ice-cap were the stamping ground of great herds of reindeer, aurochs, bison, horses and other large mammals. Cave art is predominantly zoological. Man populated the dark corridors with the images of the beasts outside.

We may infer from this that many of humanity's early magico-religious conceptions were concerned with living creatures rather than with the heavenly bodies, seasonal changes and weather phenomena. Man's interests were bound up with the animals he hunted. He desired alike the abundance and vulnerability of "meat on the hoof." Wishful thinking and magico-religious ideas have always been closely related. Probably it was not until later that men attached importance to the influence on their livelihood and well-being of rain and thunder, the phases of the moon and the movements of the sun. In Mesolithic times, when the forest, advancing from the south, forced men to live on its fringes and exploit its food resources, and still later when primitive horticulture and agriculture began, it became more apparent that man's prosperity depended on the weather and seasonal changes.

As it is now generally accepted that these Palaeolithic representations of animals were believed by their designers to possess magico-religious efficacy there is no need to do more than mention a few relevant considerations which support this view. Instead of being placed where they could be most readily seen, cave paintings and engravings are often situated deep in caverns, as if executed there for some esoteric purpose. Although these grottoes and passages offered safe retreats at an equable temperature they were not used as dwellings. They were evidently reserved for the performance of ritual. A group depicting nesting snowy owls is engraved on a wall in the final passage of the Trois Frères cave (Plate 1, p. 16). The bird at El Pendo, which is still sometimes erroneously called a penguin, due to misunderstanding of the French *pingouin*, is now more plausibly identified as a great auk, though it may be a Brünnich's guillemot (Fig. 2, p. 5). It is hidden away at the end of a winding fissure. The "birdman"

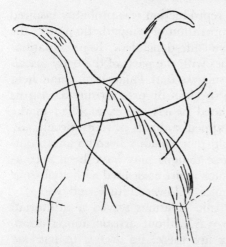

FIG. 2. Engraving on rock of auk-like bird, possibly Brünnich's guillemot or great auk, with another unidentified species. El Pendo. (After Alcalde del Rio *et al.*, 1911).

scene at Lascaux is painted on a stone boss near the bottom of a vertical shaft (Frontispiece). The rock at the top edge of this cleft, polished by the bodies of those lowering themselves into it, indicates that in Palaeolithic times access presented some difficulty. At Font de Gaume the frescoed procession of mammoths and other animals is encountered after squeezing through the narrowest section of the passage. So men throughout the ages have tried to conceal the sacrosanct from the prying eyes of the vulgar and have striven to shelter objects potent with magical *mana* from the gaze of those unable to appreciate their significance or unlikely to comport themselves correctly in relation to them.

In this art there are two motifs which provide clues to the understanding of the impulses which inspired it. Many of the animals are depicted as gravid, and a number, such as the famous bisons in clay at Tuc d'Audoubert, the bull and cow of *Bos primigenius* on a wall at Teyjat, the stallion following a mare at Font de Gaume, the pair of reindeer engraved on schist at Laugerie Basse and another similar group at Font de Gaume, show the male in rut or about to mount the female. A pair of elk engraved at Kløtefoss in Norway appear to be copulating. A megalithic stone sculpture in Sumatra represents two tigers *in coitu* and an engraving at Kisese in East Africa depicts a female rhinoceros chasing the male. Such is the normal method of courtship in this species. Rock paintings in southern Andalusia show a male bird apparently treading the female.

Prehistoric man's emphasis on reproduction was probably inspired by a longing to stimulate, by the operation of sympathetic magic, the increase of animals on which human life depended. Representations of human coitus and female figurines with the parts of the body associated with maternity emphasized suggest that Palaeolithic man held similar ideas in regard to his own species. By exteriorising a wish its fulfilment could be attained. Related beliefs are exemplified in the pictures showing wounded or trapped animals (Frontispiece). By picturing what was desired it would more readily become an accomplished fact. The execution of these designs may have been accompanied by incantations and rituals such as are associated with analogous artistic representations among peoples of lower cultures today.

To stress that early man's artistic creations served a utilitarian purpose is not to suggest that he was without artistic appreciation. Animals carved on spear-throwers are there, no doubt, to increase their effectiveness. Would not the carved beast seek its affinity and a decorated weapon acquire some of the speed and strength of the creature portrayed? The hunter could not have chosen more agile creatures to speed his weapon's flight than the chamois and birds depicted on the spear-thrower depicted in Fig. 1, p. 3, but the artistry seems to go beyond utilitarian needs. A duplicate of this design has been found. Perhaps its artistic merit inspired the making of copies. The animal may be shown defecating because this act in some animals precedes flight.

Primitive folk do not feel the superiority to animals which is characteristic of the modern civilised adult—but not of his untutored children. The conviction expressed in Genesis that man was granted dominion over the beasts of the earth is sophisticated, springing from a milieu in which domesticated animals were commonplace. Communities which live by hunting usually have respect for large quadrupeds, in some ways more efficiently adapted than man for their mode of life. Hunters, therefore, endeavour to assimilate themselves to the nature of the animals they pursue—mimicking their movements, eating their flesh, drinking their blood, wearing their skins, antlers, feathers or claws, and naming individuals after them. Characteristic of this outlook is the saying of the Micmac Indians: "In the beginning of things men were as animals and animals as men." Thus the Ainu and the Gilyak treat the bears they slay with great reverence. Probably Palaeolithic man's attitude to animals was based on the assumption

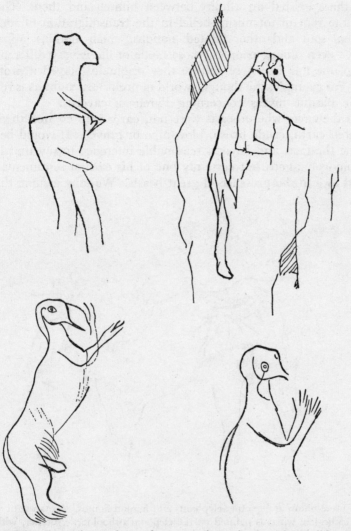

FIG. 3 (*top left*). Engraving on bone of man wearing animal mask, possibly engaged in magical fertility ceremony. Pin Hole Cavern, Derbyshire. (After the original in the British Museum. E.A.A.).

FIG. 4 (*top right*). Engraving on rock of man with animal mask. Los Casares, Guadalajara. (After Graziosi, 1956).

FIG. 5 (*bottom left*). Drawing on rock of zoomorphic human figure with bird-like head and bear's legs. Altamira. (After Cartailhac and Breuil, 1906).

FIG. 6 (*bottom right*). One of several graffiti on wall of cavern representing a human figure with bird-like head. Altamira. (After Cartailhac and Breuil, 1906).

that there existed an affinity between himself and them. This idea is at the root of totemism, belief in the transmigration of souls, the external soul and other related notions. Such notions apparently survive even among peoples whose mode of life is very different from that of the folk in whose culture they originally played a prominent role. For example, the thought-world of prehistoric hunters is reflected in the Basque myths concerning Pyrenean caverns.

In the caves where beasts were not, early man created them with coloured earth, crude brush, blow-pipe or graver. It would be going outside the facts and beyond reasonable inference to say that he had theriomorphic gods but certainly one of his earliest sentiments was a fearful awe in the presence of great beasts. We may assume that this

FIG. 7. Cave painting depicting elephants and human figures. A man with a snout and penguin-like wings is painted on the elephant's shoulder. Another, with head and bill, resembling those of a duck is shown head downwards on the right. The bodies of the human figures are pierced by lances or darts. On the rock face are marks daubed with fingers and over the elephant's body an enigmatic mark has been made, perhaps indicating a wound intended by the operation of sympathetic magic to render the animal more vulnerable. The horns of an ibex are painted over another elephant's head. A third elephant is indicated below the feet of the central elephant. Cougnac. (E.A.A., after Méroc and Mazet, 1953).

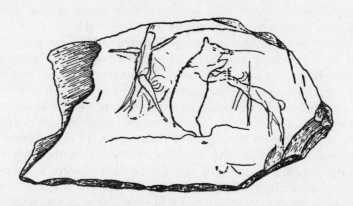

FIG. 8. Incised drawing on schist apparently representing a man coming to the rescue of another who is being overthrown by a bear. Péchialet. (After Breuil, 1927. *Rev. anthrop.*)

was one of the roots from which magic and religion sprang.[1] Along with the animals this primitive response has been domesticated but it is in the shadowy background when the firelight glows on the faces of pyjama-clad children as they listen to tales of Peter Rabbit, Badger and his crew, or the older and less sophisticated stories of Aesop and Grimm. As we shall see, there are some of our birds which have not been entirely dispossessed of the strange powers they wielded many centuries ago.

Associated with the magico-religious character of Palaeolithic cave art was its ceremonial importance. Probably some of the designs related to the performance of initiation ceremonies. Nearly all peoples mark the attainment of puberty with special rites. During the proceedings those being initiated are secluded from most of the other members of the community, especially those of the other sex. Among Ice Age peoples the caves would serve this purpose admirably and

[1]As we are concerned here with the inferences which may be drawn from the art and artifacts of prehistoric times no account is taken of the anthropological evidence brought forward by Wilhelm Schmidt and his school concerning belief in "high gods" among primitive people. It should also be noted that "primitive" is used here without introducing any value connotation, and the term "magico-religious" is employed because it is improbable that early man differentiated clearly between magical and religious ideas.

their mural decorations would be appropriate to the special concerns
of initiation rites—reproduction and the chase. In the cave of Tuc
d'Audoubert one may still see the heel marks of the boys who danced
around the animals. Footprints lead to other parts of the cave where
there are phallic symbols. The famous "sorcerer" of the Trois Frères
cavern wears a deer's hide and antlers, and the painting is so placed
that a man adorned thus could step out in front of it from a place of
concealment and suddenly appear before a group of neophytes.
Chagga boys living on the slopes of Kilimanjaro in recent times were
taught, during initiation, the meaning of designs on the rock at the
traditional meeting place. In the Californian deserts I have seen
petroglyphs made by Red Indian initiands. The initiation ceremonial
of Australian aborigines includes the interpretation of drawings to the
boys. At the initiation of girls in Rhodesia the meaning of highly
conventionalized designs painted expressly for the ceremony is dis-
closed. The "guinea fowl" is a sexual symbol and the "owl" stands for
the transition from ignorance to wisdom. A rock painting by bushmen
in Basutoland depicts Basotho initiates with owl masks and wings
(Plate 3, p. 32). Initiated Basotho boys still try to frighten younger
boys by running around masked as owls, uttering shrieks. Among

FIG. 9. Coffin of Tungus shaman with wooden figures of birds on posts at each side.
After Harva, 1938).

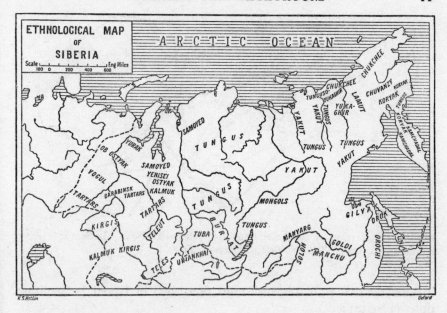

FIG. 10. Ethnological map of Siberia showing the location of tribes mentioned in the text. (After Czaplicka, 1914).

many peoples those who officiate at initiation ceremonies wear masks, sometimes of animals, as many human figures in the caves are depicted as doing. In some prehistoric designs faces are drawn so crudely that it is not easy to decide whether they are beaked or snouted, but the bird-headed man at Lascaux, beside a post on which a bird with head similarly outlined perches, proves that at least some of the other human figures are indeed bird-headed and presumably wearing bird masks (Frontispiece, Plate 4, p. 33, Figs. 3, 4, 5, 6 and 7, pp. 7, 8).

Although a considerable number of representations of birds appear in Palaeolithic art they are rare compared with the designs showing large mammals. There are also some fish and reptiles, including snakes, as well as a few insects. Until Lascaux was discovered in 1940 it seemed that birds occupied a very minor role in the beliefs and ritual of the Old Stone Age. The strange scene, called by some "The Prehistoric Tragedy" but which might more appropriately be named "The Death of the Bird-man" raises more problems than it solves but

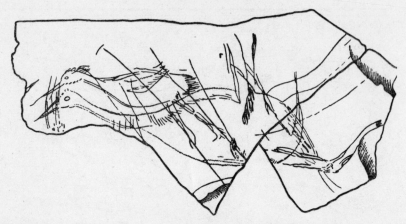

FIG. 11. Engraving on stone depicting two heron-like birds. Labastide. (After Simmont, G., 1947. *Bull. Soc. Préhist. Française*, 44).

it indicates that probably bird cults flourished in Upper Palaeolithic times (Frontispiece).

The visitor, descending into an eerie fissure finds a vivid painting on a rock cornice. A man is falling, or has fallen, on his back between a bison confronting him and a rhinoceros, (probably Merck's and not the woolly species) which is lumbering away. At his feet lies his spear-thrower, and the weapon which he has discharged has apparently pierced the bison's body obliquely. Through a gaping wound in the beast's belly a great gory mass of entrails protrudes. The animals are represented naturalistically but the man is shown in an odd schematic convention. He has but four digits on one hand and his bird head is crudely but vigorously delineated.

Perhaps the scene may be interpreted as commemorating an incident in which a hunter, endeavouring to give the *coup de grâce* to a bison wounded by a rhinoceros, was attacked and killed by the bison. It is not certain that the rhinoceros, which is slightly around the cornice from the man and bison, belongs to the same scene. The terrible gash in the bison's belly is such as could have been caused by the horn of the rhinoceros rather than the man's lance. The most closely comparable design in Palaeolithic art depicts a man being overthrown by a bear while another comes running as if to rescue his comrade (Fig, 8, p. 9).

In the Lascaux scene the bird on the post is of special interest. It

FIG. 12. Engraving on bone of ptarmigan. Isturitz. (After Passemard, 1922).

is difficult to believe that if the artist had wished to portray a living bird perched on a tree he could not have painted the tree more realistically. Probably, therefore, the representation is of a cult object. The bird may be carved in wood and affixed to the pole. The similarity between its head and that of the man suggests that the artist intended to indicate an affinity between the man and the bird.

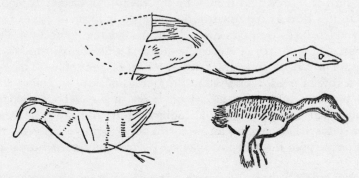

FIG. 13. Engravings of birds. *Upper:* Swan on stone (Gourdan): *Lower left:* Unidentified species on stone (Lourdes): *Lower right:* Goose or duck on antler (Gourdan). (After Alcalde del Rio *et al.*, 1911).

FIG. 14. Rock engravings at Lake Onega, North Russia. Among the subjects represented are swans, elk or reindeer, a boat, a snake and two figures—apparently men in animal masks engaged in magic. (After Raudonikas, 1936-38).

Some totemic notion may have been involved but a more likely hypothesis is that here we have a representation of the external soul— which in later cultures was so often visualised as a bird. If any particular bird is represented it may be the raven, for Basque legends still refer to this bird as the spirit of the prehistoric hunters' caves.[1]

Wooden birds on poles are placed around the coffin of a Tungus shaman (Fig. 9, p. 10) or erected beside a sacrificial platform (Plate 16, p. 95). The Voguls sometimes depict a bird on the coffin. The Yakuts erect a row of trees, representing the storeys of heaven, before a sacrificial platform and place model birds on them. Wooden effigies of mythological birds, including a double-headed bird and a raven, are set on posts where a shaman performs the "flight to heaven" ritual. For this purpose the Dolgans may set up nine bird-surmounted poles.

[1] A bird perched at the summit of a tree, pole or pillar is common in ancient Egyptian and Mesopotamian art and also occurs in Crete. The symbol sometimes had solar significance or associations with thunder but might also be connected with funeral rites as in the scene on the Hagia Triada sarcophagus (Plate 21, p. 116).

FIG. 15. Rock paintings of birds in flight. S. Andalusia. (After Breuil and Burkitt, 1929).

Apparently the birds are believed to accompany him. Holmberg, commenting on the double-headed bird on the "world-pillar" among these people and worn as an emblem by Ostyak shamans, remarks, "This bird has flown here from the mythology of the ancient peoples." It appeared on Hittite seals, and probably the Scythians were responsible for its reaching India. The diffusion of the "bird on pole" symbol from the Middle East would not be incompatible with its being a Stone Age symbol adopted and reinterpreted by these civilisations.

FIG. 16. Rock paintings of birds including a great bustard displaying, swans in line and birds disputing a stick or other long object with one another. S. Andalusia. (After Breuil and Burkitt, 1929).

FIG. 17. Engraving on reindeer antler of bird resembling lesser bustard. Laugerie Basse. (After Breuil, 1936).

FIG. 18. Engraving on obverse of the reindeer antler shown in Fig. 17. The bird would seem to be a less successful representation of the same species. It has been suggested that it is depicted as if incubating. Laugerie Basse. (After Breuil, 1936).

The Great Mother of these cultures is derived ultimately from the Old Stone Age. The bird on pole is used by the Eskimo and some North American Indians to mark a grave. Arguing from this custom the Abbé Breuil has ventured the suggestion that the bison's victim may lie buried in the unexcavated recesses of the Lascaux cavern. Since Palaeolithic art reached North Russia and artifacts resembling Danish Maglemosian finds have been found in Alaska it would not be surprising to find some Palaeolithic cult practices lingering in the Palaearctic and Nearctic regions.

More recently another remarkable Old Stone Age picture has been discovered in a cave at Addaura near Palermo (Plate 4, p. 33). A group of people, delineated with striking naturalism, including apparently bird-masked officiants, surrounds two men whose necks are attached to their feet apparently by hide thongs. The scene probably represents men being strangled in a sacrificial rite involving

Plate 1. a. Blackcock (or closely related species) carved on Palaeolithic spearthrower. Parts of the bird's head and feet have been restored. Mas d' Azil. Cf. pp. 3, 18. (*Maringer and Bandi*)

b. Pair of nesting snowy owls, with owlet. Engraving on rock face, Trois Frères. Cf. pp. 4, 17. (*Centre d'études et de documentation préhistoriques*)

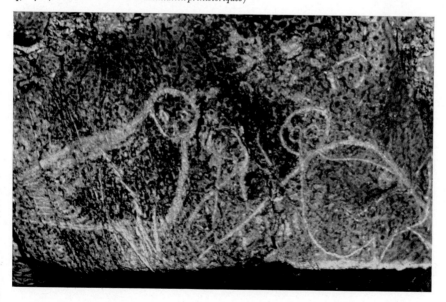

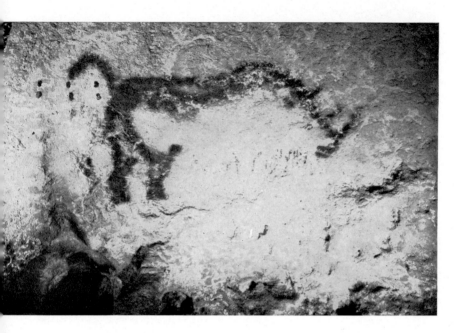

Plate 2. a. Rock painting of a rhinoceros at Lascaux. The animal is depicted immediately to the left of the scene shown in the Frontispiece. Cf. p. 12. (*Courtesy French Vogue*)

b. Rock painting of enigmatic horned beast in the main cavern at Lascaux. It is represented as gravid, suggesting its significance in fertility magic. Cf. p. 5. (*Courtesy French Vogue*)

FIG. 19. Engraving on stone of a young bird and a bison's head. The chick might be a young bustard. Puy-de-Lacan. (After Ridder, L.&H., 1936. *L'anthrop.* 46).

an association between death and reproduction (p. 104). The full argument for this view need not be stated here.

At Cougnac, in another recently discovered cave, there is a painted scene depicting three elephants. Over the shoulder of one of these a snouted human figure equipped with penguin-like wings and pierced by darts or lances is traced. Another figure with a duck-like head and bill, also pierced by darts, is falling headlong near the elephant's rump (Fig. 7, p. 8).

Apart from these scenes the most outstanding bird picture on a cavern wall is the group of nesting snowy owls at Trois Frères (Plate 1, p. 16). The parents perch on either side of the half-grown owlet. Although the engraving is in crude but vigorous outline it gives a vivid impression of the nest on the tundra. We know, through the evidence of bones scraped by Palaeolithic men, that snowy owls were eaten. Small models of a snowy owl and what is considered to be an eagle have been discovered at Vestonice in Moravia.

A fragment of reindeer antler found at Andernach is shaped like a bird's head and a peculiar relief of a bird with a powerful beak was dug up at Raymonden in the Dordogne. A bird-headed spear-thrower from Trois Frères bears the outline in relief of another bird.

FOB—C

At Gargas, on the roof of a cave is the likeness of an egret or heron, probably Aurignacian. An engraving showing two heron-like birds was found at Labastide (Fig. 11). At Altamira there is a queer design which has been conjectured to represent some kind of composite bird-fish. Perhaps the nondescript, composite creatures sometimes depicted by primitive folk witness to the absence of clear distinctions in thought between man and beast which has already been mentioned.

In addition to the blackcock or other grouse-like bird carved on a spear-thrower (Plate 1, p. 16) there is an engraving of a ptarmigan on a reindeer antler found at Isturitz in the Pyrenees (Fig. 12, p. 13). Three swans are beautifully etched on an antler from Teyjat and there is another on a stone from Gourdan in Cantabria. On a stone from Lourdes there is a big-beaked bird (Fig. 13, p. 13). Another bird, identified as a goose, is depicted on a rock face at Labastide. At Lake Onega in North Russia swans are carved on rocks and a rock engraving at Hammer in Norway illustrates a brood of goslings or cygnets with their parents. Files of birds are depicted in the later rock paintings of Andalusia. In some of these, which breathe a different spirit from the cave art which we have been considering, we find illustrations of birds in flight, fighting or displaying (Figs. 14, pp. 14, 15 and 16 p. 15).

A well-carved bird on a fragment of reindeer antler found at Laugerie Basse belonging to the period dated Magdalenian IV resembles the little bustard but climatic conditions there at this period would scarcely have been suitable for this species (Fig. 17, p. 16). However, an engraving of what appears to be a panther from the same rock shelter is a reminder that we have much to learn concerning the distribution of animals and their adaptation to conditions in the Ice Age. Another engraving on the reverse side of this antler fragment depicts a somewhat similar bird (Fig. 18, p. 16). The chick of a large nidifugous species is represented on a stone from Puy de Lacan (Fig. 19, p. 17).

Objects carved in mammoth ivory found at Mézine in the Ukraine were at first identified as birds but later found to be conventionalised figures of women! Many female figurines, mostly naturalistic, have been found. In front of a small, obese, stone female effigy the Neolithic miners at Grimes Graves in Norfolk laid an offering of antler picks and set a stone phallus beneath. Perhaps they hoped that fertility magic might bring them better fortune in their labours for this "shrine"

FIG. 20. Hellenistic relief showing a sleeping man being assailed by a winged and taloned Siren—apparently representing the nightmare. (After Saglio, E. Dict. des Antiquités, 4).

was at the end of a worked-out seam of flint. This figurine and engravings of deer on bone also found in these workings indicate the continuity of Palaeolithic traditions into later times.

Old Stone Age representations of figures which are partly bird and partly human can be classified into two categories. Firstly, figures which are definitely human but apparently wearing bird masks, such as at Addaura (Plate 4, p. 33); secondly, figures of a composite character exemplified by the drawings from Altamira (Figs. 5 and 6, p. 7). It is sometimes difficult to decide whether or not these are masked human beings. Perhaps in some of these the artist has merely taken the line of least resistance and avoided the difficulty of delineating the face. However, as cave art shows us men masked as a mammoth, a reindeer, chamois and other animals it is not surprising to find bird-masked figures also, as at Lascaux, Addaura and elsewhere.

Some sub-conscious impulse may be responsible for the tendency in many cultures from the Palaeolithic to the present day to represent human figures with avian characteristics, especially with beaks, wings or claws. Female beings of this type, or with birds perched on head or hands, are particularly common—goddesses, sirens, harpies, angels, and so forth. Man's ambivalent attitude to woman seems to find expression in this imagery embodying contrasting attributes—soft feathers and sharp beak and claws, songs and shrieks, amorousness and cruelty, devotion and fickleness. There is a strange procession down

FIG. 21. Carving on Moone Abbey Cross, Ireland. This has been interpreted as the Temptation of Saint Anthony but is a form of a motif depicted on the Sutton Hoo purse, and found in Merovingian and Western Asian art. (After Allen, 1887; Cf. also Henry, 1940).

FIG. 22. Design on the Cross of Papil, Isle of Burra, Shetland, apparently representing a development of the motif in Fig. 21. (After Allen, 1887).

FIG. 23. Figure of a Dekan from a 15th. century MS at Cracow. A Dekan was conceived to be the sinless soul of the just transferred into an immaterial spirit of the spheres. (After Ameisenowa, 1949).

the centuries of these personifications from the ambiguous figures of the Palaeolithic to the nude, clawed goddess of Sumeria (Plate 5, p. 48), the bird-footed Nightmare of Greek art (Fig. 20, p. 19) and culminating in the Madonna with a Bird of mediaeval Christendom (Plate 31, p. 192). On the Cross of Moone in Ireland St. Anthony is shown being tempted by two snouted women—according to the usual explanation—but this is a rationalisation of a misunderstood motif which can be traced into the past through Anglo Saxon art, as in the ornament found in the Sutton Hoo ship burial (Fig. 21, p. 20; Plate 7, p. 64) to Byzantine decoration and designs in Babylonian art. On the

FIG. 24. Christian Evangelist, presumably St. John, from 13th. century Prayer Book, St. Gall. The device of representing the Evangelists zoomorphically originated in Coptic art and was adopted in Visigothic Spain, France and Ireland. Examples appear in the illuminations of the Book of Kells. (After Ameisenowa, 1949).

Papil stone from Shetland the flanking figures are beaked and pecking at a human skull—as if the artist had been confused as to what he was representing (Fig. 22, p. 20).   Male bird-like or bird-headed figures also follow one another through successive civilisations—Assyrian bird-masked beings of the ninth century B.C. (Plate 6, p. 49), silver images of gods from Ras Shamra with huge beak-like noses, men with bird heads such as the Dekans of Jewish iconography and Christian saints (Figs. 23 and 24, p. 21), down to the modern Chinese thunder god, equipped with wings, beak and claws.

The motives, conscious and subliminal, which underlie these symbols would repay investigation.   Certain characteristics of birds have always impressed men—their swift motion, sudden apparition and disappearance, and the suggestion of communion with higher powers implicit in their powers of flight.   Impressions thus gained have led to ideas concerning the visits of winged gods or their aerial ambassadors and, on the other hand, to concepts of the soul as a bird. Men seem to have experienced a vague and disturbing sense of affinity between themselves and these other bipeds, some of which could look

FIG. 25. Rock painting representing hunting magic. The human figures are adorned with feather head-dresses. Frieze of Alpera, Cueva de la Vieja, Albacete. (After Obermaier, 1916).

FIG. 26. Rock engraving of Neolithic hunting scene. The archer, aiming at an ostrich is apparently receiving magical power from his wife. She holds up her arms in a gesture resembling that of the men in the Addaura engraving (Plate 4). Tiout, Atlas. (After Frobenius and Obermaier, 1925).

him straight in the face with binocular vision and make quasi-human sounds (p. 113).

Birds and human figures alike become more frequent in the later Stone Age art of Spain. Some of the men wear feathers in their hair as a head-dress (Fig. 25, p. 22)—a custom still maintained with variations in style, by Siberian shamans, North American Indians, men of the Tyrol and women of fashion. Prehistoric people fletched their arrows, probably sometimes using eagle feathers. At a site in the province of Cadiz 178 birds are depicted on the rocks, most of them species still to be found in the neighbourhood. The naturalism of these paintings is impressive (Figs. 15 and 16).

There is an immense contrast between the art of the Upper Palaeolithic and this later Spanish art. When we think of the former we picture naked hunters drawing their magical designs in the bowels of the earth; the latter we see out in the open, conducting ceremonies in scanty garments adapted for decoration rather than warmth, robbing bees, hunting and fighting in a landscape where birds were numerous, the marshes resounding with their cries and the sky traversed by a multitude of wings. Perhaps their dances, like those of many modern peoples, imitated the birds. The scene is sunlit and we feel that the beliefs of these folk must have been very different from those of the northern hunters. In later North African rock pictures we see a further flowering of the ideas which underlie this Iberian art. An archer aiming at an ostrich is aided by magical power from a woman, perhaps his wife, streaming to him and to his arrow (Fig. 26, p. 23), and in contrast to the Aurignacian, Magdalenian and Perigordian pictures of wounded beasts we have a rock engraving in which an elephant is shown protecting her calf from a lion.

Clearly early man was interested in birds, held magico-religious ideas about them and probably assimilated himself to them to some extent in cult practices. The scenes depicted suggest that he found a connexion between birds and death—an association continued in historical times and which still persists strongly in folklore. There are also hints of an association between birds and reproduction, as in the phallic bird-man of Lascaux and the sacrificial scene at Addaura, perhaps also apparent in the engraving of the owls with their young. On the other hand there are no indications in Upper Palaeolithic art of birds being connected with the heavenly bodies as they so often are in the early art of the Fertile Crescent. It may be presumed, too, that birds were not regarded as weather-changers or prophets, at least to the extent to which they occupied these roles in later times. Concern about the weather and techniques designed to change it probably became prominent when man learned to cultivate plants. In short, to man in the Old Stone Age birds were not merely acceptable as food but symbolised mysterious powers which pervaded the wilderness in which he hungered, hunted and wove strange dreams.

CHAPTER 2

THE MICHAELMAS GOOSE

IN the previous chapter we have briefly reviewed some of the earliest evidence of man's interest in birds and noted the possibility that some ideas about them dating from the remote past may survive in more or less modified form into the present. In this and subsequent chapters we shall, in the main, follow the reverse course and starting from modern customs and beliefs trace them as far as possible into the past. We should find, if the views already suggested are sound, that some of these beliefs originated in prehistoric times.

In spite of the gastronomic havoc wrought during this century by food standardisation there are still some localities in England where the traditional custom of dining on roast goose at Michaelmas or Martinmas continues. At first glance it might seem absurd to suppose any further explanation necessary than the obvious fact that geese are in season then:

> So stubble geese at Michaelmas are seen
> Upon the spit; next May produces green;

as King's cookery book of 1709 reminded the careful housewife.[1]

Indeed, when the Gregorian calendar was introduced on 2 September, 1752, one of the objections raised was that geese would not be in their greatest perfection when Michaelmas was celebrated eleven days earlier, according to the new reckoning. As recently as 1 January, 1954, Compton Mackenzie, writing in *The Spectator*, "regretted that the traditional fat goose at Michaelmas is hardly ever attainable because it is difficult to fatten a goose satisfactorily by September 29th."

The sceptic who doubts that feasting on goose could have had a ritual origin has a variety of other explanations from which to choose.

---

[1]"Green geese" were birds fed on spring pastures. Cf. *Love's Labour's Lost*, IV, iii.75.

It was said that Queen Elizabeth I heard the news of the defeat of the Armada while dining on goose on Michaelmas Day and therefore commemorated the victory annually in the same way, her people following suit. This story, which is still sometimes quoted as the correct explanation, is easily discredited. The battle with the Spanish fleet was fought at the end of July, 1588. Moreover, Englishmen were celebrating the feast of St. Michael and All Angels by dining on goose long before Philip of Spain tried to invade these shores. In the tenth year of the reign of Edward IV, "John de la Hay was bound to render to William Barneby, Lord of Lastres, in the county of Hereford, for a parcel of the demesne lands, one goose fit for the Lord's dinner on the feast of St. Michael the Archangel." In 1575 George Gascoigne wrote:

> *And when the tenauntes come to paie their quarter's rent,*
> *They bring some fowl at Midsummer, a dish of fish in Lent,*
> *At Christmasse a capon, at Michaelmas a goose;*
> *And somewhat else at New Yere's tide, for feare their lease flies loose.*

Two other explanations of the custom appear in verses published in 1709 in the *British Apollo:*

> Q. *Yet my wife would persuade me, (as I am a sinner,)*
> *To have a fat goose on St. Michael for dinner;*
> *And then all the year round, I pray you would mind it,*
> *I shall not want money—oh! grant that I find it.*
> *Now several there are that believe this is true,*
> *Yet the reason of this is desired from you.*
> A. *We think you're so far from having of more,*
> *That the price of the goose you have less than before;*
> *The custom came up from the tenants presenting*
> *Their landlords with geese, to incline their relenting*
> *On following payments.*

Thus one of these explanations amounts to little more than the common explanation of customs whose origin has been forgotten— that they bring luck. There was a saying, "If you eat goose on Michaelmas Day you will never want money all the year round." The other explanation, taking account of the payment of rents at Michaelmas, attributes the origin of the custom to the desire to keep landlords in good humour. Another story—an Irish version recorded by Lady Wilde which may have had only limited currency—explains that geese are killed at Michaelmas because the son of a king was enjoying a feast when he began choking on a goose bone. Fortunately St. Patrick came on the scene in the nick of time and saved the prince's life.[1]

So the king ordered geese to be sacrificed every year on the anniversary of the event to commemorate it and in honour of St. Michael. This tale is of unusual interest in view of the prejudice in some Celtic areas against eating goose. It may be a rationalisation in which the intervention of the patron saint of Ireland is invoked to explain and condone the abandonment of an ancient food tabu. The incident of the prince nearly dying through being choked by a goose bone recalls the revulsion and nausea felt by primitive people when threatened with having to eat tabued food.

The most sophisticated explanation is that quoted in Blount's *Popular Antiquities*, published in 1679. It was said that the "common people" interpreted the ending of the Latin collect for Trinity XVI— *ac bonis operibus jugiter praestet esse intentos*—as a reference to a goose with ten toes! Brand dismissed the problem by remarking, "Probably no other reason can be given for this custom but that Michaelmas Day was a great feast, and geese at that time most plentiful." In place of the romantic and fantastic the antiquarian gives us a douche of the prosaic.

The number of these explanations weakens the plausibility of any of them but we can learn from their variety one of the characteristics of what we may call, for want of a better term, the folk mind. Its uneasiness when unable to account satisfactorily for a custom whose origin has been forgotten impels it to manufacture rationalisations— just as a man who performs some action suggested to him under hypnosis concocts an explanation. Moreover, when the stories of a custom's origin are various and mutually exclusive or absurd there is usually reason to believe the custom to be of considerable antiquity. To attribute the Michaelmas goose feast to a great national heroine is a typical folk rationalisation, illustrating how legends accumulate around eminent personages. But this story, for all its falsity, has an element of truth not contained in the down-to-earth views of the

[1]St. Blaise, who had cured a boy with a fish bone stuck in his throat, was the saint usually invoked in such predicaments. The goose bone story may have been inspired by the ancient tale of King Cormac choking on a salmon bone.

antiquarian. It assumes rightly, as we shall see, that the celebration
was connected with important events in the past.

Even if there were no other evidence than the holding of the goose
feast at festival seasons we would have good reason to suspect that it had
ritualistic antecedents. In England, as the quotations show, the goose
feast was usually held at Michaelmas but in a few localities the roasted
bird was served at Martinmas, 11 November. Thus in Farndale,
Yorkshire, according to a writer in the *Yorkshire Evening Post* of 14 November, 1934, it was, and presumably still is, the custom to eat goose on
Martinmas Sunday. This dale, he says, "has been noted for ages for
its goose pies." The date links the practice with observances on the
continent, for it is mainly at Martinmas that goose is eaten there. In
Norway the day is honoured with roast goose and the gourmandising
is justified by relating how the modest St. Martin, being unwilling to
accept a bishopric, concealed himself, only to have his hiding-place
betrayed by a goose.[1]

In Denmark a roasted goose is eaten on St. Martin's Eve and in
Germany geese are included in the celebrations of Saint Martin's
Day. In Paris geese were eaten then as well as on Twelfth Day.[2]

Early documents attest the eating of goose at Martinmas on the
continent. In 1171 Othelricus of Svalenburg presented a silver goose
to the monastery of Corvei on the feast of St. Martin. "Unblessed is
that house which has not a goose to eat that night" wrote Sebastian
Franck (1500-1545) in his *Weltbuch*. Dr. Hartlieb, physician to Duke
Albrecht of Bavaria, writing in 1455, mentions that goose was eaten on
St. Martin's Day or Night. This authority gives what is apparently the
first reference to divination by the wish-bone. As this is one of the
few ritual acts concerned with birds still commonly maintained amongst
us it deserves comment. Hartlieb remarks: "When the goose has been
eaten on St. Martin's Day or Night, the oldest and most sagacious
keeps the breast-bone and allowing it to dry until the morning examines

---

[1]The motif of the bird which discloses the presence of a person or persons occurs in
other old traditions, such as that of the Capitoline geese. The converse—the bird which
conceals a person or deflects pursuers—appears in a variety of forms, as for example, St.
Bride's bird, the oystercatcher, which according to Scottish legend concealed our Lord
under seaweed. Another story relates that an owl which perched above the hiding place of
a Mongol chieftain deluded his enemies into thinking he was elsewhere.

[2]The custom of killing a black cock on St. Martin's Day in Germany finds a parallel
in Ireland where a sheep, goose or fowl was slaughtered and its blood sprinkled in the house
(cf. p.165).

it all round, in front, behind and in the middle. Thereby they divine whether the winter will be severe or mild, dry or wet, and are so confident in their prediction that they will wager their goods and chattels on its accuracy." Hartlieb describes a conversation with an officer who asked him on St. Nicholas' Day what sort of winter he supposed it would be. He replied: "Lord Saturn goeth this month into a fiery sign, likewise other stars are so arranged that in three years no harder winter shall have been." "This valiant man, this Christian Captain drew forth out of his doublet that heretical object of superstition, the goose-bone, and showed me that after Candlemas an exceeding severe frost should occur, and could not fail. What I had said he endorsed and told me that the Teutonic knights in Prussia waged all their wars by the goose-bone; and as the goose-bone predicted so did they order their two campaigns, one in summer and one in winter."

Such importance was attached to the goose as an oracle that it was said that a goat and a goose led all Christendom in the First Crusade of 1096 A.D. The goose-bone oracle is mentioned in the *Calendarium Oeconomicum* of J. Colerus, published in 1591, and other works of about this date. In the seventeenth century Protestant German preachers inveighed against the custom as a superstitious heathen practice. The *British Apollo* of 1708 contains the query: "For what reason is the bone next the breast of a fowl, etc., called the Merry Thought, and when was it first called so?" The answer given shows that the origin of the custom had been forgotten: "The original of that name was doubtless from the pleasant fancies that commonly arise from the breaking of that bone, and 'twas then first certainly so called, when these merry notions were first started." Some, however, took these prognostications seriously, for a writer in *The Spectator*, quoted by Brand, stated: "I have seen a man turn pale and lose his appetite from the plucking of a Merry Thought." The custom of scrutinising a breast-bone and deducing from it the nature of the coming winter continued well into last century in Hampshire, for a contributor to *Notes and Queries* in 1875 stated: "In Richmondshire some persons say that the breastbones of ducks after being cooked are observed to be dark coloured before a severe winter, and much lighter coloured before a mild winter." Yorkshire folk predicted the weather by examining the flesh of geese. Similar prognostications were made in France. Welsh people carried about a small bone called the "goose's tooth" to ensure good luck and prevent toothache but this custom may not have been derived from the wish bone tradition.[1]

Thus this ritual, which has become a dinner-time children's amusement, can be traced back to its performance as an act of augury to determine the auspicious time to wage war. As belief faded the duck and the chicken took the place of the lordly goose. The sequence illustrates the process whereby oracular traditions become weather-forecasting and eventually pastimes. Many rites have followed a somewhat similar course.

Ancient sources furnish further evidence of the ritual importance of geese in western Europe. The Swedes and some other peoples of the time of the Germanic invasions made use of the bird as a grave offering. Goose bones found in a Swedish ship burial may have been sacrificed or intended as food for the dead. The ancient Germans sacrificed geese to Odin at the autumnal equinox and there seems to have been a cult of a goose goddess at Cologne.[2] Undoubtedly the modern goose feast is connected with, and is probably a survival of, the practice of sacrificing animals at pre-Christian festivals. Pagan rites in which geese were concerned survived well into the Middle Ages. During the thirteenth century Pope Gregory IX preached a crusade against the Stedingers of Friesland, declaring that they worshipped the devil under the name Asmodi, and that during their rites he appeared to them in the form of a duck, a goose or a youth.[3] After the worshippers had kissed him and danced around he enveloped them in darkness and the people gave themselves up to sexual orgies. The description is strongly reminiscent of the proceedings at a witches' sabbath, which appears to have been essentially a gathering where fertility rites of pre-Christian origin were celebrated. The goose has had erotic associations for many centuries. We may interpret the Stedingers' ritual as a fertility ceremony presided over by a pagan divinity.

Perhaps the tangled mythology of "Bloody Bertha," called in Germany Perhta, Berchta and Perchta, embodies reminiscences of a supernatural goose. This personage has one goose- or swan-foot and

---

[1]Divination by means of bones is extremely ancient and widespread. Highlanders still divine with a sheep's shoulder blade and Mr. T. C. Lethbridge tells me of a man in East Anglia who recently "sold his soul to the devil" to obtain power over animals by procedure which involved swimming a frog's bone upstream.

[2]Some of the place-names in this area are of Slav derivation.

[3]Apparently a corruption of "Ashmadai," the king of the demons in Hebrew mythology.

is associated with the Wild Hunt (p. 221). In ancient times the goose was said to be a holy bird which flew in front of the earth-mother Berchta. This seems to link it with the early mother goddesses. The explanation of her large flat foot as a deformity caused by working the treadle of a spindle seems to be a late rationalisation. She is closely connected with fertility, and in South Germany, her dancers, the Berchten, wear masks representing mammals and birds and jump in the fields to ensure their fruitfulness. At Shrove-tide in the Erz mountains bird masks are worn (Fig. 27). During Bloody Bertha celebrations on St. Nicholas' Eve a boy wearing a hideous mask

FIG. 27. Shrovetide masqueraders representing a stork and a bear. Erz Mountains. (After a photograph by Berliner Illustrations Gesellschaft).

goes around in Czecho-Slovak villages sporting goose wings on his shoulders and threatening children with a wooden knife. In Basque villages boys escort one of their number masked as an ogre from house to house singing and begging much as Irish "wren boys" do at the same season—the winter solstice. In Germany Bertha's festival is on Twelfth Night, corresponding with the winter solstice before the change of the calendar. Freya was goose- or swan-footed. In the cult of this goddess German warriors undertook vows while partaking of a sacred meal. French folklore also tells of women with one goose foot, notably *la reine pédauque*. The House of Cleves was said to be descended from the offspring of a woman and a swan.

Evidence is lacking of goose sacrifices among the ancient Celtic peoples but the bird was held sacred by them. Julius Caesar (*De Bello Gallico*, v. 12) noted that the Britons "may not eat hare, domestic fowl or goose but kept these animals for entertainment." He misunderstood the significance of these customs. The hare and the goose were tabu, and perhaps the fowl also.[1]

Many later observers in other parts of the world have made similar mistakes and supposed dances and other celebrations to be merely for diversion when in fact they were religious or magical. Prejudices against eating goose flesh still persist in Celtic areas, such as some parts of Ireland. Thus D'Arcy Thompson remarks that "geese were kept, but not eaten, by the Celtic inhabitants of Britain—very much as at the present day." Similar prejudices in regard to the hare, a highly magical, lunar animal, survive in parts of Ireland, Wales and Brittany. Across Eurasia and into the New World it is regarded as having supernatural qualities. The disfavour with which horse flesh is viewed in Britain probably lingers from the time when this animal was ritually important among the Indo-European peoples. As late as 1185 Giraldus Cambrensis described the remarkable ceremony at the enthronement of an Irish chieftain. He walked on all fours and then ate slices from a white mare while sitting in a bath of broth made from its flesh.

Before tracing goose lore further a few comments are needed on the dates of the seasonal celebrations. Why should the feast be held usually at Martinmas on the continent and at Michaelmas in England, apart from a few exceptions such as the festivities at Farndale? This question raises the complicated issue of the division of the year in early times but the essential fact is that Michaelmas is a more recent festival than Martinmas. It was not until 813 A.D. that the ecclesiastical festival of St. Michael and All Angels was instituted. Martinmas is the successor of an early Germanic festival, probably alluded to by Tacitus (I.xliv) and it has been kept as a Christian festival from about the middle of the sixth century. The pagan festival coincided with the slaughter of domestic animals which took place, owing to the scarcity of fodder, in the first half of November. The Venerable Bede refers to November as the month in which cattle used to be offered to the

[1]In Cambridge Ethnological Museum there is an exhibit of the objects found in the grave of a Belgic chieftain at Snailwell. These include the skeletons of a pig and a decapitated fowl. The presumption is that these were sacrificed.

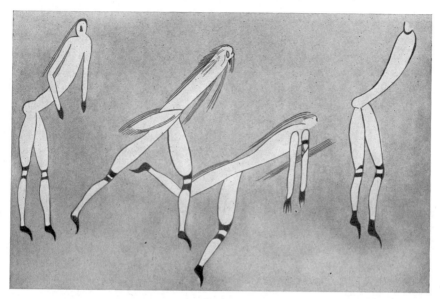

Plate 3. a. Bushman rock painting showing Basotho boy initiates masked and decorated as owls. Tosing. Basutoland. Cf. p. 10. *(Copy specially made by James Walton)*

b. Bushman rock painting in cave at Leeuwfontein, S. Africa. A medicine man is depicted adorned with feathers and wearing a mask representing a bird's head. Creatures half-animal and half-human suggest that some magical myth or ritual is represented. These ambiguous figures are reminiscent of similar types of representation in Palaeolithic art. Cf. p. 19. *(Stow and Bleek)*

Plate 4. Palaeolithic sacrificial scene engraved on the wall of a cave at Addaura, Palermo, Sicily. Bird-masked figures surround two sacrificial victims. Compare the hieratic posture of the men with the posture of the woman in Fig. 26. Cf. pp. 11, 16, 19, 23, 104. (*Cav. Giuseppe Lo Cascio*)

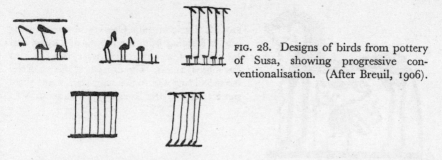

FIG. 28. Designs of birds from pottery of Susa, showing progressive conventionalisation. (After Breuil, 1906).

gods before being killed (*De temporum ratione*, xv). Until as late as the reign of King David of Scotland (1124-1153) cattle, sheep and swine were slaughtered from Martinmas until Christmas and these 44 days were in legal language the "tyme of slauchter." The season thus naturally became one of sacrifice, feasting and revelry—and to a considerable extent still retains these characteristics on the continent. The festival was closely connected with stock-breeding. This gives some indication of its geographical distribution and extension in time. The Germanic and Celtic years were originally determined by agricultural and pastoral activities, though there are traces of some solstitial, equinoctial and lunar observances among both Germanic and Celtic peoples. With Roman and Christian influences solar festivals received increased emphasis. Thus in some places celebrations connected with Martinmas were shifted to Michaelmas. In Gaul, under Roman rule, many of the observances of Samhain were transferred to the calends of January.[1]

Where Germanic influences prevailed we find Samhain celebrations occurring at Yule. Christianity substituted All Saints' and All Souls' Days for the Celtic festival, and Hallow Eve remains a great occasion in many Celtic areas. At my home in Ulster it was kept with festivities almost comparable with those of Christmas. On that day

[1]Samhain, now celebrated as Hallow Eve, was the beginning of the Celtic New Year. Until recently mummers in the Isle of Man used to go around singing, "To-night is New Year's Night, Hogunnau." The Germans and Celts reckoned by nights, counting the eve as part of the next day. Hence our "fortnight" and "Twelfth Night." In the Highlands and Islands St. Michael's function was considered to be "meeting the souls of the elect at the moment of death, and . . . presiding at the balance where the soul's good and bad works are weighed." This suggests the transference of some beliefs associated with Samhain to Michaelmas, and also illustrates the survival of ideas concerning the weighing of souls ultimately derived from ancient Egypt.

FIG. 29. Design from a Geometric vase showing snakes hanging from the mouth of a horse and the beak of a bird. The horse and the bird are solar symbols. The unnatural design of the horse holding the snake suggests a symbolical significance. (After Roes 1933; Heraeum, VI).

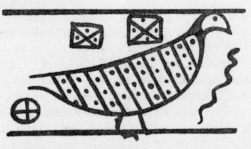

FIG. 30. Design of bird with snake on Rhodian vase, *c.* 3rd. century B.C. The bird has become modified from the anserine type, the sun symbols have also become modified and the snake has been detached from the bird's mouth. This suggests decay of the original symbolism. (After Roes, 1933; Louvre, inv. 335).

FIG. 31. Gaulish coin showing birds with modified sun symbols and a detached snake as in Fig. 30. (After Roes, 1933).

we sometimes dined on capercaillie. Perhaps, although we did not realise it, ancient prejudices prevented roast goose from appearing on the table.

Having traced the spiritual ancestors of the festive English goose from the present day to ancient Germanic altars and Celtic sacred

FIG. 32. Bird of prey on a dolphin from a coin of Sinope struck by a Persian governor. (After Roes, 1933).

FIG. 33. Bird on a fish from a vase found at Phaistos. (After Roes, 1933; Monum Ant. XIV).

FIG. 34. Carving on base of Cross of Kells, Ireland, depicting the bird-on-fish design and other eastern motifs. (After Allen, 1887).

enclosures we must now approach the problem from the other direction, seeking to discover links between the goose lore of early times and such practices as we have been considering.

Engravings found at prehistoric settlements show that at least as early as the Old Stone Age anserine birds aroused man's interest (Fig. 13, p. 13). They were probably among the first creatures to be domesticated, for some species are easily caught while moulting and newly-hatched goslings become fixated or "imprinted" on the first large moving object they see. They will follow a man who happens upon newly-hatched birds and remain permanently attached psychologically to him. Pliny (x.26) describes such geese. However, in domestication geese require more care than they would be likely to get from people before the Neolithic or Bronze epochs. The goose may have been revered before it was domesticated. Indeed, the maintenance of animals in sacred enclosures was, apparently, the first step

FIG. 35*a*. Pottery jug from Tepe Sialk, Iran. (9th. century B.C.) showing a bird on an ibex-like animal. Moussa Collection, Boston Fine Arts Museum.

b. Syro-Hittite seal (2nd. millennium B.C.) showing a bird on a horned animal. Pierpont Morgan Library.

c. Shard found in Sumeria showing a bird on an ibex or goat. (After A. L. Gourhan, 1938. *Revue des Arts Asiatiques*, *12:* 150).

d. Design showing a bird and deer on a Geometric pyxis. Fitzwilliam Museum, Cambridge. Drawn by T. Armstrong. (Cf. B. Segall, 1943. *Bull. Mus. Fine Arts, Boston, 41:* 72-76).

FIG. 36. Design on scarlet vase from Tell Agrat showing birds, fish, antelopes and trees. (After Delougaz, P. 1952. Pottery from the Diyala region. Chicago Univ. Oriental Inst.).

towards the domestication of a number of species. Geese were kept in Egypt during the New Kingdom (B.C. 1530-1050) and perhaps during the Old Kingdom (c. B.C. 3100-2500). Penelope had a herd of twenty (*Od.* xix, 538). One of the earliest religious representations in which the goose appears is a diorite statuette from Ur showing the goddess Gula the Healer seated upon four geese which bear her over waves— perhaps the ocean of the sky. She was a creative divinity, identified with the Sumerian fertility goddess Bau, the Great Mother, who was later absorbed into Ishtar. Images of Baubo, and later, shiela-na-gigs, carried this complex of ideas into the mediaeval period, as house wall paintings and carved work on some English churches show.

Anserine birds of the Proto-Elamite cultures of Susa I and Susa II are almost the first natural objects represented on pottery. They are sometimes conventionalized with excessively long necks (Fig. 28, p. 33). From these early times onwards such designs were used in culture after culture down to our own day. Because there are close associations between goddesses and water it has been maintained that these water birds represent female divinities, but this is doubtful. Their significance may have changed at an early period. It is generally considered that veneration of powers associated with femininity preceded the worship of masculine, solar powers. Anserine birds soon appear in combination with symbols, such as the fish or snake (Figs. 29, 30 and 31, p. 34). The two types of animal in conjunction may represent contrasting or complementary concepts, such as the union of earthly and heavenly powers. The history of such designs suggests that the symbols were brought together for doctrinal or ritual reasons and only later assumed a more naturalistic form. Anserine birds do not seize snakes

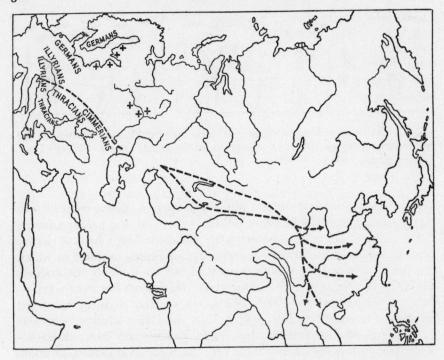

FIG. 37. Map illustrating culture streams from the Pontic area, after Heine-Geldern (1954). The diffusion westwards to Yugoslavia is added on the evidence brought forward by Kunst (1954) showing similarities between Indonesian and Yugo-Slav music, musical instruments, dances and artistic motifs. (Cf. also Heine-Geldern, 1950). The crosses indicate Scandinavian settlements about 800 B.C. The most northerly of the five arrows indicates the region of the Ordos bronzes. Their art motifs show strong affinities with those of ornamental metal-work found as far west as Sweden and Carinthia. The southerly arrows show the direction taken by culture streams to Indonesia which may have continued across the Pacific. The culture streams eastwards are shown from the point where they diverged.

or fish as they are represented as doing on early pottery, though some raptors feed on these creatures. Later symbolism appears to have adapted itself to observed fact to some extent, but no bird of prey would attack a dolphin and no goose would devour a huge fish (Figs. 32, 33 and 34, p. 35). Any interpretation of such designs in naturalistic terms is inadequate.

From Asia these anserine birds were carried over into Mycenaean and Geometric, Hallstatt and La Tène art and thus into the broad stream of European culture. In Geometric art anserine symbols are particularly common (Plate 10, p. 69) but it is when they are associated with other patterns that the probability of transmission rather than independent invention becomes impressive. Thus in Proto-Elamitic pottery of Susa II a bird perches on a goat, and similar designs occur much later in Villanovan art as well as on an object showing Hallstatt influence found in Denmark. The goat and bird motif appears also in Cappadocian and Luristan art, also on a Syro-Hittite cylinder and a sherd found in Palestine. The bird on goat and bird on deer are represented on a Bosnian tomb and the bird on deer on an Indonesian shroud (Plate 8, p. 65). The latter motif is known from ancient India (Harappa) and the bird on ibex from Sumeria. The bird and deer also occur on Geometric pottery (Fig. 35, p. 36). An Egyptian design on a coffin lid depicts the soul bird above the mummy, which is placed

FIG. 38. Designs on Cross of Drosten, St. Vigean's Forfarshire, including the bird-on-fish and other eastern motifs. (After Allen, 1887).

FIG. 39. Swastika on bird from an Argive sherd. (After Roes, 1933; Heraeum II).

on the back of a bull (Plate 9, p. 68). This type of motif, and presumably concepts associated with it, were evidently carried by one or more of the culture streams described by Heine-Geldern (Fig. 37, p. 38). That it diffused over the huge area from Yugoslavia to Indonesia is confirmed by similarities, pointed out by Kunst, between the music, musical instruments and dances of these two regions. A related design showing a bird on a horse's croup is known from Geometric and Etruscan art as well as from Gaulish coins. In later European art the bird perches on a centaur's croup as on the cross of Kells. The design includes the bird-and-fish symbol (Fig. 34, p. 35). Various combinations and permutations of these emblems occur. For example, a bird holding a fish is shown standing on an ibex-like animal painted on early pottery from Diyala near Bagdad (Fig. 36, p. 37). Such designs as appear on St. Vigean's cross in Scotland (Fig. 38, p. 39) can be traced to Byzantine and other eastern influence.

FIG. 40. Triskele designs with birds. *Left:* perched on an arm. *Centre:* goose heads terminating arms. *Right:* cock heads terminating arms. (After Roes, 1933; Brit. Mus. Lycia.).

Perhaps the stonemasons had seen eastern ivories. Although the bird-and-fish symbol probably represented the powers of sky and earth in combination or opposition its significance was so far distorted in Christian times that it was explained as "the pure soul feeding on Christ." This interpretation became possible owing to the letters spelling "fish" in Greek being construed as the initial letters of "Jesus Christ, Son of God our Saviour." Some of these symbols had astronomical or calendrical significance. A few of these motifs are found across Eurasia and even into the New World, and they are commonly accompanied by the widespread solar symbols of the swastika and the wheel. Composite symbols including birds and swastikas prove that in the cultures in which they occur the anserine bird was an emblem of the sun (Plate 10, p. 69; Figs. 30, 39, pp. 34, 40).

It is not surprising that symbols and the ideas associated with them should have travelled to the Far East from the Near East. At every prehistoric epoch for which we have a sufficient number of Chinese artifacts there is evidence of cultural influence from the west. For example, throughout an enormous area of Europe and Asia a mythology and ritual involving cutting three, or a multiple of three, furrows was associated with the introduction of plough agriculture. Again, throughout Eurasia the ideas associated with the herb mugwort are very similar. The "Crane Dances" of Crete and China were evidently derived from a common source, and ritual connected with the bull in China and the west has such similarities in detail that independent invention is out of the question. Comparison of designs used in metal work has led Heine-Geldern to maintain that a culture stream arising in Anatolia about B.C. 3500-3200 reached China. He holds that two others, one from the region of the Danube and Caucasus about the ninth century B.C. and another from Asia soon after the birth of Christ travelled to the coasts of China and eventually reached South America. Even if such views are received with some hesitation it is undeniable that the evidence for trans-Pacific culture contacts is increasing. The bottle-gourd was introduced to America from Asia or Africa not later than B.C. 2500.

At the winter solstice the ancient inhabitants of Korea, the Kitans, sacrificed a wild white goose and mingled its blood with spirits which they afterwards drank. The Chinese in the district of She Chiang killed geese, roasted them and presented them to one another at the summer solstice, which they kept as a great festival. Thus in east and

west geese were sacrificed at solar festivals. The variation in the
solstice chosen may be an indication that the ceremonies date from a
remote time.

As we have noted, the goose feast in Europe exemplifies the process
by which a cult object may become a feature of homely ceremonies
and descend from the realm of religion to folklore. In the Far East the
goose has also declined in esteem. There remain only reminiscences
of the sacrifice of the bird here and there but its widespread importance
in marriage ceremonial is well attested. The custom of giving a wild
goose as a wedding or betrothal present is very ancient, for it is mentioned in the earliest accounts of wedding ceremonial, the *Li Ki* and the
I Li. In Han times the practice was observed and the words used in
the wedding ceremony agreed largely with the Chou ritual. Still in
some parts of China live geese are among the traditional gifts from the
bridegroom's family to the bride. In other areas the girl's family sends
a pair of geese to the man's family when a betrothal takes place. The
ceremonial in Korea is thus described by Ross: "In front of the
procession is a servant on horseback, carrying a life-size likeness of a
wild goose, covered by red cotton cloth, which he holds with both
hands. When the procession reaches its destination the man bearing
the wild goose dismounts, enters and places the goose on the top of a
huge bowl of rice, and then retires." Details of the procedure vary.
The bridegroom sometimes goes on horseback and himself lays the
goose on a table in the bride's house. In China there prevailed a very
ancient custom of pouring a libation to the geese in connexion with
weddings, and a goose used to be among the presents given to a man
setting forth to Peking to sit for the literary examinations.

At all the first rites of marriage in China the wild goose was offered
at dawn, but at the nuptial rite it was presented at dusk. In one of the
Odes—which contain very ancient material—we read:

> *The call of the wild goose is heard at break of*
> *day when dawn appears.*
> *Man goes forth to seek his wife . . . betrothal*
> *should not be delayed.*

The goose also served a ritual purpose to some extent in the West.
It was presented to newly-weds in the Moscow region. The procedure
in which it figured in a district of France is reminiscent of Chinese

etiquette. A contributor to *Blackwood's Magazine* (November 1887) wrote: "We find from George Sand that at the marriage of French peasants in Berry, a goose, though a dead one, was commonly borne in the bridegroom's procession. 'Near,' writes the authoress, 'this bearer of a flowering and ribboned thyrsus is an expert spit-bearer, for under the foliage is a trussed goose which forms the object of the ceremony; around it are the carriers of the presents and the good singers, that is to say those who are clever and knowing and who are going to engage in an (amicable) quarrel with the followers of the bride'."

A cock is led at the head of some Hungarian wedding processions or carried in the bridegroom's hand. Thus another solar bird has taken the place of the goose. There are clear traces of eastern and shamanistic practices in Hungarian customs.

The association of the goose in China with ceremonies at dusk and dawn indicates that the bird had solar significance. This is supported by documentary evidence. A Tang dynasty work explains that "the goose stands for the male principle." Another source says: "The goose bestowed at a wedding attends to the *yin* and the *yang*. It waits for its time and then rises. In the winter it goes south and in summer north." Thus it is said to follow the sun and the *yang*, the male principle as contrasted with the *yin* or female principle.

All the way across Asia are areas where the goose is ritually honoured. There are thus links between the goose cults of Europe and China. The hero in the Finno-Ugric account of the deluge travels in the form of a goose. In Siberia a shaman at his initiation or at other rites may sit on a model of a goose. He is also sometimes credited with flying on one—as in mediaeval Europe witches used geese as steeds. The Votiaks sacrifice these birds to the river or heaven god. Among the Ostyaks the goose-god is one of their three great divinities and the shaman makes a nest for him of skin, fur and cloth. Each spring, Toman, the Mother Goddess, shakes feathers out of her sleeves. They become geese as they settle earthward. The Voguls believe that the Supreme Creator had seven sons, and the youngest, who was set to guard mankind, flies overhead in the form of a goose. As long ago as 1730 Strahlenberg remarked that the goose was a totem animal, tabued as food among some tribes of the Yakuts.

In the two great Indian epics, the Mahâbhârata and the Râmâyana, we have the beliefs of the folk of North India along the lower Ganges

within a few centuries of the Christian era. The period from B.C. 300
to 100 seems to be the most probable date for the Mahâbhârata, which
is later than the Râmâyana. In this mythology the wild goose is the
supreme bird, its white coloration making it an emblem of the pure
soul and of God. Varuna assumes the form of a goose and Visnu and
Kubera are drawn through the air by geese. We are expressly told
that the goose represents the sun, and this is related to its high flight.
The divine power in the universe is conceived as a cosmic gander which
makes itself known in song. The god of fire, Agnis, is called *hamsa* or
goose in one of the Vedic hymns and in Hindu mythology the god
Brahma rides on a white *hamsa*. He is called the One Goose or Swan.
When Buddhism arose the goose as a sun-bird was taken over into it
with other solar ideas. The Indian god of love Kama Deva rides on a
parrot which in some representations bears a resemblance to a goose.
Like Eros, who rides a goose or drives a swan chariot, he carries a bow
and arrow. In modern India, as in China, the duck (ruddy shelduck)
is a symbol of conjugal fidelity.

The Japanese, too, have pictured the goose as the chariot of a
divinity. A calendar print attributed to Harunobu dating from 1765
shows a Japanese girl representing by analogy Kosenko, the only
woman among the Eight Immortals, riding a wild goose (Plate 12,
p. 79). In a letter to me Mr. Basil Gray of the Department of

FIG. 41. Carving on stone of a ship of
the time of Septimus Severus found
near Ostia, the shrine on the galley is
the goose of Isis. The sailors may be
sacrificing to the goddess. (After
Lethbridge, T.C., 1952. Boats and
Boatmen).

FIG. 42. Adonis and Aphrodite riding in a chariot drawn by two swans. Design from a vase. Vulci. Brit. Mus. (After Reinach, 1899).

Antiquities of the British Museum expressed the opinion that "the point of the print is simply the power of a pretty girl over men." Thus the goose, as in India and China, symbolises the male principle. This design and its symbolism may be compared with the painting on a drinking cup found in Rhodes but made in Athens, dating from about B.C. 470. Aphrodite is seen being borne through the air on a bird which most closely resembles a goose (Plate 11, p. 76). Direct influence is out of the question. Here we have an illustration of the manner in which, where there are similar underlying concepts, strikingly similar motifs may emerge. The similarity is not due to coincidence nor to the existence of basic pictorial archetypes but is the outcome of the refinement of a widespread sex symbol of masculinity. When basic myths, rituals and symbols have diffused widely, as is known to have occurred, it is to be expected that, fundamental human impulses having much in common everywhere, the outcome should sometimes be the occurrence of rather similar patterns of symbol, ritual or myth in places far distant from one another.[1]

[1]Since this was written evidence has accumulated suggesting that the concept of a divinity or important personage borne by a goose may have diffused to Greece and Japan from the shamanistic cultures of Northern Asia. Cf. for example, M. de Ferdinandy's paper (1956) in *Ural-Altäischer Jahrbücher 28:* 18-34.

We enter the realm of speculation when we ask, where did the idea of the goose as a sun-bird arise? But we are not without some clues. Sir J. G. Frazer summed up the situation in regard to sun worship: "Among all the peoples of antiquity none adored the Sun so fervently or so long as the Egyptians." Nevertheless, the priesthood could not conceal traces of the earlier matriarchal religion.[1]

Although the concept of the goose as a solar symbol seems to have owed much to Egyptian influence the early prominence of the bird in Sumeria in connexion with fertility and creation goddesses suggests the possibility that neither civilisation derived the goose as symbol and cult object from the other but that each may have received it from a culture prior to both. Hahn has cited evidence suggesting that the bird was a supernatural being among the earliest agricultural people. It is not improbable that goose beliefs were important in late Neolithic times before the rise of city civilisations and that when these arose, with their anthropomorphic deities, goose mythology became elaborated, taking a somewhat different course in the cultures with which it became associated according as the masculine or feminine principle predominated. In ancient art there is a tendency for anthropomorphism to be more prominent in the city civilisations than among the people of the mountains and steppes.

Lunar worship preceded solar, so the goose may have had some early lunar associations, but normally, and throughout most of its history as a symbol it represents the male, solar principle. The proof, of this, which have been already mentioned, weaken the arguments based largely on its association with Aphrodite, that the goose was a

---

[1]According to a creation myth the Great Cackler, or Chaos Goose, cackled loudly to the Chaos Gander and laid an egg—the sun. This myth hints at the priority of the female principle. Ra, the sun, was identified with the egg, though the Heliopolitan priests maintained that it was made on Ptah's potter's wheel. The Gander was Seb, the goose-headed earth-god who, at the beginning, sped through the air. Eventually Amon-Ra, the combined deity of Thebes, was regarded as the Chaos Goose and Gander in one. Pausanius (x.32.16) says that geese were sacred to Isis and Osiris and were sacrificed to them in autumn. Their priests ate their flesh. On a goose-prowed Roman galley we see the sailors apparently sacrificing to Isis (Fig. 41, p. 44). Ovid (*Fasti*. i.454) mentions these sacrifices, identifying Isis with Argive Io, who was a moon goddess (iii.658). Hera, who had associations with the cuckoo (Plate 29, p. 176) transformed Io into a wryneck—the bird known as the "cuckoo's mate," Rotated on a wheel the wryneck was a love charm. Perhaps this hints that the wheel was occasionally a lunar symbol. Diodorus Siculus (i.70.84) mentions that goose flesh was fed to the sacred cats and eaten by the Egyptian pharaohs as part of a rigidly determined regimen. This rule of life had similarities to that of the Chinese emperor and indicates that the ritual patterns of the Divine Kingship formed the basis of Chinese ceremonial.

female symbol—though in its decadence its significance may have been confused. In Greece and Rome it became an erotic symbol, representing sex or sexual union. Sometimes, as on Greek tombstones, it stood for marital love, and in Rome it could signify fertility and perhaps conjugal fidelity—symbolism which the goose and mandarin duck acquired in China. The bird's fat was considered an aphrodisiac (Pliny, *Nat. Hist.* xxviii.261). A 2nd or 3rd century Indian ivory, now in the Kabul museum, showing a lively goose with a nude woman, suggests that this motif may have reached India through Roman influence (Plate 13, p. 82). In Greek and Etruscan art the goose, swan or duck appears with nude goddesses and through the influence of classical myths, such as that of Leda, the association continued in Renaissance art and up to modern times (Plate 14, p. 83; Fig. 42, p. 45).

Aphrodite has many oriental and avian affinities. The sparrow and partridge, as well as the goose, were her sacred birds and the two latter were sacrificed to her. The dove was also associated with her. Farnell wrote: "In the cult of Aphrodite the Greek religion was mainly conservative of Oriental ideas; the ritual, the attributes and most of the characteristics of the goddess are derived from the East." Her ancestry can be traced back through the Mother Goddesses of the ancient civilisations to Neolithic and Palaeolithic figurines (p. 16). How widespread was this cult, and how basic to the evolution of later magico-religious ideas is indicated by the finds of Aurignacian female images from southern France to Siberia and the records of clay figurines resembling Asian examples in Mexico. Over an enormous area there was substantial identity in early times between certain fundamental magico-religious ideas, and with them the goose was associated at a remote period.

Our enquiry into the origin of the English goose-feast and the custom of breaking the wish-bone has led us to some of the earliest magico-religious ideas known to have been cherished by man. As we proceed we shall find further evidence that modern folklore is derived from ancient fertility conceptions which were once widespread throughout Europe and Asia, and even further afield.

CHAPTER 3

BIRD-MAIDENS

IN ancient literature, art and ritual the rôles of the swan and goose are not clearly distinguishable. It is often difficult to decide whether designs on early pottery represent geese or swans, or even cranes, flamingoes or other long-necked birds. Probably the goose preceded the swan in attaining supernatural status over a wide area but at various periods and places beliefs and customs concerning one were transferred to the other. When a belief spreads into an area where the relevant object is missing, rare, or for some reason unsuitable, a surrogate is commonly found. Thus, as we have seen, the duck sometimes acquires the symbolism of the goose in Europe and Asia. Similarly the inspiration of Bronze Age duck designs was probably originally from goose motifs (Plate 15, p. 94).

The swan is such a spectacular bird that even if we were without the evidence of Stone Age art (Figs. 13 and 14, pp. 13 and 14) we could be confident that it attracted man's attention very early. Its size, shape, white plumage, powers of flight and migratory movements combine to render it conspicuous. The trumpeting of the whooper and the wing music of the mute swan attract attention when the birds pass overhead.

In Ireland, styled "the swan-abounding land" by a seventeenth century poet, and to a lesser extent in Scotland, the swan is still a bird of mystery and magic. The mute swan has acquired the respect which may have been restricted in earlier times to the whooper and Bewick's swan. Bad luck attends the swan-killer. It was believed that the souls of people became embodied in swans. In Co. Mayo folk said that at death the souls of virtuous virgins dwelt in these birds and he who interfered with them would lose his life before the year was out. Mr. Tom Henn, Senior Tutor of St. Catherine's College, Cambridge, tells me that the folk at Corofin, near Lough Inchiquin, Co. Clare, say that if a swan on the lough were to be killed one of the villagers

Plate 5. Sumerian cult plaque in baked clay representing Lilith, a goddess of the underworld (*c.* 2300-2000 B.C.). She is crowned with a domed head-dress on which are set four bovine horns and is holding measuring ropes, symbols of judgment. The clawed feet and the spur on her leg suggest that she is demonic. The name of Lilith is rendered " screech owl " in the Authorized Version (Isaiah, XXXIV. 14). The Gilgamesh Epic mentions that she built her house in a hollow tree, as owls do. Cf. pp. 21, 106. (*Col. Norman Colville*)

Plate 6. Assyrian bas-relief from the frieze in the palace of Ashur-Nasir-Pal at Nimrud showing a ritual anointing scene. The eagle-masked figures are probably ministers of a god, perhaps Ashur, whose emblem was an eagle. Cf. p. 22. (*British Museum*)

would die. There is a local tale that the chieftain of the Quins, who owned the castle of Inchiquin on the lough married a mysterious lady whom he found in a cave near-by. She stipulated that no O'Brien should ever be allowed to enter the castle. When this happened she sprang with her child through a window into the lough. This is a variant of the swan-maiden legend. In the Hebrides, according to Kenneth Macleod, "No good Islesman would put taunt or hurt on that same Wild Swan although evil men did both, leaving a woman-lord to keen over her mate." Writing in 1716 Martin Martin noted that in the Western Isles it was considered unlucky to kill a swan. In Uist the naturalist Gray was told by an old woman that a wounded swan on Loch Bee which uttered melancholy cries was the ghost of her grandmother.[1]

Similar ideas are cherished by Siberian tribesfolk. Many believe that he who kills a swan will soon die. Even to point at one is to risk calamity. Among the Buriats to slay a swan is a dreadful sin and to handle a feather is reprehensible. These people offer a libation to the swans when they arrive and women pray to the first which they see in spring. A legend tells of a swan which brought fire and burnt the tent of the man who had robbed its nest. In certain groups of the Yakuts the swan is a totem and its flesh is not eaten. Hawks and swans are said to know the Zado root which has power to alter the weather. The Tungus erect a wooden model of a swan on a pole, place a wooden fish near its base and sacrifice reindeer there (Plate 16, p. 95).

Although Ireland and Siberia are a long way apart it should be borne in mind that the Finno-Ugric area extends into Norway and Sweden. These swan beliefs provide further evidence, confirming

[1]Space is lacking to discuss the various forms of belief in which the human soul is thought to take the form of a bird, or persons are believed to become birds (Folklore Index Motif D 150) though forms of the belief are considered later (p. 211). Such notions are ancient and widespread. The Babylonians and Assyrians believed that the dead were clothed in feathers, and apparently the souls of early Greek kings were thought to depart as birds (Plate 30, p. 177). In parts of Russia there was a belief that dead children returned as swallows. Some Finno-Ugric peoples say that the departed appear as birds. Similar ideas prevailed among the Aztecs and Australian aborigines. In Brittany it was said that children who died unbaptised became birds. The ritual employed by a Siberian shaman to make a childless woman conceive involved letting fall model birds on her recumbent body. Miss Christina Hole tells me that there is a remarkable series of well-attested accounts, from the fifteenth century to 1911, of birds appearing at the death of Bishops of Salisbury, culminating with a manifestation of them to Miss Moberly of the "Vision of Versailles" fame. In mediaeval paintings of the Annunciation a bird sometimes has a significant place.

FOB—E

that in the previous chapter, of an early culture which influenced Europe, including the British Isles, as well as much of Asia.

Myths concerning swans are numerous in Ireland. In "The Wooing of Étaíne," dating probably from as early as the eighth century, we are told how Midir appeared in the banqueting hall "while Tara was surrounded by all the champions of Ireland, ring within ring." He boldly claimed the forfeit which King Eochaid had promised him if he lost a game of chess—to clasp his wife, Étaíne, in his arms. With his weapons in his left hand and the woman on his right arm Midir made for the smoke-hole—and, looking skywards, the assembled host saw them as two white swans circling over Tara. They took refuge in a fairy mound but after nine years Eochaid secured Étaíne and bore her back in triumph. The story has points of resemblance with the Indian tale of Damayanti and Mala. There are so many similarities between Indian and Irish traditions that Dillon has suggested that "the first Celtic invaders of Ireland brought with them a special system which had its root in Indo-European times." Further evidence of culture contacts at a remote epoch is provided by comparison of other folktales. Scandinavian scholars, notably Libjeblad, have shown that to explain the close agreement between Gaelic and Slavonic stories one must conclude that they go back to a direct connexion between Slavs and Celts before the Celtic expansion (c. 600 B.C.).

Another tale of Étaíne's grandson, King Conaire Mor, whose father came in a bird-skin to woo his bride, relates how he pursued great white-speckled birds in his chariot and followed them into the sea. They turned into armed men and told him that to kill birds was tabu for him but that if he walked naked to the bull-feast at Tara carrying a sling and stone he would become king.[1] When he drew near to Tara kings awaited him with royal raiment and a chariot. In written form this story dates from the eighth or ninth century.

Swans are not mentioned in another myth containing many primitive elements concerning the magical birth of the hero Cú Chúlainn but details therein, especially the linking of the birds with chains, indicate affinities with swan legends even if the behaviour of the birds seems more appropriate to geese. A flock used to come to Emain Macha, destroying all that grew in the fields, so King Conchobar of

---

[1] It is widely believed that nakedness endows a person with magical power and ability to ward off evil (p. 114).

IG. 43. Apollo bearing off Kyrene in a swan-drawn chariot to the Hyperboreoi. An engraved *smáragdos* of Roman work, Leningrad. (After Overbeck, J. A., 1871. Gr. Kunstmyth.).

Ulster set out with a hunting party of nine chariots to pursue the birds, which associated in nine groups assorted in pairs linked with golden chains.[1]

At nightfall they find themselves at Brug na Bóinne, the most renowned fairy stronghold in Ireland and the dwelling of the Dagda, the foremost of magicians.[2] The warriors enter a cottage which miraculously enlarges itself to accommodate them all. During the night a son is born to the woman of the house and at the same time a

[1]The motif of swans joined by golden or silver chains (D536.1) appears in so many legends that one might suspect that it arose from some magical belief or ritual. In a Tibetan story a hunter catches a swan-maiden by throwing a chain around her. Juno's swans "went coupled and inseparable." In Greek art swans are depicted harnessed, illustrating the well-known myths (Figs. 42 and 43) and the needlework on the silk found in St. Cuthbert's tomb, dating from about the sixth century shows pairs of geese or ducks wearing decorated breast-bands. The traditional design seems to be of eastern, probably Persian, provenance. A French mediaeval legend refers to six brothers and sisters whose transformation into swans depended on the possession of golden chains. This has affinities with Grimm's tale of "The Six Swans" in which a golden chain is placed around the neck of the swan-maiden. Variants attained wide popularity as the story of Le Chevalier du Cygne in France and Lohengrin in Germany, culminating in the presentation of the legend on the operatic stage by Wagner. When Edward I swore to destroy the Scots who had revolted under Robert Bruce two swans with trappings of gold were brought into Westminster Abbey as part of the ceremonial. The references to gold in the swan-lore of Ireland may indicate that these stories ante-date the Iron Age conquest of Ireland, for by the time these invaders arrived the gold was exhausted.

[2]Dagda means "the good god" but not in the moral sense. He was "good at" various activities, a capable craftsman and artificer. The weather was under his control.

mare gives birth to twin foals which are presented to the child and become famous in the annals of Cú Chúlainn. The boy is given into the care of Dechtire, the King's sister. (Another version relates that Dechtire and her maidens in the guise of birds ravaged the crops but after three years she was discovered in the cottage).

In the morning the house has disappeared and only the foals and the child remain. He dies—but he will be reborn. Dechtire dreams that a stranger, who is none other than the god Lug, approaches her. She bears a son who, according to the variant we choose, is Lug himself reincarnated or his son. Dechtire brings about an abortion but becomes pregnant again and Setanta, later called Cú Chúlainn, is born. Among the later exploits of Cú Chúlainn was the bringing down, first of eight swans, and then sixteen, with single stones from his sling. He led them to Emain Macha tied by ropes to his chariot.

There is also an ancient story relating that when the Ultonians had gathered for the festival of Samhain a flock of most beautiful birds alighted on the lake. Cú Chúlainn slew them and gave birds to all the women of the court except his wife. To appease her he promised that the next time the birds came she should have the two loveliest. Soon there appeared two birds on the lake, linked with chains of red gold. They sang so sweetly that sleep fell on the assembly. All Cú Chúlainn's efforts to slay them failed.

The sea-god Manannán mac Lir, whose name is borne by the Isle of Man and who also appears in Welsh mythology, had a son Mongán of whom it was said:

> He will be in the shape of every beast,
> Both on the azure sea and on land,
> He will be a dragon before hosts . . .
> He will be a wolf of every great forest.
>
> He will be a stag with horns of silver
> In the land where chariots are driven,
> He will be a speckled salmon in a full pool,
> He will be a seal, he will be a fair white swan.

We hear of other transmigrations in Irish folklore—as, for example, Tuan mac Coirill who lived 100 years as a man, 20 as a pig, 30 as a stag, 100 as an eagle and 30 as a salmon. Fintan claimed to have been

500 years a salmon, 50 an eagle, 100 a falcon, and then God restored him to human form.

. It will be apparent that although these traditions have run the gauntlet of Christian expurgators they retain archaic ideas recalling the time when men did not make a clear distinction between themselves and the animals. The association between large birds, geese or swans, and the realms of fairyland is surely significant, for the Tuatha Dé Danann are the people of the fairy strongholds and there are some grounds for thinking that the fairy belief embodies reminiscences of a subjugated race and their culture. They were great magicians and craftsmen, and were conquered by the Sons of Miled whose exploits are recorded in the Book of Conquests. According to Macalister these were Iron Age Celtic invaders of Teutonic extraction who became a ruling aristocracy. If this somewhat daring theory be correct we have an explanation of the abhorrence in which fairies hold iron, and perhaps also a hint that the supernatural swan belonged to the Bronze Age predecessors of these conquerors.

Among the "Three Sorrows of Storytelling" of the Irish shanachies is the lovely legend of the Children of Lir—a tale based on a theme which apparently reached Ireland from the British kingdom of Strathclyde in the eighth century. Françoise Henry, commenting on the two swan-like birds carved on an eighth century slab at Inishkeel, Donegal (Fig. 44), remarks: "One cannot help thinking of the Children of Lir." But swan designs are too widespread for a definite assumption

FIG. 44. Swans and human figures carved on the Inishkeel slab, Ireland. (After Henry, 1940).

FIG. 45. The bird sun-ship symbol. *Top:* From a necklace found at Allancourt, Haute Marne; *Centre:* Catalauni, Marne: *Bottom:* From amphora found at Prenzlauvitz, Lower Weichsel, Urnfield period. These designs illustrate the association between anserine birds and the sun. They suggest the transference of anserine solar symbols from the urnfield culture to later cultures. (After Sprockhoff, 1955).

of a connexion between this particular legend and the carving to be justifiable (Figs. 45 and 46, pp. 54 and 55).

According to the story the daughter and two sons of the king were turned into swans by their wicked stepmother and doomed to spend nine hundred years on the sea between Ireland and Scotland. They sang such sweet fairy music that a spell was on all who heard them and bird flocks gathered around to listen. The tale describes how Fionnuala gathered her young brothers about her, striving to shelter them under her breast and wings from the fury of the Waters of Moyle. When the enchantment had run its course, the swans, having found sanctuary with a Christian monk and been linked with silver chains, were restored to human shape, wizened and decrepit, and baptised just before they died. Doubtless the ending of the story indicates that, with some emendations and additions, an ancient myth was approved by the church. Similarly in a Russian ballad a swan-maiden will only marry the hero after he is baptised, and a German forester, according to a Hessian legend, lost a swan-maiden because he did not say a Paternoster for her every Sunday.

The story of the Children of Lir is related to the swan-maiden theme (Aa 400; D 361.1) which is among the most widespread of all legends. The following Irish version contains a number of ancient elements. Oengus, the son of the Dagda, dreamed that a surpassingly beautiful girl visited him, and he fell into a wasting sickness because of her. With the help of the troops of Ailill and Medhb, king and queen of Connacht, the men of the Dagda overran the fairy hill where lived Ethal, the father of Caer. When the king threatened to behead Ethal unless he would divulge how Caer might be approached he was told that next Samhain she would be at Lough Bél Dragon in the form of a bird with three times fifty swans wearing silver chains and coronets of gold on their heads. He called to Caer. When she drew near he embraced her and they fell asleep in the form of swans. Then after swimming around the lake three times they flew off to New Grange tumulus on the Boyne and chanted a song that set sleep upon those who heard it for three days and three nights.

The most usual form of the swan-maiden story describes the arrival of a flock of swans at a lake. They divest themselves of their feather garments in order to bathe in the form of maidens. A man who has been spying on them steals a garment and so secures the maiden as his wife, but years later she finds it, and having donned it, disappears.

Whatever archaic features occur in some variants the versions which contain the theft of the maiden's clothes seem rather sophisticated compared with the legends which tell of the revenge wreaked by Athene and Artemis on those who saw them naked. The garment-stealing incident suggests that this motif, at least, was contributed in a patriarchal society. It is a man's wish-fulfilment story, as Cinderella is a woman's, and in many of its variants expresses the realisation,

FIG. 46. Variation of the bird sun-ship symbol from Ireland. (After Sprockhoff, 1955).

lightly come, lightly go; the bird of happiness is always liable to take wing. It is incredible that such a story had a Palaeolithic setting. At what epoch, then, may we date it?

The oldest known recorded variants are Indian but this does not necessarily imply, as has been supposed, that it originated in the subcontinent. According to an ancient tale the heavenly Urvasi deserted her husband when he broke a tabu. He found her at last with nymphs, all in the form of swans, swimming on a lake. They assumed their normal shapes but in spite of her husband's entreaties Urvasi would not return. The stealing of the maiden's clothes is missing here, but it appears in another Indian legend which does not mention swans. Krishna was seated under a fig tree—a tree which in mythology has sexual symbolism—when he heard the sound of singing. Peeping out he saw some girls bathing. He slipped along to where they had left their clothes, tied them in a bundle and went back to sit in the tree and await events. When the maidens discovered what had happened they begged Krishna to return their garments but he told them he would not do so until they approached with their hands clasped together. In another legend Marabhuti is told by a hermit to steal the clothes of a heavenly nymph while she is bathing. She is only able to regain her garments when she gives the hermit certain information. This she does, and becomes "in virtue of a curse, the wife of that ascetic." She gives birth to a child and then informs the hermit that if he wishes to be united with her he must cook and eat the child—a motif which appears in a number of folk-tales. On doing so the hermit acquires the power of flight and is thus enabled to join the nymphs. Penzer, who quotes these tales, points out that together they contain all the elements of the swan-maiden motif, and he agrees with Holmström that the story radiated from India to other regions in Asia and the south with the expansion of Hinduism and Buddhism, and reached the West with the advance of Islam. Thus, Mediterranean versions have affinities with the tale "Hassan of Bassorah" in *The Arabian Nights*.

Although this reconstruction of the tale's travels may explain the propagation of some of the variants it omits consideration of some of the facts and it is more probable that the Indian stories are fragments of the tale in disintegration than the originals of it. Leaving out of account what may be a version among the Arawak Indians of Guiana, the occurrence of the tale among such peoples as the Eskimo of Greenland and the Samoyedes suggests that its diffusion ante-dates that of the great religions.[1]

This is supported by study of a closely related folk-tale, the Magic Flight (Aa 313) in which the hero is pursued by an ogre and helped by the ogre's daughter. According to Irish, French and Spanish versions the hero fetches an egg from a tree but carelessly leaves a joint of the lady's little finger at the top. This story, part of which is incorporated in the tale of the Argonauts, embodies motifs which occur in the swan-maiden theme and has much the same geographical distribution. This coincides closely with the colonisations of the megalith builders. Von Sydow believes that these people disseminated both tales. If so, they may be 4500 years old. Megalith building did not originate in the north but probably the swan-maiden story evolved in a northerly climate where swans were common and nakedness was unusual.

In northern Europe the story seems to have been current earlier than Penzer's theory would allow. On the Franks Casket, carved from walrus ivory in Northumbria before the Danish invasion, Egil, the brother of Wayland Smith is shown catching the birds to make wings (Plate 17, p. 96) and Wayland himself is depicted on the cross now in Leeds Parish Church (c. 1050 A.D.) clad in the feather garment which, according to one tradition, Egil made for him. The carving illustrates the episode when Wayland appears to King Nithudr, by whom he has been ill-treated (as King Minos ill-treated Daedalus (Diod. Sic. iv.76-79)) but whose daughter had fallen in love with him—a motif of the Magic Flight story. He is shown "holding in his arms the princess,

[1]Seal-maiden stories are more general around our Gaelic-speaking coasts than among Arctic peoples whose economy is largely dependent on seal hunting. We may infer that seal-maiden traditions arose where seals were not systematically slaughtered. The earliest literary record of a seal-maiden is the story of the nereid Psamathe who turned herself into a seal while unsuccessfully trying to avoid ravishment by Aeacus (Apollodorus, iii.12.6; Pindar, *Nemean*, v.13). Her son was Phocus=seal, who founded a colony at Phocis. The mythographers seem to have tried to harmonise two strands of legend for another Phocus, son of Ornytion, had already established a colony in this region. Phocis (Daulis) has bird associations and Graves has suggested that it was the centre of a bird cult. At all events, here we have transformations of human beings into both birds and seals. In spite of some approximations between the appearance and calls of seals and those of human beings general considerations which cannot be discussed in detail here, make it improbable that swan-maidens are derived from seal-maidens. Legends tell of horse-maidens in Wales and wolf-maidens in Croatia. Until a century ago men masqueraded in horse heads and hides in Wales and cow hides in Scotland. The Abbots Bromley dancers adorn their heads with antlers as did the shaman of the Trois Frères cave. As we noted earlier, the endeavour to exploit supernatural power by wearing parts of animals is among the oldest known and most widespread magico-religious procedures.

FIG. 47. Panel at base of cross-shaft in Leeds Parish Church showing Wayland holding the swan-maiden aloft. Wings are attached to his body and the tools of his trade are depicted. (After Collingwood, 1912-14).

high above him in the clouds" as the myth relates (Fig. 47). The story represents a variant or elaboration of the swan-maiden theme and has points of contact with "The Wooing of Étaíne." Even if Penzer were correct in regarding the swan-maiden as an annotator's addition to the Lay of Wayland in the Elder Edda (*c* 900 A.D.) the witness of the Franks Casket is sufficient to prove that the story was extant earlier. The Leeds cross shows a similar tradition maintaining itself later.

We must conclude that bird-maidens are of very ancient lineage throughout Eurasia north of the great mountain ranges. Thus it seems more probable that the swan-maiden motif originated as an explanation of bird ancestry than as a merry tale. Apparently the only people who enact a ritual associated with the myth are the Buriats of Siberia who look on the eagle as their paternal forbear and the swan as the mother of their race. They explain their ceremonies by a tale which conforms to a standard type of legend; One day three swans arrived at a lake to swim, leaving their feather-garments on the bank. A hunter seized the cloak belonging to one of them and married her. After many years he allowed his wife to try on the garments, whereupon she flew out of the smoke-hole of the tent—as Étaíne and Midir escaped from the smoke-hole of the hall at Tara—and cried, "Every spring when the swans fly north, and every autumn when they return south you must honour me with ceremonies." Usually where myth and ritual are conjoined we have a more archaic survival than where one occurs without the other. Even if this were not so here and the garment-theft motif had been incorporated late into the cult we have among these Siberian peoples, with their many bird-beliefs and animal-human identifications, the type of culture out of which the full swan-maiden legend might have arisen.

A frequent element in swan myths and related legends is the association of iron as an element in some way opposing the interests of the supernatural creature, and there is the curious motif in the Spanish and some other versions of the wearing of iron shoes by the hero until they are worn out. (The goose-wife's husband in Siberian tales wears out ten pairs of shoes in pursuit of her). The Buriats, who honour the swan so highly, believe in one-legged dwarfs dressed in skins and living in caves, who possess mineral treasures and precious metals. These beliefs are related to the myths about Vulcan, Wayland and other lame smiths and may, perhaps, be derived from the practice of incapacitating smiths to prevent their absconding with their mysterious knowledge and magical craftsmanship to enemy peoples. The travelling tinker is a man with a long and chequered past. Nomadic smiths lived a life apart among Arabian tribes, some metal-workers speak a different language from that of the people among whom they dwell, and the Masai and other tribes would not inter-marry with the smiths on whom they depended for weapons. The tinkers in the West of Ireland are a nomadic people with distinctive customs.

A Welsh legend related that Wastin of Wastniog watched during three moonlit nights (as swan-maiden espousers are sometimes said to have done) and saw groups of women in the oatfields. When he followed them they took refuge in a pool where he overheard one of them saying to another, "If he did so-and-so he would catch one of us." He secured a maiden who told him that she would serve him until he struck her with a bridle. Later he unintentionally did so and she flew to the lake with her children to plunge in. Her husband was just in time to rescue one child. In another Welsh story, the earliest recorded version of which appears in Walter Map's *De Nugis Curialium* (1182) we hear of a man who wedded a wife on two conditions—that he should never know her name and that he must never strike her with iron. One day when catching a pony she called to her husband for a bridle.

The iron bit of the halter he tossed struck her. She flew through the air and vanished in Corwrion lake. There are other rather similar legends. As bits were not made until comparatively late in the Iron Age the story in its present form cannot be earlier. An Irish tale relates that a man who lived near Lough Sheelin, Co. Clare, noticed that corn disappeared night after night, so he sat up to watch. A number of horses came out of the lake driven by a beautiful woman. He seized her and induced her to marry him, but stipulated that she must never see the lake again. Twenty years later she caught sight of it and rushed to plunge in and disappear.[1]

In many variants of the swan-maiden legend horses and twins are associated. Also, the wearing by the hero of a pair of iron shoes occurs in tales from the Caucasus, the Tyrol and Spain. In the Caucasian tale and a Catalonian version we hear of the identification of a person through the lack of a little finger. Such clues give indications of where variants have diffused. In several southern European versions we have dove-maidens, in Greenland a goose-maiden, and there is even a magpie-maiden variant. Underlying the twin legends is the belief in double paternity and the idea that when a god intervenes twins result. Until recently in Scotland and Denmark it was said when twins were born that one was mortal, the other immortal. The intervening divinity is often thought of as appearing in animal form. Such beliefs are derived from totemic ideas and notions of human kinship to animals.

As a consequence of her union with Zeus in the guise of a swan Leto bore twin children, Apollo and Artemis, who had a sanctuary in common at Troy (*Il.* v. 445-448). Apollo also had twins by the Cretan woman Akukallis. Leda—another form of Leto—laid two eggs after consorting with Jupiter. Out of one came Castor and Pollux, out of the other Clytemnestra and Helena. In classical art Leda and the Swan are represented with the Heavenly Twins. The latter appear with Aphrodite and the goose on an Etruscan mirror in the Fitzwilliam Museum, Cambridge (Plate 14, p. 83). The swan's erotic symbolism among the Greeks was transferred from the goose. Leda's swan was originally a goose. On a wine jar in the British Museum Adonis and Aphrodite are depicted in a chariot drawn by two swans

---

[1]This legend has some similarities to the story of the birds which raided Emain Macha and also with the Finnish, Lapp and Scandinavian tales about three brothers who kept nocturnal watch at midsummer to discover the birds which were damaging the crops.

(Fig. 42, p. 45). In his swan-drawn chariot Apollo flew northwards for a sojourn of at least three months in a land of youth, music and feasting. He was associated with music and had connexions with the North Friesian coast. The absence of his name from the recently deciphered Linear B inscriptions gives additional reason to believe that he did not come to Greece from Asia. Tennyson, quoting the classical tradition, makes Ulysses refer to,

> *That strange song I heard Apollo sing*
> *While Ilion like a mist rose into towers.*

May not the swan-song tradition have come to Greece originally from the north? D'Arcy Thompson, who considered it an astronomical myth, dismissed it as baffling. But the swans of northern legends sing in their own right. The Children of Lir sang in swan-shape on the Waters of Moyle and the chanting of Caer's companions on Lough Bél Dragon was so sweet that all who heard it fell into a slumber for three days and nights. How much more probable that northern folk, so much more familiar than southerners with the wild clamour of swans and their mysterious appearances after migration, should weave tales of their magical music-making!

What conclusions may we draw from this brief survey? Our swan legends are linked with others throughout Eurasia and some of the elements in them are very old. Designs on pottery and metal objects bear this out (Figs. 45 and 46, pp. 54 and 55). The frequent occurrence of swans and other anserine birds in Bronze and Iron Age art, especially such designs as twin-headed or -bodied horses together with sun symbols suggests that early swan beliefs were modified by successive waves of cultural invasion, and that metal-using, horse-riding and sun-worshipping peoples incorporated swan-beliefs into their cults. We have seen that there is reason to connect the swan-maiden tale with the megalith builders, and one can hardly doubt that swans were important in beliefs before this form of culture started its distant travels. Swan beliefs may thus be regarded as dating from not later than fairly early in the Bronze Age.

CHAPTER 4

THE RAIN-GOOSE

IT is still a popular belief in Shetland that the red-throated diver, locally called the "rain-goose," is particularly vocal before bad weather. No evidence of this has ever been adduced and my own observations in the haunts of three species agree with those of other naturalists who have studied divers intensively that their calling is mainly connected with courtship, conjugal or aggressive activities.

Suspicion that belief in the red-throated diver's capacities as a weather prophet is based on tradition rather than observation is increased when we find that in Shetland it is believed that its comings and goings, as well as its cries, prognosticate changes in the weather. There is a popular rhyme:

> If the rain göse flees to da hill,
> Ye can gang to da heof when ye will;
> But when shö gangs to da sea,
> Ye maun draw yir boats an flie.

One is left to imagine what weather the Shetlander should anticipate when the divers are noisy and also "flee to da hill."

The difficulties involved in taking divers seriously as weather-prophets increase the more we consider the traditions about them. We have to believe that all species are similarly endowed, for in Norway the cries of both the great northern and black-throated divers are believed to predict stormy weather or rain. There is not necessarily any contradiction in this but, considering how easily beliefs become transferred from one bird to another in folklore, it would be more easily explained as due to the diffusion of beliefs rather than independent observations. However, a real problem is presented by the Faeroese belief that before wet weather the red-throated diver mews like a cat or cries *varra-vi-varra-vi,* while if fine weather is imminent it calls *gaa-gaa-gaa* or *turkatrae-turkatrae.* In Shetland no such fine distinction is drawn. Thus if the Faeroese were correct the Shetlanders would frequently be misled. To them all noisy calling, including *turkatrae, turkatrae* which announces good weather to the Faeroese, portends rain and storm.

When we abandon the attempt to interpret diver lore in terms of accurate meteorology we find that those elements which are most difficult to reconcile with one another, or with the facts, are the most illuminating. What the more detailed Faeroese folklore suggests is, not that the Faeroese are better observers than other people, nor that their divers behave differently from those elsewhere, but that they have retained more of a tradition which has reached almost the limit of decay in Shetland. Norwegians believe that the diver's calls foretell that someone will be drowned and attribute the strange sounds to ghosts and water-spirits. The Faeroese say that when red-throated divers call overhead they are following a soul to heaven. As we have already noted in connexion with augury by the wish-bone, magic which has lost nearly all its power is apt to become limited to weather forecasting—as one of the few remaining realms where contingency reigns. This association between the diver and the dead raises the questions whether the bird in time past may have been a magician rather than a meteorologist.

Since the diver does not predict rain it is improbable that this belief could have arisen through independent observation in Britain, the Faeroes, Scandinavia and even in North America. For example, the Thompson Indians say that the calling of the great northern diver—the loon—portends rain. These folk also believe that imitating the call—which is easy to do as the bird's voice has a very human quality—will bring down rain. Thus among them the diver has a higher status than in sophisticated Europe. He does not merely predict rain. He makes it. If an imitation of the bird's voice can cause a downpour the loon's actual utterance must be more powerful. Human rain-makers not infrequently exert their magic by mimicking the utterances of creatures which they honour as possessing rain-making powers.

According to North American legends the loon has a strange past. The Ahts say that not all the animals were made at the general creation. The loon and the crow were once men. It happened that two fishermen quarrelled when they were out at sea in their canoes. The man who had been unsuccessful in his fishing knocked the other on the head, cut out his tongue and stole his catch. When the wretch reached shore he could only cry like a loon and the Great Spirit transformed him into one of these birds and his assailant into a crow. When the loon is heard uttering its quasi-human wails from the lake those who hear know that the wronged fisherman is trying to tell the sad story of his cruel treatment.

The loon is the messenger of the Algonquin culture-hero Kuloskap or Glooscap. This personage, who is also called "The Master," was pursuing his enemy, Winpe, a gigantic wizard, when a flock of loons circled around. Kuloskap asked their leader, "What is thy will, O Kwimu?" The diver replied that he wished to be Kuloskap's servant and friend. So Kuloskap taught the loons their strange cry so that they should call him when they needed help. According to the sequel they became men.

> Now it came to pass long after, the Master of Uktakumkuk
> (The which is Newfoundland) came to an Indian village,
> And all who dwelt therein were Kwimiuk, who had been
> Loons in the time before, And now they were very glad
> As men to see once more The Master, who had blessed them
> When they were only birds. Therefore he made them his huntsmen,
> Also his messengers.

Here we have the diver becoming a man, instead of, as in the previous story, the man becoming a diver. Once again folklore reveals the primitive mentality which makes no clear distinction between man and animals, and regards shape-changing as normal.

At first glance it might be supposed that queer stories assimilating divers to human beings originated independently in different parts of the world because of the human-sounding wails uttered by the great northern diver, but legends in Asia and America are so similar that there is no room for doubt that they were carried from one continent to the other. In the myths of both continents we are told of a water bird (or other creature) which helped with the work of creation by bringing mud from under the water. This tale is not recorded in the West apart from the area within the ancient boundaries of the Russian empire, some Balkan countries and in gypsy lore, but it is known from East Finland and Latvia across Asia and into North

Plate 7. a. Decorations on the shield found in the Sutton Hoo ship burial (*c.* A.D. 655), Suffolk. The bird of prey motif travelled to Europe from Asia. Cf. pp. 21, 83, 86. (*British Museum*)

b. The Sutton Hoo purse, set with gold frame, fittings and ornamental plaques, decorated with garnets and mosaic glass. The motifs of the bird of prey and interlaced beasts have affinities with designs as far east as Inner Mongolia (Ordos) and China. The human figure flanked by upright beasts occurs in the art of the ancient Middle East, Indian sculpture and Merovingian designs. Cf. pp. 20, 82, 86. (*British Museum*)

Plate 8. a. Left: Greek bronze of the Geometric period showing a bird perched on a deer. Cf. p. 36. (*Boston Museum of Fine Arts*)

b. Above: Bronze whetstone handle from Luristan. Cf. p. 36. (*Private Collection. After B. Segall*)

c. Portion of a shroud from the island of Sumba, Indonesia. (From the collection of J. and L. Langeweis, Zaandam, Holland.) The souls of the dead, represented as birds, are riding on deer to the Country of the Dead. Comparable designs appear in Sumerian and ancient Indian art. Cf. pp. 35, 36. (*J. Kunst*)

d. Ancient tomb at Ubosco, Bosnia. The souls of the dead, represented as birds, are shown riding on deer (and a goat) to the Country of the Dead. Cf. pp. 35-39. (*J. Kunst*)

America. In South America we hear of animals concerned with creation but the mud-fetching assistant bringing material from the primae-
val waters does not seem to occur. In the European creation stories
some other being tends to take the place of the bird. Sometimes the
creator-bird is a swan or duck, as among some Siberian tribes and the
Chippewas, but on both sides of Bering Strait divers figure in these
legends. In Asia the red-throated diver is often the species which
fetches mud, as among communities on the Yenesei. According to a
tale told there the bird succeeds at the third attempt. The Buriats say
that the diver was ordered to bring up black earth and red mud and
the Yakuts attribute the habits of the white-billed diver to the punishment inflicted on the bird by the Mother Goddess for deceiving her.
When ordered to bring up mud it returned declaring that it could
find none, but the Mother Goddess noticed mud on its bill and condemned it thenceforth to live in the water. As the tale refers to the
Tree of Life it would seem that it owes something to Semitic traditions.
The Samoyedes connect the story of the Flood with the activities of the
diver. Seven men escaped in a boat and after seven years the bird
brought up mud which the men threw into the water, so causing the
earth to appear. Again, the prominence of the number seven suggests
Semitic contacts. In America the Chippewas describe the diver's efforts
to fetch mud from the bottom after the Deluge. It dies in the attempt
but is subsequently resuscitated. Another Chippewa story tells of the
failure of the beaver, otter and musk-rat to obtain clay. Then the
great northern diver succeeds in bringing some up on its feet. According to the related Ojibwas the loon failed but the musk-rat, after being
restored to life, succeeded.

These similarities between Asian and American myths show that
the tales migrated across Bering Strait, as earlier data suggests and
facts quoted later confirm. Although, as we shall see in the next chapter
there was probably a "backwash" of mythology from North America
into Asia, the main stream of culture transference has been in the other
direction. There can be no reasonable doubt that the myths in which
birds are connected with the Creation and the Flood arose in Asia.
The earliest recorded versions of what we may call the mud-fetching
theme are Indian. According to a story told in the Râmâyana (xi. 110)
and at greater length in the Visnu Purana, Brahma, awaking from
sleep, took the form of a boar, plunged into the ocean and raised the
earth to its surface. With delightful artlessness the tale concludes with

FOB—F

the statement that "the Earth floated because it was so huge." We cannot assume because the motif is first recorded in India that it must have arisen there. The typical Indian type is confined to this region. Many considerations suggest as its place of origin somewhere in the area including Babylonia and India. Excavations in the Indian sub-continent at Harappa and Mohenjodaro have shown that there were cultural relations between these two centres of civilisation. If the myth originated in the south and spread northwards a bird would naturally be substituted for a mammal or reptile in regions where diving creatures of this type were rare and aquatic birds common, but it is most unlikely if a myth with a creator-bird in it travelled south to an area where aquatic birds are common that the boar or tortoise would have taken the bird's place in the myth. Since these animals are concerned with the emergence of the earth from the waters in India we are forced to conclude that the myth did not arise in the north. In mythology the boar is highly important over a wide area, and so is the tortoise in oriental regions and also to some extent in North American creation legends.

Many other diver legends prevail among the Siberian peoples. Wooden divers are erected on poles (Fig. 9, p. 10). Ornaments representing them are worn by the shaman (Fig. 48, p. 67) and the bird is believed to aid him on his magical journeys to the spirit world, which is sometimes conceived as lying beneath the water. There are indications that this idea may have been overlaid by later notions concerning a heavenly world. In the Algonquin myth already mentioned the loons fly around and act as messengers for The Master. The Buriats believe that spirits often appear in the shape of divers, and also as swans, ravens and eagles. Neither Buriats nor Yakuts will kill divers nor disturb their nests for fear of disaster befalling them. Among the Tungus the diver, swan, crane and sea-gull are sacred and it is considered reprehensible even to mention their names. In Europe similar ideas persist; the Norwegians consider it impious to destroy divers.

If further proof were needed that diver traditions diffused between Eurasia and America it is to be found precisely where it is most significant. At Ipiutak in Alaska graves have been discovered containing skeletons of people of early Eskimo cultures. The eye-sockets of the skulls have artificial eyes in them, giving them a gruesomely lifelike appearance. With the skeletons was found the skull of a diver treated in the same way (Plate 18, p. 97). It has been suggested that

FIG. 48. Part of a Yakut shaman's clothing showing figures of divers attached to it. (After Harva, 1938).

the purpose was to keep in the soul but against this it may be argued that this operation could not have been performed until time had elapsed since death and it is unlikely that these folk could have believed that the soul which did not escape during this interim period would need to be confined after it. As divers are believed to accompany Siberian shamans to the spirit world it is more than a possibility that these birds were thought to escort, and perhaps, guide, the dead to the land beyond. What bird more suitable than this creature which wails like a human being, at home alike in the heavens and the sea-depths, to accompany the dead seafarer to the bourne from which no traveller returns? When aged folk in the Faeroes see the noisy rain-goose passing overhead and remark that their parents told them that the birds were accompanying a departing soul their ideas are close akin to those which prompted these people far away and long ago to make certain that the diver should accompany their dead friends on the last, long journey.[1]

Some connexion may exist between the practice of equipping dead men and divers with artificial eyes and the very widespread legend of the blind man and the loon. There are a great many variants but the Copper Eskimo version gives the gist of it: A loon approached a blind boy and told him that he could cure him. The boy managed to follow the bird to a lake, and there, following the loon's example, he dived three times and so regained his sight. This tale is recorded from eastern Greenland, Labrador and the Eskimo of Central and Baffin Land as well as some Alaskan groups. The theme is also know to the Indians on the northwest coast of America and to some Athabascan peoples of the interior. Traces of it are recorded among the Plains Indians. Moreover there are elements which suggest affinities with Siberian folklore. It would seem that here we have a development of diver mythology which may have originated in north-western America and diffused more widely in the New World.

Divers are greatly revered among the Eskimo. The severed head of a diver is worn as a talisman in the belief that it endows the wearer with manly qualities and new-born babies are wiped with the skins of divers so that they may be assured of health and long life (Plate 19, p. 112).

If, returning from this excursion, we now ask why the diver is regarded as a weather prophet in Shetland, we are able, in this wide perspective, to suggest an answer. Throughout circumpolar Eurasia the diver is associated with shamanism and the shaman is believed to be able to control the weather. Until recently, indeed, British witches were credited with the ability to raise storms. The shaman has disappeared from Shetland but his associate—we might almost say his familiar—remains. The belief in the diver as weather-forecaster is a lingering relic of an element in a culture which once extended around the crown of the world. Here we have further evidence of an ancient and extensive Eurasian culture. This culture dates, probably, from Neolithic times and contained Palaeolithic elements.

Archaeological evidence confirms the existence of a prehistoric

[1]Undoubtedly the carriers of early cultures to the New World travelled by Bering Strait, whatever contacts there may have been across the Pacific. Arrow heads found in Alaska are very similar to those of the Danish Maglemose period. Designs derived from the Scytho-Siberian animal style were found at Ipiutak and still survive in modern Alaskan and Eskimo art.

Plate 9. a. Soul-bird hovering over the mummy of Ani. Papyrus of Ani. New Kingdom (*c.* 1200), XIX Dynasty. Cf. p. 22 (*British Museum*)

b. Soul-bird hovering over a mummy on the back of a bull. Base of a coffin lid of the XXVI Dynasty. Cf. p. 40. and *Plate 30.* (*British Museum*)

Plate 10. a. Chinese bronze vessel of the period of the Warring States (c. 481-221 B.C.). The bird-and-snake motif is shown in the upper panels. Beneath is a figure with wings holding a snake in either hand. Figures confronting animals, reminiscent of designs from the ancient Middle East, occupy other panels. Cf. pp. 122, 127 and Fig. 73. (*Chinese Government and Topical Press Agency*)

b. Vase from Argos of the end of the Geometric Period. The designs include sun symbols, the swastika, anserine birds and the horse. The cosmic symbol, the bird-and-fish, is also depicted. Two men fighting are shown beneath one of the handles. Cf. pp. 39, 41. (*Ecole Française d' Athènes*)

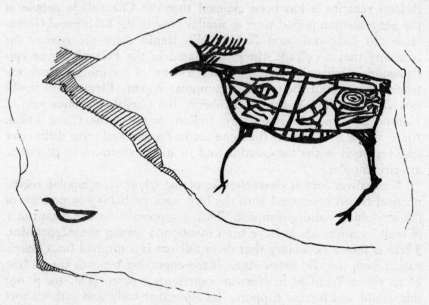

FIG. 49. Rock engraving of elk and diver (?) at Åskollen, Vestfold, Norway. (After Maringer and Bandi, 1953).

Arctic culture which extended to the British Isles. It is acknowledged that the Lapps preserved into Viking times many elements of the Baltic Bone Age and the Arctic Stone Age. They settled in the north in very remote times and their language shows that they lived on the coast before they adopted their present Finno-Ugric language. At Skara Brae in the Orkneys the flagstone industry recalls the slate industry of the Arctic Stone Age. Various writers have pointed out the analogies between the cultures of Northern Scotland and the Eskimos. For example, Piggott writes: "The earlier population of the Pictish area, from the early 2nd millennium B.C. onwards combined traditions from the ancient Eurasian hunter-fisher areas of the Circumpolar north, the builders of chambered tombs from Atlantic Europe, and the Warrior Cultures of the north European plain." In this area a non-Indo-European language was spoken.

The problem of the relationship between Eskimo cultures and those of the Palaeolithic remains controversial. Following examination of skeletal remains it has been claimed that the Chancelade people of the Magdalenian period were of similar type to the Eskimos of Greenland and Labrador, and Birket-Smith thinks there are reasons for believing that a culture which originated in the Palaeolithic or epi-Palaeolithic with the distinguishing feature of ice-fishing, once extended throughout the whole circumpolar region. Elements of it still survive among the Yukaghir of Siberia, the Caribou Eskimos west of Hudson Bay and the Algonquin Indians south of the Great Lakes. Arctic magic is essentially the same across Eurasia and some distinctive features, such as the tambourine and its use in shamanistic practices, are circumpolar.

Since diver lore is characteristic of the whole circumpolar region magical beliefs connected with the bird were probably components of the ice-fishing culture-complex. This is supported by the occurrence of such loon legends as have been mentioned among the Algonquins. There is thus a possibility that diver folklore is a survival from beliefs dating from the Old Stone Age. If the engraving beneath the outline of an elk at Westfold in Norway represents a diver (Fig. 49, p. 69) this would add further support. Its elongated body and rather short neck preclude its being a goose or swan and it is unlikely that a duck would be chosen for representation when there were bigger and more spectacular species around to which magical properties were probably attributed.

CHAPTER 5

THE BIRD OF DOOM AND DELUGE

IN British folklore, and indeed European folklore in general and even wider afield, the raven is predominantly an ominous bird, but like the cuckoo and a number of other species, it has an ambivalent character. It is sometimes good and sometimes evil. This is attributable to characteristic primitive modes of thought. Supernatural power is regarded as liable to express itself either benevolently or malevolently, and often, unpredictably. Consequently, a supernatural bird may foretell, or indeed bestow, weal or woe. Although historically the raven's ambivalence in our folklore can be traced to two conflicting strands of tradition, heathen and Christian, the ultimate explanation appears to lie in man's tendency to dread, as well as to employ and cherish, objects or organisms to which he attributes supernatural power. Also, man has a tendency to perceive or imagine exceptional characteristics in omens normally evil which alter their significance, just as it is believed that a small detail omitted from magical ceremonial may annul its effect. Thus in Ireland at the end of the seventeenth century it was considered "certain, by observation of all ages, that a raven having white on its wings and flying to the right hand of any person, croaking at the same time, was an infallible presage of good luck." The event would be sufficiently unusual for disproof to be difficult. Highlanders setting out to stalk deer regard the croaking of a raven as lucky—as if the bird which feeds where the body is gralloched could anticipate the kill.

The ambivalence of the raven is illustrated by the lines quoted by Swainson from a ballad:

> *To see one raven is lucky, 'tis true,*
> *But its certain misfortune to light upon two*
> *And meeting with three is the devil!*

We are reminded of the well-known rhymes about the magpie in which similar ambivalence is indicated by the fortunate or disastrous consequences which may ensue according to the number of birds seen. Magpie lore seems to be dependent upon, or derived from, raven traditions to a considerable extent and the folklore of the crow is confused with that of the raven.[1]

As a bird of death the raven is familiar to all readers of English literature. In *Macbeth* (I.v.39) the raven "croaks the fatal entrance of Duncan." Elsewhere in Shakespeare it hovers around "a sick fall'n beast" (*K. John*, IV.iii.153) or over a doomed army (*Julius Caesar*, V.i.85). Poole, in *The English Parnassus* mentioned that,

> *The om'nous raven with a dismal chear,*
> *Through his hoarse beak of following horror tells,*

and Peele wrote in *David and Bathsabe* of

> *the fatal raven, that in his voice*
> *Carries the dreadful summons of our death.*

In such writers we may trace the development of a trend towards the horrific and fantastic. From the observation of ravens assembling where corpses lie on battlefields imagination passed to the assumption that the birds could predict death and doom, and then to the belief that the raven not only flies "o'er the infected house" (*Othello*, IV.i.21) but that she could, as Marlowe phrased it in *The Jew of Malta*, "shake contagion from her sable wing."

All over Europe, and also in parts of Africa and Asia, a croaking raven portends death. In Britain and elsewhere its call has been held also to foretell or announce other kinds of calamity. Thus Brand quotes from an ancient source the countryman's superstition that,

> *If a raven cry just o'er his head*
> *Some in the towne have lost their maidenhead.*

---

[1]Although the magpie colonised Ireland in the seventeenth century the familiar traditions have not established themselves in the Irish-speaking west—an interesting example of a culture's resistance to intrusive elements. Von Sydow has shown that even where no linguistic barrier exists, traditions in adjoining areas may remain practically uninfluenced by each other for centuries (Cf. p. 165).

A similar belief prevailed in North and South Wales until recently in regard to the persistent screeching of owls (p. 116). Here we have exemplified the procedure by which the folk mind generalises an ominous belief and then particularises it in relation to a different sphere.

We have another curious example of the evolution of folklore in the development of the belief that ravens (and other corvine birds) peck out the eyes of their victims. This tradition, which is mentioned in the book of Proverbs (xxx.17) and by Aristophanes (*Aves*, 582) is based on accurate observation. In the ballad of *The Twa Corbies* one is overhead to say to the other,

> '*Ye'll sit on his white hause-bane,*
> *And I'll pike out his bonny blue een:*
> *Wi' ae lock o' his gowden hair*
> *We'll theek our nest when it grows bare.*'

Writing in a County Bird Report a few years ago an observer recorded without comment two human eyeballs as part of the food of a carrion crow. Bohemian peasants say that as crows pecked out the eyes of St. Lawrence, or according to some, St. Carlo Borromeo, the birds do not dare to roost in the forest from springtime up to St. Lawrence's Day (or, following the other version, St. Bartholomew's Day), but in Wales we find a curious inversion of the tradition. There they say that blind folk who are kind to ravens will regain their sight. It is odd that the raven and diver should both be considered able to cure blindness. Probably the Czecho-Slovak belief that he who eats the hearts of three ravens reduced to ashes will become an unerring shot is also a distorted form of the same tradition—ravens eat eyes and so acquire good sight, therefore by eating ravens' hearts a man acquires the birds' powers of vision and so gains the acuity of vision essential to clever marksmanship. In Northern India it is said that the crow has one eye which it can shift from one socket to the other.

It is a small step from observing a bird to be associated with death, as is the carrion-feeding raven, to connecting it with doom. The complex of ideas may then extend further and the bird be regarded as able to predict events both good and evil. Athene hated the raven because of its powers of augury. In ancient Ireland future events were divined by noticing the calls of ravens. Innumerable other examples of the attribution of oracular powers to corvine birds might be given but one further example will suffice. In the Faeroes an unmarried girl used to go out on Candlemas morning and throw three objects in quick succession at a hooded crow, a stone, a bone, and a piece of turf. If the bird flew to the sea the girl expected her future husband to come over it; if it alighted on a house or farm she would marry a man from that family, but if it remained where it was she would know that her fate would be to remain a spinster. As hooded crows are wary birds the girl would have to be a very bad shot not to gain reassurance.

Through its association with death the raven became connected with ghosts and spirits. King Arthur was said to frequent his favourite haunts in Wales and Cornwall in the guise of a raven, and it was considered unlucky to kill one of these birds. In Cornwall he was also said to take the form of a chough or a puffin. In Scotland there was a saying, "Nae gude ever cam' o' killin' black craws" but this may have arisen from the oracular powers attributed to corvine birds. The Buriats believe that anyone killing a raven will soon die. In Swedish folklore ravens are the ghosts of murdered folk who have not had Christian burial—a belief which carries the implication, which we know to be true, that the bird was revered in heathen times. The raven on the old Danish standard was said to stand erect before a victory but to indicate forthcoming defeat by bowing its head and drooping its wings. Swainson supposed that the threat to naughty West Riding children, that a black raven would take them away, was a reminiscence of the period of the Norse raids. William the Conqueror is depicted on the Bayeux tapestry under a raven banner. In Germany it was believed that ravens were damned souls or the steeds of witches, and in Russia the spirit of a witch was thought to assume the form of a crow. In Pieter Breughel's picture "The Triumph of Death" a raven is shown perched on the horse which is dragging away a waggon load of corpses. In some folktales the devil appears as a raven or crow, sometimes guarding a treasure, or one of these birds is said to act as Satan's messenger. Herodotus (iv.15) tells a strange tale concerning the poet Aristeas. He appeared as a ghost to the Metapontines and told them he had visited them before with Apollo in the form of a crow. So, on the advice of the Pythoness, they erected a statue in his honour.

The raven was the lowest order of initiation in the cult of Mithras and the bird was regarded as the messenger of the sun god. It appears

FIG. 50. Bas-relief in Rome depicting Mithras slaying the bull. The sun and the raven are shown in the left upper corner. (After Cumont, 1899).

in representations of Mithras slaying the bull (Fig. 50, p. 75). During the ceremony in which the migration and purification of the soul after death was represented "some flapped their wings like birds and imitated the cawing of ravens, others roared like lions" (Pseudo-Augustine, *Quaest. Vet. et Nov. Test.* 114). A man masked as a bird—perhaps an eagle rather than a raven—is shown on a Bosnian relief which gives a vivid representation of the communion of initiates (Plate 17, p. 96).[1] If what look like ravens on a priest's sceptre found in a Romano-Celtic temple at Farley Heath are indeed such, we have evidence that the bird had a role in local cults in England (Plate 15, p. 94).

[1]The solar associations of the raven and crow are less important than its associations with death and—due to its being connected with thunder and water-fertility. They also seem to belong to a later phase. However, in Greece as Apollo's bird it was connected with the sun and Chinese legends tell of a three-legged crow of the sun. Aelian's comment (xiii.11) that the hare, a lunar animal, detests the voice of the raven, may be an oblique reference to the latter's solar associations.

Shakespeare, true to the traditions of his time, found no difficulty in treating the raven, which was the symbol of malevolence in some of his plays, as the embodiment of beneficence in others. In *The Winter's Tale* (II.iii.186) Antigonus remarks:

> Come on, poor babe:
> Some powerful spirit instruct the kites and ravens
> To be thy nurses.

In a single scene of *Titus Andronicus* (II.iii.97, 153) the dramatist refers in one context to the "fatal raven" and in another to the saying that "ravens foster forlorn children." This theme of the helpful raven is scriptural and represents the Christian tradition as contrasted with the pagan tradition of the ominous and sometimes diabolical bird. Ravens fed Elijah (I Kings xvii.4,6) and God provides food for them (Job xxxviii. 41; Psalm cxlvii. 9; Luke xii. 24) as Shakespeare reminded his audiences (*A.Y.L.I.* II. iii. 43). These scriptural references inspired a series of legends in which ravens are said to have succoured various saints. However, in the Old Testament the raven has another role—as a symbol of desolation (Isaiah xxxiv. 11), an unclean bird (Lev. i. 15) and Noah's messenger (Gen. viii. 7).

The Biblical account of the Deluge, with its reference to the sending forth of the raven is derived from Babylonian sources (Fig. 51). In

FIG. 51. The raven returning to the ark and the Babylonian Noah leaving. (After Contenau, 1952).

Plate 11. Greek kylix showing Aphrodite riding on a
goose. Attributed to the Pistoxenos Painter (*c.* 460
B.C.). Cf. p. 45 and *Plate 12*. (*British Museum*)

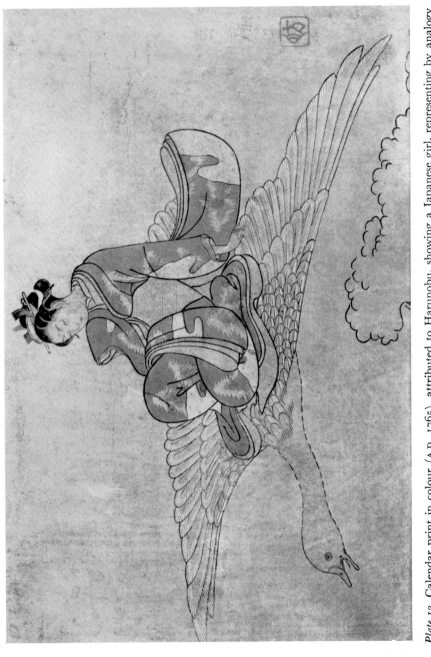

Plate 12. Calendar print in colour (A.D. 1765), attributed to Harunobu, showing a Japanese girl, representing by analogy
a young girl riding on a wild goose. Cf. p. 44. *(British Museum)*

the Akkadian myth the dove, swallow and raven are sent out in turn to discover whether the waters have subsided, but in the account in Genesis, which combines two sources, the raven goes first and does not return. Noah then sends the dove; but not until its third mission does it find dry land and stay away. It has been assumed, as, for example in the fourteenth century manuscript, *Cursor Mundi* that the raven did not return because there were abundant floating carcasses for it to feed on but this realistic explanation takes no account of the bird's supposed supernatural powers and association with storms and rain in many other contexts. On a Babylonian tablet appears the following incantation:

> *A raven, the bird that helpeth the gods,*
> *In my right hand I hold:*
> *A hawk, to flutter in thine evil face*
> *In my left hand I thrust forward.*

Among all Semitic peoples ravens embodied strange powers. In Syriac stories devils driven out of men take the form of these birds, and evil spirits assail saints in the form of "black stinking ravens." The Arabs say they foretell death and disaster. In such places as Timgad in North Africa where the ravens perch on the broken columns of the ruined city it is not difficult to believe that the raven is a sinister bird.

Although little is definitely known of Minoan beliefs the raven perched on the double-axe in the cult scene depicted on the Hagia Triada sarcophagus hints that it was connected with death, and perhaps also, the sun. As elsewhere, it may have been the messenger of the gods or have represented the external soul. (Plate 21, p. 116).[1]

Painters from the Asian mainland evidently went to Crete, and there were other cultural contacts, so Minoan bird traditions were probably modified forms of Asian, and perhaps to some extent also, Egyptian beliefs.

The raven's death associations need no further emphasis. They are primary in importance, and probably also in time, but they should not be allowed to obscure the bird's importance as a messenger.

---

[1] These birds have been identified by some scholars as woodpeckers or cuckoos. Others consider them to be ravens. My own close scrutiny of the original paintings before restoration work was done on them leaves no doubt in my mind that such they are.

Odin's two ravens, Hugin and Munin, flew abroad every day over the whole world to gather news, and returned to whisper what they had learned as they perched on his shoulders, while the two wolves, Geri and Freki, lay at his feet (Plate 20, p. 113). We are reminded of the raven which brought news to Apollo of the unfaithfulness of Koronis (Hesiod, fr. 125 (142) *ap. schol.* Pind. p. 48 (28); Ael. i.47) and of the Irish phrase "raven's knowledge," meaning to see all and know all. In the Hebrides the phrase meant knowing the whereabouts of a dead body and a boy could obtain such insight by drinking out of a raven's skull. In Ireland the raven and the grey crow "tell the truth." The Irish saying is: "The raven told it, the grey crow told it." It is a common remark: "He's in the book of the black raven." According to a Celtic legend ravens carry messages to the enemy but in Tibetan mythology the bird is the messenger of the Supreme Being. Czecho-Slovak children used to be told that crows brought babies. As the baby-bringing stork was once thought to be the gods' messenger, the original belief may have been that children's souls are their gift (Cf. p. 49).

These notions, indicating the raven's close touch with the gods, suggest that the raven may himself have been a god. How could such a divinity be more politely evicted than by making him the ambassador of his supplanters?

Connected with the raven's function as messenger is its ability to speak or understand the language of men, and of men to acquire understanding of its speech. When a Siberian shaman conjures up a spirit it talks in its own language unless it is a wolf, fox or raven, which have human speech. In an Icelandic tale we hear of a bishop who understood raven language. The German legend of Faithful John who overhears three crows talking and is thereby forewarned of three dangers is paralleled in India by the story of Rama and Luxman. The Buriats relate that a man learned how to cure a Khan's daughter by overhearing the conversation of two ravens.

A messenger may also act as a guide, so the raven was believed to lead men to towns and havens. Ravens guided Alexander to the temple of Jupiter Ammon (Plut. *Vita Alex.* c. 27) and led the Boeotians to the site for a new town (Photius s.v. *ès kôrakas*). Pliny states that the mariners of Taprobane (Ceylon) carried birds in their ships and set their course to land by following them. There are allusions to this practice in Indian sources of about the fifth century B.C. The Vikings

FIG. 52. Drawing by a Haida Indian depicting Raven in the whale's belly—an episode in a myth current on both sides of the N. Pacific. (After Niblack, A.P. 1888. *U.S. Nat. Mus. Rep.*).

made use of ravens in this way, as in their discovery of Iceland. The Emperor of Japan is said to have been provided by the sun-goddess with a sun-crow to guide his army.

We shall see presently that belief in the wise raven which serves mankind and acts as a go-between or emissary for gods and men prevailed throughout the greater part of the northern hemisphere, but what evidence is there that he was once a god?

Lug and Odin have so many similarities that we may regard them as having a common origin. As Krappe has shown, they are both talented, masters of many crafts, inventors and orators. Each wields a magic spear. These resemblances are not surprising as the cult of Odin evidently arose among Germanic Rhineland peoples in close touch with the Gauls.[1]

[1]Mythology furnishes so many examples of associations between ravens, the loss of an eye and magical craftsmanship that the possibility suggests itself that the raven's habit of eating eyes may have contributed to this association. Odin was one-eyed. Lug went around an army "on one foot and with one eye" chanting incantations. Tochmarc Étaíne came to Mac Oc with his eye in his hand. One of Setanta's eyes receded into his skull and the other protruded on his cheek. The crow and the hawk quarrelled as to which had plucked out Fintan's eye. The hawk also claimed to have struck out the eye of the dying Cú Chúlainn. Ogmios on Armorican coins is shown with one eye in the middle of his cheek. The Gauls identified Heracles and Ogmios (Lucian, *Herakles*, i). Polyphemos was one-eyed. The Cyclopes were also one-eyed. The custom of smiths to wear a shade over one eye to keep off flying sparks may have had an influence on these notions; so also may fears concerning the evil eye. The Cailleach had an eye in the middle of her forehead and "Black Annis" was one-eyed.

FIG. 53. Chinese bronze vessel in the shape of an owl. A conventionalised face is represented on the bird's breast. Probably Shang dynasty. (After Hentze, 1941).

FIG. 54. Chinese bronze vessel of the Shang dynasty. A human figure is shown apparently within the monster. (After Hentze, 1941).

FIG. 55. Shamanistic bronze figure from the Ischimka graves, Perm culture, Siberia. Apparently it illustrates a form of the Bear-Mother myth, known on both sides of the Pacific. (After Rostovtsev, M.I., 1922. Iranians and Greeks).

As evidence that Lug was a supernatural being, regarded as a god, it may be noted that Pseudo-Plutarch (*De fluv.* v) tells us that Lyons (Lugdunum) was named after him. A crow appears on the city's coat of arms. Leyden and Louvain are also said to owe their names to this Celtic divinity. In the Irish sagas Lug is the father of the hero Cú Chúlainn on whose shoulder perched a scald crow as he perished defying his enemies (Plate 20, p. 113). Now, according to MacNeill, he survives in fireside tales as Lugh-chroman (Lugh-cherpan—Luprachan), the fairy craftsman, "little stooping Lugh."

Lug appears in a myth which has every appearance of being very ancient. He transformed himself into an insect which flew around and eventually fell into the cup of Dechtire, the sister of King Conchobar. As a result of swallowing the creature she gave birth to a child who grew with miraculous rapidity and was indeed Lug *redivivus* (p. 52). It is also related that when Étaíne became the wife of Midir, his first wife Fuamnach turned Étaíne into a pool of water, which became a worm, from which Étaíne emerged as a large and beautiful purple fly. Oengus rescued her but Fuamnach stirred up a great wind which blew her around until at last she came to rest on the roof of an Ulstef house and fell into Étar's cup. She was reborn as Étaíne, daughter or

FOB—G

Étar, after her birth as the daughter of the fairy Ailill. Later in the narrative we have the episode to which reference was made earlier in which Étaine and Midir fly off as swans (p. 50). This tale apparently has affinities with the motif Hiding from the Devil (Aa 329; D 641) in which the hero conceals himself first in a raven's egg, then in a fish and finally turns into an insect. There are North American myths of a similar character. According to one of these the raven knew a chief who possessed the sun, so he transformed himself into a pine needle and fell into a well where the chief's eldest daughter drew water. Changing next into a raspberry he was swallowed by the girl. She, too, gave birth to a miraculously growing son who eventually possessed himself of the box containing the sun. When he opened it the sun escaped. (We are reminded of Pandora). In another Siwash version a maiden swallows a leaf while drinking from a stream. The miraculous child she bears opens a box in which the tribe keeps the sun and moon. He tosses them up into the sky and, in order to escape the wrath of the tribe, changes into a raven.

Strong confirmation that the Celtic and North American tales are variants of a story which was carried across the northern hemisphere is furnished by the occurrence among the Chukchee in Siberia of a similar myth in which the child which results from the swallowing of a leaf is none other than the Raven. The Koryak describe the swallowing of the sun by Raven and its rescue by Big Raven's daughter. To complete these stories of miraculous swallowings in which Raven is involved it may be mentioned that tales describing the swallowing of Raven by a whale and his subsequent escape are found on both sides of Bering Strait (Fig. 52, p. 79).

The evidence that techniques of making objects of stone and metal travelled across Eurasia to America is now very strong. A design showing a human face or figure on a bird's or beast's breast (Figs. 53, 54 and 55; Plate 23, p. 124) which is known from Russia, China and among Kwakiutl Indians of the American North Pacific coast suggests either the merging of identity of bird and man such as occurs in raven myths or the bird's activity as a protective genius. Few artistic motifs have a more notable history and extensive distribution than the snake-bearing bird which has already been mentioned (p. 37). It is found in ancient China with other motifs evolved in the Middle East and in the Americas, Polynesia and New Zealand—where snakes are absent (Fig. 73, p. 121). The Master of Animals motif, in which a

Plate 13. Ivory engraving representing a woman and a goose found at Begram, Afghanistan (*c.* 3rd century A.D.). The works of art discovered during excavations at Begram show classical influence through contacts with Roman culture. Cf. p. 44 and *Plate 14.* (*Musée Guimet*)

Plate 14. Etruscan mirror representing Aphrodite and the goose, Athene and the Dioskuroi. Cf. pp. 47, 60, 120. (*Fitzwilliam Museum, Cambridge*)

figure grasps creatures of the same species in either hand (Figs. 56, 57 and 58, pp. 84 and 85) is widespread and the design of a personage between two beast- or bird-headed figures (Figs. 21 and 22, p. 20) also occurs over an enormous area, including Polynesia. A conventionalised bird of prey with strongly recurved beak is also found across Eurasia from England to China (Plate 7, p. 64; Figs. 59-64, pp. 86 and 87).

In Celtic legends supernatural beings or men transform themselves into, or are regarded as, ravens. The war-goddess, the Badb Catha "Raven of Battle" appeared to Cú Chúlainn; the Morrigu, goddess of slaughter and queen of demons alighted in the guise of a bird beside the Bull of Cuailgne uttering an incantation, and the wife of Tethra, king of the Fomorians was the grey, or scald, crow. These dreadful creatures still linger in Scottish folklore as the Cailleach who may appear as a raven or hooded crow, or even a gull, cormorant or heron. She is a terrible hag who feasts on the bodies of men. The fertility aspect of these ancient goddesses is apparent in the legend told alike of the Morrigu and the Cailleach—each had a cow which gave great quantities of milk. Moreover, the Badb had sexual significance and was associated with childbirth. Cailleach Day is the 25th of March. Until December 1599, this date was New Year's Day. It is now Lady Day. The bloodthirsty goddesses were vanquished but they have not been completely forgotten.

We have already noted the associations of the god Lug with the raven. His cult was, in part, an Earth cult, and in part connected with the Heavens and the powers of Day. Owein's band of fighting ravens, mentioned in the *Mabinogion* may have been a raven clan. Troops of warriors are called "ravens" in Aneurin's *Gododin*. In the tale called *The Begetting of the Swineherds* in *The Book of Leinster* the swineherds spend two years in the shape of ravens. Such references indicate bird totemism or some other form of identification with birds. The indications that the supernatural raven was important in Celtic thought are impressive.

The *Mabinogion* also mentions that Bran's head was buried on Tower Hill to guard London from invasion. Bran means "raven" and Branwen, his sister, was the "white raven". Among the Celts the personal name Brannogenos means "son of the raven." People still take a lively interest in the tame ravens kept in the Tower of London. A letter to *Country Life* in 1955 commented: "There is a vivid tradition that the loss of the Tower ravens would presage Britain's downfall.

During the war there ran around a rumour that for five days no raven had croaked in the Tower, and it is a queer thing that all the six birds are young ones."

The anti-Christian role in which the raven appears in folklore supports the view that in earlier times it was revered and feared. In Languedoc it was believed that wicked priests and nuns became ravens and crows respectively after death and there was a Danish tradition that when a raven appeared in a village it foretold the death of the pastor. The very ancient and widespread legend that the raven was once white but was turned black on account of its wickedness, has received a Christian twist in the Tyrol where the Holy Child is said to have condemned ravens because they fouled the water He was about to drink. In such legends in which Christ condemns or punishes birds, the inconsistency of their themes with the teaching of Him who spoke compassionately of the sparrow is disregarded so long as a compromise is reached between the old and the new, between heathen and Christian ideas. Folk thinking is associationist rather than logical. Like our dream thinking it is careless of contradictions. Probably both types of thinking are therapeutic because in them the lightly buried, partly repudiated, past finds expression.

One further topic with which the raven is closely associated requires mention—the weather. Odin was Hrafnagud, the raven-god, and his son Thor, the thunderer. Odin led the Wild Hunt which raged

FIG. 56. Design from Boeotian Geometric vase depicting a goddess with birds flanked by beasts. (After Nilsson, 1955).

FIG. 57. Ivory found at Laconia, Sparta, believed to represent a primitive goddess such as may have influenced the conception of Artemis. (After Dawkins, R. M., 1905-07. *Brit. School Athens*, 13). Cf. Plate 22, p. 117.

FIG. 58. Carved stone figure holding two birds by their necks at White Island, Lough Erne, N. Ireland. (After Lethbridge, T. C., 1953. *Journ. Royal Anthrop. Inst., 83*).

tempestuously through the night sky (p. 221). Aratus (*Phaen.* 963-969), Theophrastus (*Sign.* vi.16) and other Greek writers mention the raven as foretelling storms. Antigonus Carystus (*Hist. mir.* 15) states that at Krannon in Thessaly there were two ravens and never more. This is based on observation, for, as Pliny (x.15) noted, ravens are strongly territorial, but the Krannon birds had a ceremonial significance. Fourth century coins show two birds on a cart which contained a jar of water and had pieces of metal hanging from it. When it was jolted it simulated a miniature thunderstorm (Figs. 65 and 66, p. 88). Related beliefs prevailed elsewhere. In Pedasa in Caria two such birds lived in the temple of Zeus (Arist. *Mirab.* 844b 8). We also hear of pairs of ravens in Egypt (Aelian, vii. 18) and, according to Ktesias, in Ecbatana and Persia. The thunder cart at Krannon had a parallel in China under the Han

FIG. 59. Bird Design from Seven Brothers Grave. Compare the bird on the Sutton Hoo purse, Plate 7. (After Rostovstev, 1922).

FIG. 60. Design from a Chinese bronze vessel in the style of the West Chou dynasty. (After Hentze, 1941).

dynasty. The Genius of Thunder was represented holding a hammer and mounted on a cart furnished with two or four drums which were beaten. According to a Chinese legend a raven flies through the woods causing a storm and so warning creatures that the gods are about to ride past. They should go to their homes and not pry into the secrets of supernatural beings. So in days gone by the people shut themselves

FIG. 61. Eagle on proto-Corinthian lékythos of early 7th. century B.C. It is accompanied by sun-symbols. (After Cook, 1940, Fig. 893).

FIG. 62. Eagle from Melgunov's Barrow, Lower Dnieper. Scythic style. (After Minns, E. H., 1942. Art of the Northern Nomads. *Proc. Brit. Acad.*).

FIG. 63. Bird of prey depicted on bronze die. Garchinovo, Bulgaria (c. 500 B.C.). (After Minns, 1942).

FIG. 64. Chinese mask with representations of heads of birds of prey as eyepieces. (After Salmony, 1928).

in their houses when the Emperor went in ceremonial procession to sacrifice.

The numerous legends which connect the raven with water are evidently derived from its association with storms and rain. We hear of its being sent by Apollo to fetch water, and being condemned to everlasting thirst for loitering on the way to eat ripening figs (Hyginus, *P. Astr.* xl; Paus. ii.26.6). The crow was called *ombrophorus* because of the belief that its calling portended rain. There is a European belief, derived from classical sources, that rain is imminent when crows stalk at dusk into water. It must be quite unusual for crows to behave in this way, and apparently we have here an instance of natural facts being forced to conform to folklore traditions (Cf. pp. 94 and 198). The fable of the thirsty crow, which obtained a drink by dropping pebbles into a pitcher, also belongs to this circle of ideas. In an Indian legend

FIG. 65. Coin of Krannon (4th. century B.C.) showing a raven perched on the rain-making cart. (After Cook, 1925).

FIG. 66. Coin of Krannon (4th. century B.C.) showing a pair of ravens on the rain-making cart. (After Cook, 1925).

the crow announces to a thirsty prince where water is to be found. Among the Koryak it is said that the culture hero Big Raven and his son were obliged to change themselves into ravens and fly up to heaven, and, by a stratagem, stop the incessant rain pouring down from Universe's wife's vulva—a tale which seems to be a variant of the myth that Thor threw a rock to block the vulva of a giantess. This story must only be told when it is necessary to put an end to rain or a snow-storm. Like many other primitive myths it is supposed to have positive, creative value. So fishermen who whistle for the wind carry on a tradition from a time when seafarers believed that they made the wind by whistling. The association between ravens or crows and rain continues across Asia into the New World. As Odin stole the mead and escaped in the form of a bird so the Amerindian culture-hero Yetl assumed the shape of a raven when he stole fresh water, and tried to escape with it. From being white he became black, but he managed to fly to earth and disgorge the water to form rivers and lakes. Later we shall hear how the woodpecker's plumage was changed because it refused to help in this way (p. 96).

It should be noted that the roles of the raven and eagle tend to overlap or become confused, as if in certain areas one or other had become pre-eminent and when cultures came into contact accommodation had to be reached between them. At Delphi the pair of eagles represented perching on the *omphalos* seem to have been supplanted by Apollo's ravens. In Siberia and North America the thunderbird is sometimes identified with the eagle or some eagle-like gigantic bird and sometimes with the raven. Both have been widely regarded as solar birds, but with the eagle this symbolism is primary (Cf. p. 126), while so far as the raven is concerned it seems to be secondary as the raven is more a storm bird than a sun bird. Nevertheless, the raven (or crow) is a solar bird in China, Japan, N.E. Asia and N.W. America. Though the fame of both birds is widespread, the eagle was most honoured in sunlit southern regions, the raven in the stormy north.

The *locus classicus* of the raven's association with rainstorms is, of course, in the narrative of the Flood. Here it also figures as a messenger, and in a sense, an oracle, so the ancient Middle Eastern Flood myths may be regarded as containing in essence much that appears in modified form in the legends we have been considering. We must therefore discuss whether stories concerning Creation and the Flood from other parts of the world show any indications of having been derived at some remote time from these Babylonian myths. It does not seem very likely that people in widely separated parts of the world should independently manufacture tales in which the raven is associated with a Flood, so that if these two elements are found in association we may suspect the diffusion of the myth.

The Mandan Indians of North America performed regular cere-monies in connexion with a wooden structure, a kind of sacred tub, which represented the canoe in which the only man who escaped the Flood saved himself. The officiant who impersonated him wore a robe of white wolf skins and a head-dress of two ravens' skins. The extent to which these ceremonies were integrated with the social life of the people renders it impossible to believe that they were due to Christian influence. The extensive Algonquin group of Red Indian tribes relate a myth (which was recorded in 1634) describing how, when Michabo, the sun, was hunting with wolves acting as his dogs he disappeared into a great lake. As he entered the water the lake overflowed and inun-dated the world. At Michabo's bidding the raven went to find some earth to remake the land but returned with the news that none was to be found. The otter tried but also failed. Then the musk-rat was sent, and with the mud which it brought Michabo re-made the earth. His offspring by union with the musk-rat peopled the world. The Hare Indians say that the raven caused the deluge in order to punish Wise Man who threw him on the fire. The raven appears in other such myths in America, as in the creation story of the Loucheux Indians of Alaska, and the Kwakiutl legend which tells of Raven's activity after the Flood in showing how to obtain water by chewing wood and digging. Like Lug their raven is a culture hero.

Returning to Eurasia, the Voguls associate the raven with divers in the making of the world. They say that while the white-billed and red-throated divers toiled to bring up mud the raven flew around, returning at progressively longer intervals. As Dähnhardt points out this myth has a North American counterpart (A 812). The version of the Vogul myth quoted by this writer combines Creation and Deluge legends. The raven's rôle is to estimate and report on the increasing size of the emerging earth. As a punishment for feeding on corpses it is condemned to change its white plumage to black. It is very significant that motifs such as this not only occur in Eurasia and America but in the same place in the tales. In another tale from southern Siberia quoted by Dähnhardt, we hear of God and a man in the form of black geese flying over the watery waste. At God's command the man dives for mud, with which God makes the earth, but later the man dives again and returns with some mud in his hand which he gives to God, but retains some in his mouth, intending to become a creator himself. He nearly stifles, but God saves him and he spits out the mud to form mountains. A variant comes from Latvia. There, the devil, who lives in the water, dives for mud and spits it out to form mountains. In the northern myths the rôle of birds tends to diminish as we come westwards. In other words, anthropomorphisation seems to have advanced further in the west.

The emphasis on the raven as a culture-hero or as active in some related capacity alike in Siberia and North America constitutes a strong argument for the diffusion of culture across Bering Strait, and, indeed, for a homogeneous cult around the northern latitudes. Although the culture stream set mainly eastwards there are indications of some movements in the reverse direction. Thus we find a culture hero called Raven or Big Raven figuring in North American legends. The Kamchadal said that Raven left them to go to the Koryak and Chukchee, but the Koryak stated that Big Raven came to them from the east across the sea and went away again. We could hardly be told more plainly that this lore had been passed from tribe to tribe. Moreover, that Big Raven should be for the Koryak an emissary of the Supreme Being to carry out reforms while the raven itself figures in their legends as a droll and despicable character suggests two layers of tradition. It seems as if the anthropomorphisation of the raven may have proceeded more quickly in America than in northern Asia and that a cultural backwash influenced northeast Siberia. Thus, working from North America eastwards, we find the Amerindian raven humanised to a considerable extent and possessing great supernatural powers as a culture hero, then in north-east Siberia concepts influenced by such ideas. In other northern Asian myths birds are concerned to some extent with the work of creation, which involves bringing earth out of the waters, but as we have seen, further west a man or the devil more frequently takes the place of the bird. The southern Siberian version shows us what appears to be a kind of a compromise in which black geese merely fly over the waters, just as in the Vogul legend the raven plays a secondary rôle. We get the impression that in earlier forms of these stories birds may have been more prominent. It has been suggested that the non-dualistic forms of this myth in America may be the earliest and that the dualistic variants date from the early centuries of our era.

A great mass of evidence ranging from Palaeolithic art to the aetiology of mythology suggests that animal or theriomorphic gods preceded anthropomorphic gods; or to put it more accurately, that man thought of supernatural powers in terms of animal qualities before he pictured God in his own image. Therefore Creation and Deluge myths in which animals are creators or co-creators are probably earlier than those in which anthropomorphic powers are concerned. The accounts of Creation in Genesis are more sophisticated than the Babylonian myth in which it is recorded that Tiamat, the personification of watery chaos, was cut in two, the one half being stretched across the sky and the other under the earth and sea. But this story, too, is patently the result of priestly reflection and syncretism. The creation myths in which an animal brings earth from the water approximate much more closely to the kind of explanation which would occur to primitive folk, for it involves merely the extrapolation of the observed behaviour of animals to cosmic dimensions. Abstract notions were alien to early man and his myth-making was pedestrian, mainly consisting of association thinking in which cause and effect were often incorrectly linked.

If, then, we are correct in regarding myths involving an animal creator as earlier than those in which anthropomorphic divinities appear, the Babylonian and Hebrew Deluge myths may conceal an early Creation myth; the birds sent out over the waste of waters may be the wraiths of those which in earlier legends were active in creating land. It will have been noticed that the mud-fetching bird myths presuppose a primordial lake. In the version of the Babylonian myth, which we owe to Berossus, priest of Bel, we are told that the birds sent out returned with mud on their feet, as do some of the birds in Creation myths. The olive branch brought by the dove would seem to be a modification of this detail; similarly the muddy feet of the reconnoitring birds may be a reminiscence of a bird which brought mud to create land. The sending forth of the birds in turn is perhaps a vestige of an earlier form of the story in which, as in so many creation myths, animals were commissioned to fetch land, not merely to find it. Thus in the Middle East the raven may have been a coadjutor in the work of creation.

Babylonian cosmology originated at Eridu, the seaport on the Persian gulf where silt piled up rapidly. Thus the belief was formulated that by an increase of the amount of mud on a great scale, the world had arisen. To connect increasing land with the activities of living creatures in bringing material from the water would be very natural, especially where multitudes of birds gathered to feed on the mud-flats and in the shallows. We must suppose that with the development of priesthoods and cults which accompanied the rise of town life in this region, and the syncretism in religious ideas characteristic of the changing relationships between city states, this myth was greatly modified. Some inundation such as is known to have occurred at Ur may have stimulated the elaboration of the Deluge myth, and the prominence of the raven in the story may be due to influence from the north rather than from the coast. If we postulate the simple mud-fetching form of the myth diffusing outwards in northerly and easterly directions among people having great regard for animals as super-natural beings, and then being followed and supplemented in many areas by a more elaborate version, practically all the facts can be explained. The main routes of this diffusion have already been out-lined by Dähnhardt.

This discussion has revealed evidence that the raven was a com-ponent in a very early magico-religious culture-complex which ex-tended from Ireland to Kamchatka and beyond into a great area of North America. With the data considered in previous chapters it confirms the existence in northern Eurasia of a cult which was dominated by beliefs about animals. These beliefs are just such as we should expect to emerge from Palaeolithic man's relationship to the animal world. Raven mythology shows considerable homogeneity throughout the whole area in spite of differences in detail. The raven peeps forth from the mists of time and the thickets of mythology as a bird of slaughter, a storm bird, a sun and fire bird, a messenger, an oracular figure and a craftsman or culture hero. First, perhaps, it achieved prominence as a death bird, then as a storm and rain bird it became associated with creation and deluge. With the anthropomorphisation of supernatural powers and the invention of more elaborate tool- and weapon-making techniques men thought of it as an artificer and messenger of the gods.

In tracing the history of the raven we have seen how folklore grows and decays. How are the mighty fallen! Yet the activities of the Tower ravens are still regarded as indicative of the prosperity of the realm, and the fairy shoemaker of the poets, the Leprachaun whose gold turns to withered leaves, lives on in literature and legend. Eyes sparkle at the *céilidhe* or in the nursery as his tricks are told. Great Lug, the crow or raven god, is not entirely forgotten and more of the past survives than we realise. Many thousands of years after a painter at Lascaux depicted a bird—possibly a crow or raven—beside a dying hunter a statue representing another dying hero with a similar bird on his shoulder was erected to commemorate those executed in the Irish rebellion of Easter Week 1916 (Plate 20, p. 113).

CHAPTER 6

THE THUNDERBIRD

IT is still fairly generally believed in England that frequent calling by
the green woodpecker is a sign of coming rain. Swainson comments:
"The constant iteration of its cry before rain (which brings out the
insects on which it feeds) gives it the name of Rain bird; Rain pie;
Rain fowl." The parenthesis is an interesting example of arguing from
folklore to fact and falling into the snare of an *ex post facto* explanation.
The underlying assumptions are: Since a belief is widespread it must
be true; since it is true the facts must be so-and-so. Thus it is inferred
that increased calling by the woodpecker precedes rain, that the bird
vocally announces an anticipated plenitude of food and that rain does
"bring out the insects on which it feeds." These beliefs are all unsound.
Observation indicates that there is no correlation between the green
woodpecker's volubility and rainfall, nor does an imminent downpour
attract wood-boring insects, ants or larvae to the surface; and to
imagine that the woodpecker yaffles in anticipation of abundant food
is to think in anthropomorphic terms which students of animal
behaviour have shown to be mistaken.

Despite the lack of foundation for the belief that the woodpecker's
calling foretells wet weather credence is, or has been, given to it
throughout most of Europe. Aubrey wrote that they were "much
esteemed by the Druides for divination" and remarked: "To this day
the country-people doe divine of raine by their cry." In many
languages the woodpecker is called the equivalent of "Rain bird."
Two of its Welsh names imply that it foretells storms. In Shropshire
it is the "Storm cock," in France *pic de la pluie, pleu-pleu* or *le procureur du
meunier.*" The latter nickname is based on the notion that it pleads for
rain as ardently as the owner of a watermill in time of drought. In
Germany it is called *Giessvogel*, and in Austria and the Tyrol *Gissvogel*
and *Regen Vogel*. The Danes name it *Regnkrake* or Rain Crow. In

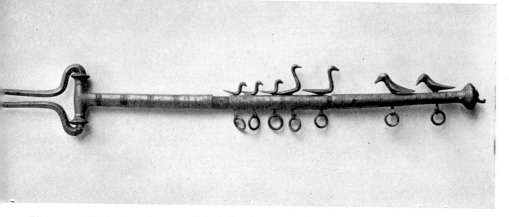

Plate 15. a. Shaft-mounting, possibly belonging to a goad, found at Dunaverney, Co. Antrim. The decorations of anserine and other birds are in Hallstatt style. Cf. p. 48. (*British Museum*)

b. Embossed bronze binding strip from a priest's sceptre found in a Romano-British temple at Farley Heath, Surrey. The birds have been supposed to be wrens but are probably ravens. The symbols are connected with the cult of Jupiter-Toranis and related cults. Cf. p. 75. (*British Museum*)

Plate 16. a. Wooden swans erected on poles above a platform on which a reindeer had been sacrificed by Reindeer Tungus. N.W. Manchuria. Cf. pp. 14, 49, 112. (*E. J. Lindgren-Utsi*)

b. Wooden fish placed beneath a sacrificial platform close to the swan-poles in the companion picture. Similar wooden fish are carved by Indians on the North-West coast of America. Cf. pp. 49, 112. (*E. J. Lindgren-Utsi*)

North America, on Vancouver Island, the Indians call the pileated woodpecker the Rain Bird.

Couplets in various languages also proclaim the woodpecker's qualities as a forecaster of bad weather. In France they quote,

> Lorsque le pivert crie
> Il annonce la pluie.

The Milanese used to say,

> Quand el picozz picozza
> O che l'e vent, o che l'e gozza.

As we shall see, it is interesting that in Italy, as this proverb indicates, it is "when the pecker pecks" rather than calls, that storm or rain follows.

The woodpecker's close association with rain also appears in legends right across Europe. This story is told in the Gironde: At the beginning of things, when God had finished creating the earth, He ordered the birds to excavate with their beaks the hollows that were destined when filled with water, to become seas, rivers and pools. All obeyed except the woodpecker, who, in sullen obstinacy sat still and refused to move. What was the result? Why, that when all was completed the good God declared that as she was unwilling to peck up the earth, her lot should be to be ever pecking at wood; and moreover, that, as she had nothing to do with making the cavities in which water was to be stored, she should drink nothing but rain and get that as she could. Hence it is that the wretched bird is ever calling to the clouds "Plui-plui," and that she always keeps an upward, climbing posture, in order to receive in her open beak the drops which fall from the sky.[1]

A German tale relates that the cock woodpecker was cursed because he refused to soil his beautiful raiment digging a well as God commanded; he was forbidden to drink, from a pond and must ever call *giet, giet* (*giess, giess*) for rain.

In Esthonia another version is current: When God had finished the heavens and the earth, He ordered the birds and beasts to set to work and excavate a vast ravine (the Embach, near Dorpat). All

---

[1] In Russia a somewhat similar story is told of the lapwing.

obeyed except the woodpecker, who flew lazily from bough to bough piping her song. Thereupon the Almighty asked her, "Hast thou nothing else to do but show off thy fine raiment and give thyself airs?" The bird replied, "The work is dirty. I cannot discard my bright golden coat and shining silver hose." "O vain creature!" cried the Lord, "Henceforth thou shalt wear naught but a garment of sooty black, neither shalt thou quench thy thirst from brook or stream. Raindrops falling from the sky shall be thy drink and thy voice shall only be heard when other creatures are hiding themselves through fear of the approaching storm."

Leaving aside, for the moment, our discussion of the woodpecker as rain-bird, we notice that these legends bring it into association with the manifold myths found practically all over the world, examples of which were cited in the previous chapter, describing how birds or beasts helped in some way with the work of creation. As we noted then, these stories of animals with superhuman powers hark back to very ancient beliefs. It is not surprising that birds should figure prominently in these myths, for in early times men must have noticed that they were more competent than themselves in manipulating material. Even today, with all our technical ability we marvel at the dexterity with which weaverbirds, tailorbirds, and even such common European species as the chaffinch and long-tailed tit, weave their nests. Perhaps man's first attempts at basket-making were in imitation of the nests he robbed. (In a Stone Age painting of a man robbing a bee's nest he appears to be carrying a basket). Early pottery—basket-work reinforced with clay—may also have been inspired by the finding of birds' nests approximating to this type.

In these narratives the reluctance of the woodpecker to dig is of interest. This feature, and the reference to its dark plumage in some of the stories, suggest that the great black woodpecker is the villain, and not the green woodpecker. The black woodpecker frequently digs when seeking ants. As we shall see, the green woodpecker is associated with ploughing in some myths. Thus when the woodpecker appears in mythology one or other of these birds, or a generalised woodpecker may be denoted.

In these tales the woodpecker acts contrary to the commands of the Almighty. It behaves like, and is treated as, one who defied God, or even as an ousted divinity. We have support for this in a Mongol tale describing how Moses, whose servant the bird was, punished it for

Plate 17. a. **Panel of the Franks casket** (*c.* A.D. 700) with scenes of the Adoration of the Magi and Wayland the Smith, surrounded by runic inscriptions. On the left Wayland is seen at work and his brother Egil is seizing birds to provide wings for Wayland. Cf. p. 57. (*British Museum*)

b. **Relief representing a Mithraic ritual banquet.** Konjica, Yugoslavia. On either side are masked participants, the figure on the right representing a lion, the figure on the left a raven or, more probably, an eagle. Cf. p. 75 (*Warburg and Courtauld Institutes*)

Plate 18. a. Human skull from a grave at Ipiutak, Alaska. Ivory eyes with jet pupils are inset into the eye-sockets as in the loon's skull in the companion picture. The ivory nose plugs are carved to represent birds' heads. The mouth cover is of ivory. Cf. p. 66. (*American Museum of Natural History*)

b. Loon's skull with inset eyes and other grave furnishings from the prehistoric Arctic Ipiutak culture. *Top:* Antler masks (with cleats) placed over faces at burial. *Centre:* Loon's skull set with ivory eyes and jet pupils. The skull was evidently buried with skin and feathers in place. *Right:* Ivory eyes from human skulls. *Left:* Ivory nose plugs in the shape of birds' heads with inlaid jet eyes. *Bottom:* Ivory cylinder found with loon's skull and mouth covers. Cf. p. 66. (*American Museum of Natural History*)

thieving by forcing it to live on wood. So, too, in a Russian legend, the woodpecker is a man whom God changed into a bird because he worked on Sunday. Christianity evidently superseded beliefs in which the woodpecker held a place of honour. The conflict between the old and new faiths is illustrated in these stories and in the following Norse legend: In the days when our Lord and St. Peter wandered upon earth, they came to the house of an old woman and found her baking. Her name was Gertrude and she had on her head a red mutch. They had walked far and were both hungry, and our Lord begged for a bannock to stay their hunger. "Yes, they should have it"! So she took a very tiny piece of dough and rolled it out; but as she rolled the lump grew until it filled the griddle. "Nay, that is too big; you can't have that." So she took a tinier bit still but when that was rolled out, it covered the whole griddle just the same, and that bannock was too big, she said. They couldn't have that either. The third time she took a still tinier bit; but it was the same story all over again—the bannock was too big. "Well," said Gertrude, "I can't give you anything, you must go without, for all these bannocks are too big!" Then our Lord waxed wroth, and said, "Since you loved me so little as to grudge Me a morsel of food you shall have this punishment. You shall become a bird and seek your food between bark and bole, and never get a drop to drink save when it rains." Hardly had He said the last word when she was turned into a black woodpecker, or "Gertrude's bird" and flew from her kneading trough right up the chimney. And to this very day you may see her flying about, with her red mutch on her head, and her body all black, because of the soot of the chimney; and so she hacks and taps away at the trees for her food, and whistles when rain is coming, for she is ever athirst, and then she looks for a drop of water to cool her tongue." The conclusion of the story seems to carry a reminiscence of the parable of Dives and Lazarus. In Norwegian the woodpecker is *Gjertrusfugl* and in Swedish *Gjertrudsfugl*. If Rendell Harris is correct St. Gertrude took over some of the functions of Freya who, in his opinion, was a rain goddess.

A similar story is told in North Wales. Christ, having walked a long way, was very tired and asked a woman for food and water, but she refused and was thereupon condemned "to feed of the stuff to be found between wood and the bark of the tree" and to drink only when it rained. When Ophelia crazily remarked "They say the owl was a baker's daughter" (*Hamlet*, IV.v.41) it was a variant of this tale that she,

FOB—H

or rather Shakespeare, had in mind. The legend is also told of the cuckoo (p. 209).

If, as these stories confirm, the woodpecker was revered in pre-Christian times, the question arises, what kind of being was it supposed to be? In discussing this problem it will be convenient to begin with a consideration of the evidence from northern Europe.

Harris pointed out that the name Pikker or Pikné, the title of the son of thunder who appears in Finnish and Esthonian fairy tales, is similar to woodpecker names such as *Trepikka* in Norway, *pic* in France, *Specht* in Germany, and *Pickatree* in Yorkshire. In these stories Pikker uses bagpipes as his weapon. In one of them, the thunderclap, in the shape of the bagpipes, is stolen, and no rain falls on the earth. When the thunder instrument is sounded there is a downpour of rain. Apparently the bagpipes were used in rain ceremonies. their music being considered an imitation of the wind and thunder. Etymological similarities being notoriously deceptive the connexion between Pikker and the folk names of the woodpecker must be regarded as speculative. A document which has been quoted in this connexion has been shown to be suspect. It is the prayer of an old Esthonian farmer which appears in Johann Gutslelf's *Kurtzem Bericht* published in 1644: "Beloved Pikker, we will sacrifice to thee an ox with two horns and four hoofs, and want to beg you as to our ploughing and sowing that our straw shall be red as copper and our grain as yellow as gold. Send elsewhither all black clouds over great swamps, high woods and wide wastes. But give to us ploughmen and sowers a fertile season and sweet rain." The Esthonian scholar Loorits denies that Pikker was ever a personal god in the mythology of his country. He dismisses him as a poetic creation of Renaissance times. However, it is not impossible that we have a glimpse of the supernatural woodpecker in the Finnish epic, the *Kalevala* (XIV):

> *O Nyrikki, mountain hero,*
> *Son of Tapio of forests,*
> *Hero with the scarlet headgear,*
> *Notches make along the pathway,*
> *Landmarks upward on the mountain,*
> *That the hunter may not wander.*

Thus Tapio's son, the minor wood-god whom Lemminkainen calls on to help him capture the magic elk, wears a red cap like Gertrude in the Norse folk-tale and the woodpecker itself, and blazes a notched path across the forested hills.

The mediaeval German notion that a woodpecker flying to the right is a lucky sign might conceivably be connected with an old belief in the woodpecker as guide. It must have been derived from much older sources for Horace (*C*.iii.27) and Plautus (*Asin*.ii.1.12) mention omens derived from the direction of its flight. The woodpecker was certainly regarded by some folk as an oracular bird endowed with special insight as a guide, for we are told that when the Sabines (or Picentes) migrated to Picenum (Woodpecker Town) it was a woodpecker which led their chieftains (Strabo, V.iv.2), as a wolf guided the Hirpini, and a raven led the Boeotians (p. 78). The name Picenum persisted to commemorate the beneficence of the supernatural woodpecker.

As Gertrude was transformed into a black woodpecker, so Picus, King of Latium, was metamorphosed by Circe in revenge for his refusal to respond to the enchantress's amatory advances (Ovid, *Met*. xiv.320 ff.) (751A). Vergil (*Aen*. vii.187 ff.), describing the interview between the messengers of Aeneas and the aged Latinus in the palace-sanctuary of Laurentian Picus, where successive divine kings had received the sceptre, says: "There sat one, holding the Quirinal staff and girt with a short robe, his left hand bearing the sacred shield—even Picus, tamer of steeds, whom his bride Circe, smitten with love's longings, struck with her golden rod, and with drugs changed into a bird with plumes of dappled hue." Such is the tradition but there is much to suggest that in this and other such tales the transformation is in the reverse direction from the real one. The sacred or supernatural bird which has become humanised is represented as returning to its original form and function. They point to the time when chieftains ruled by virtue of being supposed to possess some bird attributes. Thus many transformation tales have a secondary, more esoteric and deeper significance. They depict the transformation of beliefs as well as of birds and human beings.

Quirinus, Rome's first Augur, was Romulus, one of the twins who were cared for, not only by the she-wolf but also by the woodpecker (*Met*. iii,531) (Fig. 67, p. 100). This type of tradition is very old. Minoan and Mycenaean seals show a child being suckled by a goat and there are many legends of this kind. Wolf children are still believed in though the rearing of an infant by a wolf is biologically impossible.

FIG. 67. Denarius of Sextus Pompeius Faustulus showing Romulus and Remus suckled by the wolf with the woodpecker in the tree above. (After Babelon, E. Traité 2. 336).

But of all creatures to be thought of as caring for an abandoned baby one could hardly find a more incongruous than the woodpecker. Obviously there was some important mythological reason why the woodpecker should have this function attributed to it. Its appearance in the legend is more readily understood when we notice that the lives of the twins, Romulus and Remus, were regarded as being bound up with certain sacred trees. We are told that when the trees were in danger the woodpecker and the wolf came to the rescue (Ovid, *Fasti*, iii.37). So behind the façade of the classical legends we catch a glimpse of the divine king in the sacred grove guarded by the oracular woodpecker.

Dionysios of Halicarnassus (*Antiq.* I.14) viewing Roman manners through Greek eyes and remarking on customs which might not have attracted the attention of a Latin, gives us an important piece of information supporting this reconstruction: "Three hundred stadia further (in the country of the Appenines) is Tiora, called Matiene. Here there is said to have been an oracle of Mars of great antiquity. It is reported to have been similar in character to the fabled oracle at Dodona, except that, whereas at Dodona it was said that a dove perched on a sacred oak gave oracles, among the aborigines the oracles were given in like fashion by a god-sent bird called by them Picus (the Greeks name it Dryokolaptes), which appears on a wooden pillar."

The god-sent woodpecker in the ancient sacred grove seems to belong to the same tradition as the bird which guarded Romulus and Remus. It was probably not unique though we have no means of knowing exactly how widespread was the woodpecker cult. In addition to the vestiges in Europe which we are considering the bird is worshipped by the Ostyaks, Voguls and Ainu. In India the woodpecker was one of the victims at the horse sacrifice and, as the Romans regarded the bird as a transformed king so in Indian legend he is a Raja who lost his throne. However, we cannot be quite sure that all these beliefs and customs sprang from a common root.

Dionysios' comparison of Tiora with Dodona is interesting. At both we have the sacred bird perched on the sacred tree. At Dodona the divine king is Zeus, at Tiora Matiene he is Mars. So tenacious is tradition that in the village of Monterubbiano in the Abruzzi there is still celebrated a strange ancient ceremony which is undoubtedly a survival of the cult of the oracular woodpecker at Tiora Matiene.

We have pictorial as well as literary evidence of the importance of the woodpecker among the Romans. On a denarius of Sextus Pompeius Faustulus, we see the wolf feeding the twins and two woodpeckers perched on the sacred fig tree (*Ficus ruminalis*). An engraved carnelian preserved in Corpus Christi college, Cambridge, depicts a warrior consulting the oracular woodpecker of Mars on a post or pillar up which a serpent climbs (Figs. 68–69, pp. 100, 102). Ovid refers to the woodpecker perched, not on a pole or tree, but on a young man's head (*Fasti*, 312 ff.). (This motif, a bird perched on a head is frequent in ancient art). Thus there is ample proof of Plutarch's remark that the woodpecker was specially honoured and worshipped by the Romans.

The association between the woodpecker and Mars is very ancient. There is a reference to *Piquier Martier* in an Umbrian inscription. The bird and the god are still linked in the scientific name of the black woodpecker, *Picus martius* and one of its French names, *grande marte*. Probably because of an etymological misunderstanding it is called

FIG. 68. An engraved carnelian at Corpus Christi College, Cambridge showing a warrior consulting the woodpecker of Mars at Tiora Matiene. (After Cook, 1925).

St. Martin's bird in France. Mars was the father of Romulus and Remus by the Vestal Virgin Rhea Silvia. No doubt the association goes back to the time when Mars was an agricultural deity. Cato (*de Agri. cult.* 141) quotes a farmer's prayer addressed to him at the lustration of the fields. The connexion which exists between war gods and rain gods may be due to the thunderstorm being viewed ambivalently as destructive and also as the bringer of the fertilising rain.

Professor Pollard, who thinks the rôle of the woodpecker in antiquity

FIG. 69. Carnelian in Berlin Museum depicting a warrior at the shrine of Mars with a woodpecker perched on the sacred pillar and a ram sacrificed beneath. (After Harrison, 1927).

has been greatly exaggerated admits that it was held to be a prophet of rain, as Jane Harrison had pointed out, but concludes that "Picus belonged to folklore rather than cult." This is doing less than justice to the facts and is based on the assumption that folklore of the kind we are considering is not, as this work is concerned to emphasize, cult in decay. The Latin evidence alone is sufficient to show that wood-pecker beliefs were once serious and important.

The evidence for a woodpecker cult in Greece is rather scanty and equivocal but in Aristophanes' *Birds* (480-485; Cf. 979) we find Euelpides declaring,

Zeus won't in a hurry the sceptre restore to the woodpecker tapping the oak.
In times prehistoric 'tis easily proved, by evidence weighty and ample,
That Birds and not Gods were the rulers of men, and the lords of the
  world, for example
Time was that the Persians were ruled by a cock a king autocratic, alone;
The sceptre he wielded or ever the names, Megabazus, Darius, were known;
And the Persian he still by the people is called, from the Empire that once
  was his own.

This is dismissed by Pollard as a reference "to some legend about Zeus and the woodpecker." After discussing the allusions in Greek to a number of birds, he concludes, that there is "no reason to suppose the references to the woodpecker, cuckoo and cock were intended to be anything more than mere fairy tales."

Aristophanes' allusion to the woodpecker was such as could be understood by the crowd and evidently referred to a current tradition. Even sophisticated Athenians cannot be supposed to have concocted, purely from imagination, a fantastic fairy tale about the chief deity in their pantheon having once been a woodpecker. This would have some plausibility only if there were no evidence elsewhere of the bird having in some sense "wielded the sceptre." On the contrary, as we have seen, the woodpecker emerges as something more than a weather prophet wherever ancient beliefs about it are preserved. If the Athenians showed their reverence for kites by bowing to them, as Aristophanes' play shows, it is more than a possibility that there were still reminiscences of a time when the woodpecker was given greater honour.

Antoninus Liberalis tells a queer story which he picked up in the

Ornithogonia of Boeus (Boios), who at an early date had been priestess of Apollo at Delphi. It is a Cretan tradition of the visit of Keleos ("green woodpecker") with three companions to the sacred birth-cave of Zeus with the intention of stealing the honey which nourished the infant god. As Themis and the Fates prevented Zeus from striking the intruders dead he turned Keleos into a green woodpecker. This tale is obviously very old. It has been discussed by several writers but we need only ask, Why, when Zeus might have vented his anger in so many other ways should he punish bold Keleos by turning him into a green woodpecker? There must be some mythological reason for this. It may well be that Zeus regarded the bird, so closely connected with Zeus' special tree, the oak, as a pretender to his authority.[1]

Who was Keleos? According to the Athenians he was the father of Triptolemos. He, in turn, was the Inventor of the Plough and the First Ploughman. The *Hymn to Demeter* tells us that he was a king or chief whom Demeter instructed in mystic rites in order to procure the fertility of the soil. Apparently he was named after the three furrows traced in the holy field to initiate the annual ploughing. Anybody who had closely observed the green woodpecker searching for ants, which it does more frequently than any of our other woodpeckers, thrusting its bill into the earth in similar fashion to the prong of wood which served as share on a primitive plough, would be impressed by the similarity between the action of the bird and the ploughshare. To simple folk the bird's green garb might confirm the inference that it was engaged in fertility magic. The myth tells us in so many words that the bird was regarded as having inspired the invention of the plough. There has been a long association between the activities of hoeing or ploughing Mother Earth and sexual intercourse. The ithyphallic sacrificial victims surrounded by bird-masked men at Addaura, and the bird-headed man at Lascaux (Frontispiece and Plate 4, p. 33) suggest that from the Old Stone Age birds have been thought of in connection with reproduction as well as death.

The view that the woodpecker's activities inspired its association with ploughing is supported by a story told by the Lettish folk of Polish

[1]Perhaps we may find recorded in this legend the information that when forest-dwelling people moved away from the oak woods and established sacred places in the mountains, the woodpecker, dweller in tree cavities, lost much of its dignity, but the bees, which can nest in rock crevices as well as tree trunks, retained their association with the anthropomorphised god, now dwelling in a cave rather than the thunder tree.

Livland. "Once upon a time God and the Devil were good fellows together, and each of them had a field to plough. The Devil was ploughing with horses, but God with a woodpecker. By day's end the Devil had ploughed much ground and God very little; so at night God took the Devil's horses and got his field ploughed. When the Devil saw the result next morning, he said, 'Goodman God, let us change over: you take the horses and give me your woodpecker.' For he thought it would be less trouble to feed a woodpecker than a pair of horses. The exchange being made, the Devil harnessed his woodpecker, who couldn't stir the plough. Enraged, the Devil struck at him and broke his head. So now the woodpecker is dappled and his head is red."

Thus although in the Greek myths only traces of the supernatural woodpecker can be detected these are sufficient to justify the belief that at one time the woodpecker had a place in Greek magico-religious beliefs, or, more exactly, perhaps, in the cultures ancestral to those of which we have detailed records.[1]

Tracing the mystic woodpecker to the remotest epoch preserving in its literature any hint of its presence we find a few slender clues. In Babylonia it was known as "The Axe of Ishtar." Evidently this refers to the green woodpecker for it is described in a syllabary as green. "Pilakku" or "hatchet bird" possibly is woodpecker. In Syriac *palka* is hatchet, and the woodpecker was called "axe-bird" by the Greeks— *pelekas, pelekán, spelektos*. Thus we can identify the bird called after Ishtar with fair certainty as the green woodpecker. There is no other green bird which could so naturally be regarded as an axe-bird. Ishtar was, of course, a fertility goddess tracing her ancestry back to the Palaeolithic female figurines. Like the woodpecker she was a woodlander to the extent that she possessed sacred precincts within a cedar forest. In the ancient Sumerian liturgies which bewail the descent of Tammuz into the underworld a fallen cedar is the symbol of the dead god and on pre-Sargonid seals a figure is seen cutting down a tree on a mountain. We thus learn that there was seasonal ritual originating in the mountains. It cannot have arisen in the plains of Sumer where the

---

[1]Graves, who, in his interpretation of Greek bird myths goes to the opposite extreme from Pollard's scepticism, writes of the myths concerning Io: "Io's Argive priestesses seem to have performed an annual heifer-dance in which they pretended to be driven mad by gad-flies, while woodpecker-men, tapping on oak doors and calling 'Io!' invited the rain to fall and relieve their torments." His methods are imaginative and his bird identifications sometimes incorrect.

only trees are palms. So these early gods originally dwelt in the forests overlooking the Babylonian plain.

The Babylonians and Assyrians did not deify or worship birds in their official ritual but this does not imply that bird cults did not precede such ceremonial and leave their traces in it. Excavations at Nippur some years ago revealed a clay plaque representing a very graceful nude female figure with wings and claws. Like the woodpecker she has a red crown. She is also shown on the plaque depicted on Plate 5, p. 48 and is known to have been an important deity. Most scholars identify her with Lilith, goddess of death. Apparently she belonged to popular rather than official state religion. Often, indeed, domestic religion retains more primitive elements than official cult, as is shown in this area by the worship of the nude goddess in popular cults—a survival from the Old Stone Age.

The traces which the supernatural woodpecker has left in Eurasia are shadowy but significant. All the evidence consistently points to the woodpecker as having been associated with fertility. If the woodpecker cult were ancient we should expect to find exactly what we do—faint traces of this superseded cult mingled with, and largely overlaid by, later sacerdotal, more anthropomorphic forms of worship.

Another strand of woodpecker lore may throw light on the status of the bird in the past. In the second half of the seventeenth century we find John Aubrey writing : "Sir Bennet Hoskins, Baronet, told me that his keeper at his parke at Morehampton in Herefordshire, did for experiment sake, drive an iron nail thwert the hole of the woodpecker's nest, there being a tradition that the damme will bring some leafe to open it. He layed at the bottome of the tree a cleane sheet, and before many houres passed the naile came out and he found a naile lying on the sheete. Quaere the shape or figure of the leafe. They say the moone-wort will doe such things. This experiment may easily be tryed again." Such were the ideas of country gentlemen less than two hundred years ago. These educated men were curious, interested in experimentation, but casual as to method and credulous as to the result. John Ray replied forthrightly: "The story . . . is without doubt a fable," yet this eminent naturalist blamed the death of his daughter from jaundice on the use of new-fangled scientific remedies instead of the old-fashioned cure—beer flavoured with horse manure.

In Germany it was believed that if the entrance to the nest of the

black or green woodpecker were plugged the bird would fetch a sprig
of springwort, a herb not known to men, and hold it in front of the
obstruction which would immediately pop out. To secure the magical
herb you had to place a piece of red cloth beneath the nest. The bird
would mistake it for a fire and let fall the sprig so that it would be
destroyed by the flames. This was the version current in the Mark of
Brandenburg, but in Swabia the story was told of the hoopoe, which is
sometimes confused with the woodpecker, as in the myth of Poly-
technos. It was said that the springwort could be secured either by
kindling a fire, setting a pan of water or spreading a red cloth beneath
the nest. The French version attributes to the plant properties which
endow with superhuman strength whoever rubs his limbs with it. The
bird uses it "to pierce the heart of the largest oak," and sometimes
treasures it in its nest. Winter and summer alike it is covered with dew.
To obtain the herb you must watch the direction of the woodpecker's
flight and when you see it rub its beak on a certain plant you may
congratulate yourself on having found the magical herb. But on no
account must you use an iron tool to uproot it.

What is the significance of this odd group of ideas? A bird which
knows a magical herb capable of opening closed cavities—the piercing
of the oak—fire and water—the colour red and the characteristics of
always being dew-covered? Is there a suggestion here that we are
dealing with a bird connected with the weather and in particular with
the thunderstorm which rends trees, drenches the countryside and is
accompanied by lightning? The caution against using iron to obtain
the herb reminds us of the abhorrence in which fairies hold iron objects
and hints that we are concerned with ideas pre-dating the use of this
metal.

The springwort legend originated in the east. Aelian, Pliny,
Plutarch and other Greek and Latin writers refer to it, and it appears
as the Samir legend in the Arabian nights, the Koran and the Talmud.
The ideas associated with the herb became generalised until it was
believed that it could be used magically to discover secrets and
treasures. D'Arcy Thompson thought that the belief arose from
observations of the hornbill bringing food to its mate in its walled-up
nesting cavity. This would imply that it originated in Africa south of
the Sahara, or in India—for which there is no evidence. It is much
more probable that the story is an elaboration of a common motif in
which a herb is reputed to have magical powers of healing and life-

giving—connected in turn with mythology concerning an elixir or *soma* with supernatural properties.[1]

Many of these herbs, potions and elixirs in ancient folklore were regarded as useful in easing child-birth or relieving impotence. Thus in Anglo-Saxon magical leechcraft we find the following prescription: "If a man is sexually constrained give him springwort to eat." The springwort, like the woodpecker, has fertility-giving properties and thus the plant and bird may have been brought into association.

The oak is the tree split by the springwort-wielding woodpecker. The bird has innumerable associations with the tree. The Greeks called it the "oak-tapper." In the Russian fairy-tale, "The Dog and the Woodpecker" it is described as nesting in the oak—which it often does. But a merely naturalistic explanation is inadequate. Zeus, Jupiter and Thor were closely connected with the oak; and so, too, were Perun, Perkunas and Taara, the thundergods respectively of Slavs, Lithuanians and Esthonians. Pliny (*Nat. Hist.* xvi.249) states that among the Celts of Gaul the druids "performed none of their rites without oak leaves." Thus any bird, beast or plant—such as the mistletoe—connected with the oak is apt to have some mythological association with thunder—the oak being the thunder tree. Even the stag beetle which lives on the oak is a thunder creature. It is called *Donnergueg* or *Donnerpuppe* in parts of South Germany and it is believed that if it is brought indoors lightning will strike the building. My wife tells me that as a child in London she was told that these beetles appeared before a thunderstorm.

Sir James Frazer argued that the association between the oak and thunder arose through the use of oak wood for producing and maintaining fire, but more probably it came about because of the frequency with which primitive men observed oaks to be struck by lightning. Frazer queried Grimm's estimate that the oak is struck twenty times more often than the beech but Harris quotes figures which show that in a wood in which beech predominated the oak was struck nearly ten times as often. Contemplation of a giant oak shattered by lightning, and, even more, such destruction happening before a man's eyes would readily awaken reverence for the thunder-power associated

---

[1]There is a rich literature concerning magical stones, such as the eagle- and swallow-stones, known to birds. The swallow is acquainted with a magical stone and a magical herb. These apparently represent two types of derivative from the conception of a mysterious object or substance known to a wise animal. Wise animal tales, which are abundant, are a survival of the ancient regard for animals as in some ways more knowing than men.

with the tree.[1] Frazer's explanation might account for a connexion between the oak and a fire god but not with a thunder god.

Whatever strand of woodpecker mythology we follow it reveals a rain- or fertility-bird, and when we proceed a little further we find a thunderbird. The extent to which the woodpecker was deified or divinised is not clear, but this uncertainty may be due not only to the meagreness of the evidence which has survived but to the fact that the clear distinctions which the anthropologist makes in the functions of supernatural beings were foreign to the mind of early man. He did not discriminate clearly between forecasting rain and making it, nor between the activities of the god and his messenger. When we try to define supernatural beings by the degree of respect, reverence or worship offered to them our categories break down. We may conclude that the ancient woodpecker was a thunder spirit in so far as the bird was believed to have supernatural powers because of its association with thunder and control of rain and fertility.

Why was the woodpecker connected with thunder? Not merely because of its association with the thunder tree but because it made thunder. Primitive men watched the bird using a dead branch as a resonator as he issued his invitation to a female to join him and proclaimed his defiance of other males. They watched him up there on the oak, his head a blur as he struck the branch a rapid drum-roll with his bill. As the rain-drops pattered down they perceived the significance of the woodpecker's activities. This magical creature was doing what they longed to do—and what rain-makers later, perhaps taking their cue from him, tried to do. He was making thunder and so bringing rain. The red lightning badge on his crown, typical of thunderbirds, authenticated his status as rain-maker.

Near Dorpat, where they tell the story of the recalcitrant woodpecker which was condemned to cry before approaching storms (p. 95), a rain-making procedure was enacted in which the woodpecker's behaviour was apparently imitated. When rain was anxiously desired a man would climb a tree in an old sacred grove, taking with him a small cask or kettle on which he drummed to imitate thunder.

Can we form any estimate as to when and where belief in the woodpecker as a supernatural thunderbird arose? It must have originated among a woodland people. The bird's close association with the oak

[1]Dr. R. B. Whitehead, who saw a tree shattered a few yards from him has described to me the awe-inspiring sight.

suggests that it did not become a thunderbird earlier than the period when oak forests were widespread in Europe—the Atlantic phase which began about B.C. 5000 and reached its close about B.C. 2000. There is nothing to show that Palaeolithic people were interested in woodpeckers. Thus we may tentatively ascribe the origin of the wood-pecker thunderbird to a period not earlier than the Mesolithic. The evidence we have reviewed precludes a date later than the Bronze Age. On the whole there is much to suggest that the belief arose in Neolithic times with the spread of cultivation by means of the hoe, and later, the plough. The bird's rise to supernatural status is most likely to have coincided with the time when men's interest in the rainfall was im-mensely stimulated by concern for the growth of edible vegetation. This view is reinforced by the indications that the woodpecker was con-nected with plough agriculture. The absence or meagreness of wood-pecker thunder associations in most of Asia and North America may well be due to other thunderbirds having evolved in those areas and, so far as Siberia and the more arid and tropical regions are concerned, the absence of plough agriculture or its comparatively late introduction.

A NOTE ON THE THUNDERBIRD CONCEPT

In Europe a number of other birds are associated to some extent with storms and rain (pp. 62 and 133) but the only other species which can claim to be considered a thunderbird by virtue of making thunder is the snipe. It is called "Thunder's she-goat" or "he-goat" *pehrkon-akara* or *pehrkona aksis* in Latvia, and Thunder-goat," "Weather bird," "Storm bird" and "Rain bird" in Germany. The Faeroese say that its aerial drumming or bleating portends rain (or snow, if it is heard on 25 March). In Scotland the drumming is believed to foretell frost at night and dry weather. No doubt the association with thunder arose because of the similarity which people fancied existed between thunder and the sound made by the air rushing through the birds feathers as it makes its instrumental song. Significantly, this noise, like that made by woodpeckers, is popularly called "drumming" and it is by beating tambourines or drums that Siberian shamans and rain-makers in many parts of the world claim to bring rain.

In Asia and North America other birds which make instrumental sounds are also thunderbirds. In ancient China the pheasant held this status because, as Granet points out, it "beats a drum with its

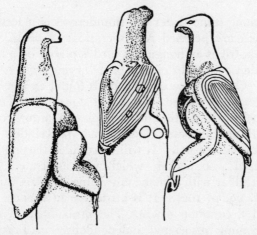

FIG. 70. Lightning birds carved in soapstone at Zimbabwe, S. Rhodesia. (After Walton, 1955).

wings" and so makes thunder. The young people danced in spring, imitating the movements of the bird and flapping their arms like wings in order to bring down the rain. In the New World the Hurons regarded thunder as a large bird. Le Jeune, writing in the seventeenth century, said that "they were led to this belief by a hollow sound made by a kind of swallow"—probably a reference to the nighthawk. The Indians in British Columbia described the thunderbird as like the ruby-throated hummingbird. Those familiar with hummingbirds will appreciate how this notion arose. They make miniature thunder with their wings.

Viewing Eurasia as a cultural area, traces of the thunderbird conception are widespread but in industrialised Europe, as we might expect, they are faint. In India the thunderbird appears to have been taken up into more sophisticated beliefs but in ancient China it was of importance in belief and custom, as it still is among some Siberian and Eskimo tribes. Over much of North America, especially the northwest, it was of considerable mythological significance. Its distribution would be consistent with an origin in Eurasia, diffusion to, and elaboration in, North America. The association of a twin-cult with the symbol of the thunderbird on a pole in Europe and Africa alike suggests the transmission of culture-patterns. In Nigeria, where twin-cults are strongly developed among some tribes the thundergod is placed between two poles on which are perched representations of birds. Among many southern Bantu tribes an image of a bird is placed on a hut to ward off lightning, which is thought of as a bird varying from a flamingo to a bird of prey. On the base of such birds found at Zimbabwe, a frog, crocodile or snake is carved (Fig. 70, p. 111). The Tungus of Manchuria, who believe in the thunderbird, place a large wooden swan on a pole with a fish near its base (Plate 16, p. 95). Reindeer are sometimes sacrificed below such a pole. It will be recalled that on a Roman gem the thunderbird woodpecker, which was associated with twins, is depicted on a pillar with a snake entwining it and a ram sacrificed at the base (Fig. 69, p. 102). It is attractive to suppose that all these practices had a common origin. The probability of such disparate elements becoming associated independently in Europe, Asia and Africa is less than that they survive in association from an earlier time when this culture-complex diffused widely.

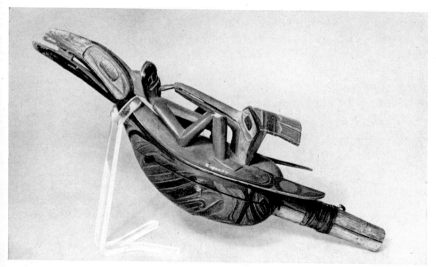

Plate 19 a. Above: Soapstone carving of a diver, Hudson Bay. Cf. p. 68 (*From the painting by Arthur Price commissioned by the pulp and paper industry of Canada*)

b. Below: Ceremonial rattle with magical attributes. Tlingit Indian of North-West America. Raven is shown carrying fire in his beak. The sun is engraved on his breast. The legend of Ka-ka-Tete, the whistling demon, is represented. This design is known from early in the 19th Century. Cf. pp. 89, 90, 93, 177. (*Cambridge Museum of Archaeology and Ethnology*)

Plate 20 a. Statue of Cú Chúlainn in the General Post Office, Dublin, erected as a memorial to the Irish patriots who fell in the Easter Week Rebellion, 1916. According to tradition a scald crow perched on the dying hero's shoulder. Cf. pp. 81, 93. (*Irish Tourist Board*)

b. Design on carved slab (*c.* A.D. 1000) at Andreas Church, Isle of Man, showing Odin, with one of his ravens, fighting the Fenris wolf. Cf. p. 78. (*Manx Museum*)

CHAPTER 7

NIGHT'S BLACK AGENTS

OUR pleasure in certain animals popular as pets appears to lie, to some extent, in the subconscious acceptance of a resemblance between their faces and our own. Lap-dogs, for example, arouse more maternal feeling than whippets. Moreover, disquiet, suspicion or fear tends to be evoked by real or imagined similarities between the characteristics of other animals and our own. People are apprehensive of anything which appears to have some human qualities without being human. Not only does the binocular vision of owls give them a resemblance to humanity but also the calls of some species are quasi-human. Their shrieks and hoots are often within the range of our own voices. Furthermore, nocturnal creatures naturally inspire fear because during darkness apprehension is increased by vulnerability to sudden attack. Some owls are among the few birds which make damaging attacks on human beings. In addition to these fear-inspiring characteristics, owls of various species frequent lonely places, such as caves, perching and calling on ruined buildings and monuments to the dead. As I was passing the Sphinx a little owl flew out of a recess and stood, bobbing, on one of its front paws, and on the island of Samothrace I found a pair of scops owls peering at me at arm's length near the massive masonry of Mycenaean times. It would be easy for simple folk to attach esoteric significance to such encounters.

Over Europe and Asia, and indeed, most of the world, the owl is, and has long been, a bird of witchcraft, death and doom. The Chinese refer to it as "the bird which snatches away the soul" and say that it sometimes calls, "Digging the grave!" It is believed to suck the blood of infants, sometimes doing so in human guise. In Morocco where the owl is said to embody the spirit of a woman there is a similar superstition. In the Indian epic Pancatantram (iii. 73) the King of the Crows likens the hostile owl to the devil. The fable of the war between

FOB—I

the owls and the crows which is mentioned by Greek and Latin writers is derived from oriental sources. It appears in the Mahâbhârata. The Rigveda (x. 165) records the supplication: "Be propitious to us when the owl emits that painful cry." Near Bombay, where it is believed that dissolute men become owls after death, propitiatory rites are enacted if one of these birds alights on the roof of a dwelling. Should this occur on a Sunday or Tuesday night the householder must pass a dark woollen thread below the cross beam. Then a naked person should add a knot for every screech. If, later, this thread is worn as an anklet the wearer need not fear ghosts, nor can he be seen by witches. Somewhat similar procedure is used in northern India to banish fever. This ritual provides an example of the accretion of beliefs around an object or event regarded as ominous. The emphasis on particular days when the ritual is effective is typical of much ceremonial. So also is the stress on the dress of the officiant—in this case the absence of it, for the belief is widespread that evil spirits are frightened by a naked body. Many nude representations in ancient art which modern taste would condemn were created, not for an obscene but for an apotropaic purpose. Transylvanian farmers walk naked around their fields before dawn to protect them from the depredations of birds. In the Indian ritual an action is performed to counteract each activity of the unpropitious object. Finally, the knotted wool is used for counter magic. In Europe, too, tying a knot in a handkerchief is believed to silence a screeching owl.

In Britain, no less than elsewhere, the owl is a death bird. Two large owls were said to warn the Arundel family that one of their connexion would die. Mr. Lethbridge informs me that he was often told as a child that when his great-aunt Lady Dorrington died "the trees were covered with owls." There is said to be a curse on the heir in this house. An owl tumbling down a chimney was an omen of death— but this superstition holds of other species entering houses. In parts of Ireland birds which come into cottages are killed lest they carry away good luck or betray family secrets. Ruskin wrote in *Praeterita:* "Whatever wise people may say of them, I at least myself have found the owl's cry always prophetic of mischief to me." W. J. Brown, writing in 1934, mentions that when he commented to an old man on the death of a mutual acquaintance he remarked: "It weren't no more nor I expected. I come past his house one night, and there were a scret (screech) owl on his roof, scretting something horrible. I always reckon

FIG. 71. Stained glass "quarry" at Yarnton, Oxfordshire, showing owl holding bell. (After Woodforde, 1944).

to take note of them things." In Shetland to see an owl or a corncrake foretells disaster, but this may be on the principle that unusual events are commonly regarded as ominous. Close to Bury St. Edmunds boys used to hunt owls and squirrels on Christmas Day. As squirrels were also ritually hunted in Germany—perhaps because their reddish coloration linked them with the thundergod—this procedure may have had affinities with other ceremonial in which some creature was hunted at the winter solstice.

The symbolism of owls in English literature is that of the Latin classics. Probably ancient Italian folklore reinforced beliefs which were already current. Shakespeare in *Julius Caesar* (I.iii. 28) follows Plutarch when he makes Casca say,

> *And yesterday the bird of night did sit*
> *Even at noonday, upon the market-place,*
> *Hooting and shrieking.*

Screeching owls are almost universally feared but this bird was especially ominous because of its unnatural behaviour.

Lady Macbeth (II.ii.3) shudderingly says,

> *Hark!—Peace! It was the owl that shriek'd,*
> *The fatal bellman which gives the stern'st good night.*

In a mediaeval painted glass window an owl bellman is depicted (Fig. 71, p. 115). Eglamour, bewailing his lost love Earine in Ben Jonson's *Sad Shepherd* (I.i) cries:

> *Not a voice or sound to ring her bell,*
> *But of that dismal pair, the scritching owl*
> *And buzzing hornet! hark! hark! hark! the foul Bird.*

Did this association occur to Jonson because he had read Dunbar's lines (*Poem* xxxiii.74)?

> *The myttane and Sanct Martynis fowle*
> *Wend he hatte here the hornit howle.*

Spenser spoke of the owl as "death's dreadful messenger" and to Chaucer (*Philomene*) it was the prophet of "wo and of myschaunce." When a bird is ominous in regard to death its predictions may be extended to other crises. Thus the owl presides also at births. "The owl shrieked at thy birth, an evil sign" says Henry VI to Gloucester (3 *Hen. VI*, V.vi.44). In Berne the owl's call may presage either a birth or death, and in Germany it can foretell a birth. There are places in the south of France where a pregnant woman hearing an owl shrieking will conclude that she will give birth to a girl. In Wales it was believed that an owl hooting around dwelling-houses signified that a girl would lose her virginity.

Shakespeare's witches were following ancient precedent when they included an "owlet's wing" in their brew (*Macbeth*, IV.i.17) for Horace's Canidia (*Epode*. V. 15, 16) and Ovid's Medea mingled owl's plumage with other ghoulish ingredients. In *The Masque of Queenes* Ben Jonson mentioned a somewhat similar potion composed of,

> *The screech owl's eggs and the feathers black,*
> *The blood of the frog and the bone of his back.*

In the *Hortus Sanitatis* we are told: "They put the ashes of owl's eyes on madmen." In England it was believed that owls' eggs, charred

Plate 21. a. Painting on the Hagia Triada sarcophagus showing sacrificial funeral ceremonies. A woman wearing a white jacket bordered with blue and a white skirt flecked with red is pouring a red liquid out of a highly coloured bucket into a large ornamental jar. The tapering pillars are clothed with green leaves. Surmounting them are double axes, symbols of power, on which representations of ravens are set. Cf. pp. 14, 77. (*Archaeology, Missouri*)

b. The painted sarcophagus found at Hagia Triada, Crete (*c.* 1400 B.C.). The figure on the right may be an effigy of the dead man. The ritual represented may have been intended to revitalize or resurrect him. These photographs were taken since the sarcophagus was cleaned. Cf. pp. 14, 77. (*Italian School of Archaeology, Athens*)

Plate 22. Gold pendant from Aegina representing the Master of Animals motif. Mid-Minoan (*c.* 1700-1600 B.C.). The figure is holding two geese by the neck. Cf. pp. 82, 84, 85. (*British Museum*)

and powdered, improved bad eyesight. Similarly it is an Indian custom to eat owls' eye-balls in order to acquire the ability to see in the dark. In Morocco a child may wear an owl's eye on a string round his neck to ward off the evil eye. The Cherokee Indians bathed children's eyes in water containing owl's feathers so that the children might be able to remain awake all night, but in India it was believed that the feathers placed under a crying baby's pillow would pacify it. Such practices were based on ideas of sympathetic magic which are still more potent in our own society than we generally realise. We have a beautiful example of this kind of thinking in the Yorkshire belief that owl broth is a remedy for whooping cough. Since the owl hoots and whoops so much without coming to harm, a concoction of its body should cure whooping cough! It will be remembered that Shakespeare's owl, true to the ambivalent concepts of folklore could sing "a merry note" (*L.L.L.* V.ii. 929) as well as portend death.

An English writer, Swan, in *Speculum Mundi*, which appeared in 1643, gave a remedy for dipsomania. He stated that if owl's eggs are broken, placed in a cup and given to a drunkard "he will suddenly lothe his good liquor." This belief is very ancient. Philostratus (*U. Apoll.*) remarked that a child who had been given an owl's egg to eat would never become a drunkard. He would dislike intoxicating liquor without ever having tasted it. According to other classical writers a toper could be rendered abstemious if he were given owl's eggs in wine for three days. The mythological origin of this type of recipe is clear. Athene, who came forth from the head of Zeus, embodied divine wisdom and she stood for qualities opposed to those of Dionysos, the god who had been brought to Greece in the eighth century B.C. apparently by Asian people from the neighbourhood of the Dardanelles.[1] He stood for ecstatic experience, mystical frenzy, inebriation and sexual licence. The antidote to the fruit of the god's vine was therefore supposed to be the egg of the goddess's bird. No doubt some other related beliefs can be explained in the same way. Cyranides (3a) declared that soup made from an owl's egg while the moon is waning cures epilepsy—a disease which was regarded as a special visitation of the gods and was confused with other forms of ecstatic or frenzied manifestations. Salted owl was considered a remedy for gout. The realisation that alcoholism may encourage gout goes back to

[1]The name occurs among the Linear B inscriptions but there is no evidence that it indicated a divine being.

classical times and was mentioned by Lucian (*Tragopodagra*) so that this belief also can be traced to the opposition between Athene and Dionysos. So, too, in all probability can the recipe in the *Hortus Sanitatis* already mentioned for the cure of madmen and Pliny's belief that "owlet" was a remedy against leech bites and insect stings. In Greek mythology gad-flies were associated with frenzied behaviour.

This odd pharmacopoeia, derived from the mythological opposition between the goddess of wisdom and the god of ecstasy and revelry, can be traced further. In Germany it is said that you can avoid being bitten by a mad dog if you place the heart and right foot of an owl under your left arm-pit. Here again the bird of wisdom counteracts madness. This belief has affinities also with the Roman notion that the ashes of burnt owls' feet were potent against snake venom, and the prescriptions for stings and bites already mentioned. Less than a century ago—in 1863—a book called "The Long Hidden Friend" was published in Pennsylvania dealing with remedies in use there. One of these is as follows: "If you lay the heart and right foot of a barn-owl on one who is asleep, he will answer whatever you ask him and tell what he has done." This can be traced to Albertus Magnus who probably obtained the information ultimately from Pliny (xxix. 82) who says that an owl's heart placed on the left breast of a sleeping woman will cause her to divulge secrets.

These beliefs take us into the realm of literary lore rather than folklore. It differs from oral folklore in that writers were usually sufficiently aware of traditions much earlier than their own time to know when they were diverging from them. It is possible for types of literary folklore to have a prolonged history in a country without influencing its oral folklore. Rather rarely literary folklore is accepted in oral folklore or the two cross-fertilise each other.

Undoubtedly the superstitious fear of owls ante-dates literary influence. We have already noted the use of owl masks to intimidate Basotho initiands. The Romans used representations of owls to combat the evil eye (Fig. 72, p. 120). The custom of nailing owls to barn doors or walls, which has only recently been abandoned in England, was too widespread to have arisen through literary influence. Ignorant countryfolk thus disposing of owls explained that they were merely getting rid of vermin, but their actions were really determined by ancient, probably prehistoric, precedent. Columella (*de re rust.* x. 348 ff.) mentions that in his time—the first century of our era—owls were hung up by country folk to avert storms, and Palladius (i.35.1) refers to their magical efficacy in warding off hailstones when nailed up with outspread wings:

> *Hence Amythaon's son, whom Cheiron taught,*
> *On crosses hung the night-birds and on roof-tops*
> *Would have them cry no more their deadly dirge.*

A similar custom prevailed until recently in Germany where an owl nailed to a door was thought to keep hail and lightning away. Englishmen believed that the owl's calling heralded hail-storms and in Glamorgan their hooting was supposed to foretell snow. Thus in Britain and elsewhere the owl was regarded as a weather prophet—a tradition which goes back to classical times.

In China, too, the owl was a thunder-averter. At the roof corners of Han houses ornaments called "owl-corners" were placed to protect the dwellings from fire, and in ancient China there were owl sacrifices as there were among the Ainu. To the Chinese the owl was a bird of the god of thunder and lightning. The Fifth day of the Fifth month—Chinese midsummer—was the day of the owl. Apparently it was the emblem of a royal clan of smiths who were "masters of the thunderbolt" and regulators of seasons.

The ambivalence of bird beliefs is illustrated by the association of the owl with Athene as emblematic of wisdom and victory. In *The Wasps* Aristophanes wrote of the defeat of the Persians:

> *Yet we drove their ranks before us, ere the fall of eventide,*
> *As we closed, an owl flew o'er us, and the gods were on our side.*

So, too, Agathokles routed the Carthaginians in 310 B.C. by releasing owls which settled on the helmets and shields of his men and thereby increased their morale. "There goes an owl" was an Athenian proverb indicating signs of victory. However, the bird still retained some of its sinister qualities for it was said that the owl which alighted on the spear of Pyrrhos of Epeiros foretold his miserable death (Aelian, *de nat. an.* x. 371).

Did Athene wield the thunderbolt of Zeus because of her association with the Thunderer or in her own right because she was descended from an owl thunderbird? Murray wrote of her: "As Glaucopis she is

FIG. 72. Roman design to avert the evil eye. An eye is shown, pierced by a lance. Around it are depicted an owl and a crow or raven as well as various animals charging. (After Cagnat and Chapot, 1920).

identified or associated with the owl that was the sacred bird of Athens. As Pallas she seems to be a thunder-maiden, a sort of Keraunia or bird of Keraunos" (Plate 14, p. 83 and Plate 24, p. 125). But Homer's Athene who appears as sea-eagle, swallow, vulture, falcon and "bird" (*Od.* i. 320; iii, 371; xxii, 239; *Il.* v. 778; vii. 58) and made herself known in the omen of a heron's call to Odysseus never takes the form of an owl. "Glaucopis" means "grey-eyed" or "blue-eyed" rather than "owl-eyed." Cook maintained that she was a pre-Hellenic rock-goddess from Anatolia who became "a mountain-mother of the Akropolis rock," and that the olive tree, the snake and the owl, inhabitants of crevices in the rock thus became associated with her as manifestations of the "life" of the goddess. Nilsson argued convincingly that she carries characteristics of the Cretan mother-goddess. Recent discoveries, notably the deciphering of the Linear B script and the identification of the name of a goddess which is patently an early form of Athene, have provided additional evidence of the influence of beliefs from Crete and the Middle East mainland on Greek religion. The Minoan goddess, arriving at Athens, apparently appropriated the

FIG. 73. Upper panels: The motif of the bird holding snake. Cf. Figs. 29, 30 and 31. Lower panel: Shaman wearing horns and wings, apparently representing an owl, holding a snake in each hand. He stands between monstrous birds holding snakes in their talons. Cf. Plate 10, p. 69. (Drawn by Miss Hallward).

owls, so common there, as her special birds. In Athens and Crete alike, the goddess was associated with snakes as well as birds.[1]

The snake-owl association also occurs in China. On a bronze vessel of the time of the Warring States (*c.* 481-205 B.C.) a horned and winged shaman is depicted holding a snake in either hand. Probably, like Siberian shamans he is garbed as an owl—a costume believed to scare evil spirits (Plate 10, p. 69, Fig. 73, p. 121). Altai shamans wear an eagle owl's skin as a head-dress. The tufts on its head look like small horns.

Somewhat inconsistently, Cook also suggested as "the remote ancestress of Athene" the nude goddess with a head-dress of horns and with taloned feet standing on two lions and flanked by owls depicted on a Sumerian tablet of B.C. 2300–2000 (Plate 5, p. 48). Whatever beliefs may have been associated with this goddess—who, as we have noted, is probably Lilith, goddess of death or kin to Ishtar "the ravisher of men"—this design is evidence against the view that Athene evolved from bird to woman goddess at Athens but supports the theory that owl traditions from this region may have contributed to the acceptance at Athens of the owl as peculiarly the bird of the city goddess. As the nocturnal owl has lunar associations, it was naturally associated with fertility goddesses who were closely connected with the moon—due, probably, to the supposed relationship between the female menstrual cycle and the phases of the moon. We may assume, therefore, that the owl attained importance in the matriarchal cultures which preceded patriarchal organisation and the domination of solar cults. Perhaps the tales in which the owl is abused by other birds, and especially the traditional enmity between owls and crows in Asian and European myths, conceal reminiscences of the conflict between lunar and solar ideas.

The problem of how Athene acquired her owl has been discussed here at some length because the relationship between gods and goddesses and their animal associates is highly complicated and yet of

---

[1] Owl representations are rare or unknown in Minoan and Mycenaean art and there is no reason to think that owls were connected with the Minoan goddess. The bird epiphany of a sea-going people might well take different forms when away from Crete. The mistaken belief of Aelian (V.2), Pliny (x (29) 41) and other writers that there were no owls in Crete may be regarded as evidence that owl beliefs were never important there. Perhaps the tradition that crows never entered the Akropolis owing to the hostility of Athene and her owls harks back to the time when the eastern goddess was accepted, with some reluctance, into the pantheon of a patriarchal people.

crucial importance in regard to the evolution of magico-religious ideas. Early man, as we have stressed, held animals in numinous awe and it is probable that, with the development of self-consciousness, more anthropomorphic theological imagery evolved. If men came to think of their gods as magnified non-natural men they were probably influenced by the prior formulation of concepts of magnified non-natural animals. Concepts of supernatural animals were transferred to, or projected upon, concepts as to the nature of human beings. Representations of Old Stone Age sorcerers show that they endeavoured to endow themselves with animal characteristics, and folklore indicates that birds with speciously human characteristics of appearance or voice were often considered supernatural. Probably, as has been maintained earlier (p. 91), the attribution of supernatural power to animals became less pronounced as the Palaeolithic gave place to more advanced cultures but this does not justify the assumption that "bird gods" gradually lost their avian characteristics and became anthropomorphised. "Bird god" is too saturated with later theological connotations to be used in this connexion. We must think in terms, not merely of a bird, such as the owl, evolving into a goddess but rather of a protracted evolution of man's formulation of magico-religions notions, during which concepts concerning the powers, natural and supernatural, of animals, merged with man's increasing appreciation of himself as different from them and his life as dependent on natural phenomena, such as the thunderstorm, the movements of the heavenly bodies and supernatural influences related to them. Thus in those comparatively few instances when some evidence can be adduced for the evolution of a bird into a humanised divinity, as in the case of Athene, this is probably due to a kind of psychological or spiritual atavism. It should not be considered proof of a straight-line evolution from animal to anthropomorphic divinity. The bird accompanying a divinity may be a symbol stressing an attribute which was given prominence at a particular epoch. It may be a sexual symbol representing the opposite sex from the figure with which it is associated or it may represent religious syncretism, the combination of two religious streams. In this matter no rule of thumb can be formulated.

The owl as Athene's companion and symbol can thus be explained by an association established at Athens between the owls of the Akropolis and a goddess from across the sea who was already believed to appear in various bird forms. However, the ambivalent notions concerning owls which bring or portend evil and yet may avert thunder have yet to be explained. We have noted that the woodpecker became a thunderbird because it made thunder, but the owl cannot be anti-thunder because it flies on noiseless wings. It has been suggested that the association arose owing to the bird roosting or nesting in the oak, the thunder tree. This is rather more plausible than the theory that its yellow eyes caused it to be connected with lightning. There is, indeed, a legend in which the owl figures as the enemy of the thunder tree, warning the birds not to let oaks grow as they support mistletoe from which bird-lime is made—but this legend seems to be of a rather late type. In remote times the owl was regarded as ominous in Semitic countries where oaks do not grow so the view that it became an averter of disaster by reason of its association with the oak is not very plausible. Moreover, since the oak is struck by lightning relatively frequently, the bird which it harbours is not obviously a thunder-averter.

The explanation of the owl's beneficent characteristics probably lies in the common belief that a frightening object is able to frighten away evil things. The owl thus acquired an apotropaic function and, as we have noted, was believed to deflect or avert the disasters which might accompany the thunderstorm. All the way across Eurasia owls are credited with counteracting evil demonic powers. Among the Chukchee it is believed that owls can become warriors, and at the Vogul bear-feast a person disguised as an owl appears to frighten the dead bear. Many Altaic peoples observe the custom of keeping an owl near a sick child's cradle in order to ward off evil spirits. An owl's talons serve the same purpose. The Ainu made wooden models of the eagle owl during times of pestilence or famine and nailed them to their houses. A communal model was called "The Defender of the Village." But the brown owl was feared as an agent of the devil. The Kazakhs look on owls as sacred but catch them to obtain the downy feathers under the tail which, in their opinion, bring good fortune. The owls are released after these feathers have been plucked.

So the owl which terrifies folk by gazing at them with its two great eyes or by wailing or shrieking like a soul in torment may be enlisted against the many powers of evil with which it is associated. The visible object of fear may be employed to inspire fear in the invisible powers which are feared. Thus the evil thing can be transformed into an ally by enlisting it against evil. But for the exploitation of this principle in the vaccines of modern medicine many of us would not be alive today.

Plate 23. Totem pole from Alert Bay, North-West America, representing the Thunderbird, the Grizzly Bear and the Woman—the myth according to which a bear and a woman marry. Cf. pp. 80, 81 and Figs. 53, 54 and 55. (*Canadian National Museum*)

Plate 24. a. Above: Perfume pot in the form of a swallow made in Rhodes (*c.* 600 B.C.). Possibly the swallow carried in the spring ceremonies may have inspired this design. Cf. p. 183. (*British Museum*)

b. Below: Kotylé depicting symbols of Athene, the owl and sprays of olive (2nd quarter of 5th century B.C.) Cf. p. 120. (*Fitzwilliam Museum, Cambridge*)

CHAPTER 8

THE KING OF BIRDS

TO trace the history of the eagle in religion, mythology and ritual would be an immense task, far beyond the scope of this chapter but a brief survey of eagle traditions is necessary if we are to appreciate the significance of the bird's folklore in Europe and these islands.

If we can base any conclusion on the rarity of representations of the eagle in Palaeolithic art the bird was not held in regard by men of this period. A design which might be meant to depict an eagle is among the many birds painted on the rocks of southern Spain (Tajo Sagura) but this Stone Age art is relatively late and there are no grounds for supposing the eagle to have been ritually important then. However, burials of falcon beaks with English archers of the Early Bronze Age and eagle talons in a Swedish grave of the Stone Cist period suggest that the bird's feathers may have been used for fletching arrows in the belief that the arrows would thereby magically acquire some of the eagle's strength, speed and skill. On similar principles eagle's talons were a talisman in war, according to Cyranides, and various organs of the bird were believed to possess medicinal qualities. In Classical times, and also among the Anglo-Saxons, "eagle's marrow" was prescribed for various ailments. As the bones of birds do not contain marrow this ingredient must have had high scarcity value. Probably the bird's association with healing is very ancient for according to the Avesta (*Yasht*, xii.17) it dwells on the tree called "All-healing." It is thus connected with the very extensive mythology of the "Tree of Life" which is too complex to be discussed here.

It can be assumed that the eagle had achieved symbolic importance before the civilisations of the Middle East arose. It must have been familiar to the mountain-dwelling ancestors of the people who founded the city-states, and it appears among their earliest symbols. For example, double-headed eagles are known from the Sumerian city

state of Lagash.   In this area as early as the third millennium B.C. the
eagle was linked with the concept of light and the activities of the god.
Ningirsu of Lagash was god of fertility, storm and war.   He sometimes
took the shape of the lion-headed eagle Imdugud who "shines on the
firmament."   A seal shows him attacking a monster.   The double-
headed eagle was adopted by the Hittites and passed on from culture to
culture down the centuries until it became incorporated into the arms
of great European states.   The crude, wooden double-headed birds
placed on poles by Siberian tribesmen of the present day were borrowed
from these ancient civilisations.

As the symbol of the eagle with a snake has been carefully studied
its history provides an excellent illustration of the transference down
the ages, not only of a symbol, but of the ideas connected with it.
In Babylonia the Etana myth describes the overpowering of the eagle
by the snake of night.   The hero Etana liberates the bird which thereupon bears him heavenward.   His mission is to obtain the herb which
will secure the happy birth of his son.   Hittite myths tell of the strife between the weather god and the serpent or dragon Illuyankas.   These
myths are part of an extensive series of observances belonging to New
Year festivals, ranging from the Zu-bird ritual of Babylonia (p. 162) to
the English Mummers' Play.   They all represent the defeat of darkness
and evil. The eagle-and-serpent motif travelled great distances, reaching
Central and South America, Melanesia and Polynesia.   It is found in
Bali, and also in New Zealand, where there are no snakes.   The symbol
is still alive.   It may be seen, to give only two examples, on the lectern
of Peterborough cathedral and the Mexican coat of arms.   Its significance has remained fundamentally the same—a representation of the
relationship between sky-powers and earth-powers.   As we noted
earlier (p. 37) this is probably the meaning of the symbol showing an
anserine bird with a snake or fish.   Perhaps this stressed the cooperation
of these powers, as the two creatures can hardly have been brought
into conjunction for naturalistic reasons.   The motif showing the eagle
grasping the snake may have represented tension or conflict.   Many
species of eagle prey on snakes.

The history of a related symbol is more involved.   An Elamite
design of the fourth millennium B.C. depicts an eagle grasping a snake
in the talons of each foot (Fig. 74, p. 127).   The British Museum has a
stone amulet from Carchemish of the seventh century B.C. on which
Lamashtu, a female demon, animal-headed and bird-clawed, is seen

FIG. 74. Babylonian seal of the 3rd. millennium B.C. showing an eagle holding a snake in each foot. (After Weber, O. 1920. Altorientalische Siegelbilder, II).

FIG. 75. Maenad dancing while holding a snake in each hand. (After Harrison, J., 1922).

with a snake in each hand. In China, as we have already remarked, the bird-and-snake appears on a bronze vessel of the period of the Warring States with a design showing a shaman dressed as a bird (probably an owl) brandishing snakes (Fig. 73, p. 121). From Greece we have a design of a maenad similarly holding snakes (Fig. 75). Probably there was some reciprocal influence between this type of design and the Master of Animals symbol depicting a personage holding two beasts or birds (Plate 22, p. 117; Figs. 56 and 57, pp. 84 and 85).

As in art, so in mythology, the eagle-and-snake association can be traced down the centuries. The Indian version of the conflict of the two creatures is contained in the Rigveda, which dates from not later than B.C. 1000. Here it is connected with the fetching of *soma*—a theme with many ramifications. The greatest feat of Indra, the god who brings rain, was the slaying of the serpent-demon Vritra. He says,

I slew Vritra, O Maruts, with (Indra's) might,
having grown powerful through my own vigour:
I who hold the thunderbolt in my arms,
have made these all-brilliant waters to flow freely for men.

RV.i.165.8

This passage is full of significance for in it the eagle-snake conflict is linked with thunder and fertility-bringing waters.

It has been suggested that Indra, who is so often associated with the eagle, was once an eagle himself—"being well-winged he carried to men the food tasted by the gods" (*RV.* iv. 26). Schrader wrote: "Even as late as the Vedas the lower deities at least are by preference thought of as being in the form of animals. But the higher gods also are repeatedly characterized as the children of animals, *e.g.* the Asvins as children of the mare. The different animals, too, which were sacred to the gods, such as the eagle of Indra . . . are unmistakable signs of these once prevalent ideas." Similarly, in writing of Greek religion Murray says: "There is a path open from the divine beast to the anthropomorphic god," and after enumerating birds and beasts which accompany Olympian divinities, "Allowing for some isolated exceptions, the safest rule in all these cases is that the attribute is original and the god is added." As our discussion of Athene's owl showed, the evolution from supernatural beast or bird to anthropomorphic divinity is not always so straightforward as these authorities suggest. We must not project into the mentality of early peoples the distinctions we make between beast, man and god. To such folk an animal, man or god could be a beast-man-god with particular characteristics or distinctions predominating in certain contexts. It is clear, however, that as this and other discussions of the magico-religious ideas of by-gone times show, the further we trace such ideas into the past the more prominent animal beliefs become, and the greater the numinous importance attached to them.

The eagle-snake myths branched out into variants as they were transmitted down the centuries. The great compendium of Indian tales, the *Jatakas*, contains the story of the Rukh, dating from not later than the fourth century B.C. The huge Roc of the *Arabian Nights* evidently evolved from this creature. Sindbad's bird, it will be remembered, was like a cloud and spread darkness over the earth. For fear of it the snakes in the Valley of Diamonds retired into cover at daylight—an indication that the eagle belonged to the powers of day and the snake to the dark forces of earth. Garuda, the gigantic Indian bird of prey, was in the same tradition. One may still see the colossal stone images of this bird and the Naga snake adorning the temples at Angkor in Indo-China. When clouds suddenly cover the sun inhabitants of Perak say, "Gerda spreads her wings to dry them." Of the same breed is the giant Simurgh of Persia. Chinese literature of the third century B.C. mentions a giant storm-bird called the *phang* which was originally a fish. "When this bird rouses itself and flies its wings are like clouds round the sky." The Chukchees of Siberia believe in the colossal Noga-bird which preys on elk, whales and men. Immense birds pouncing on animals are often represented in the lovely, vigorous art of the peoples on the northern fringes of the great Asian civilisations. Art motifs and associated tales undoubtedly travelled north and east from India and Persia. As we have seen, they also travelled westwards (Plate 25, p. 144; Figs. 21, p. 20 and 34, p. 35).

Emphasis has been laid upon the eagle-and-snake motif because of its importance in providing convincing evidence of the diffusion of culture. In regard to some art motifs there is uncertainty concerning the associated myth, but the eagle-and-snake design has remained associated with its myth in a great variety of cultures from the earliest times of which we have record to the present day.

Thus in the mythologies of Babylonia, Assyria and the Hittite empire the eagle is conspicuous. So it is also in India and Persia, Greece and Rome. Only in early Egypt, where the falcon of Horus took the eagle's place, and China, where syncretistic animal symbols, especially the dragon, became popular, was the eagle of comparatively little significance.[1] Eagles are less conspicuous in the Nile valley and the loess lands of China than among the mountains which fringe the Mesopotamian plains in which the city states flourished. In Mesopotamian and Levantine traditions the eagle and the griffon vulture are sometimes confused, as they are in our English Bible.

The Middle East may thus be regarded as the centre from which eagle traditions radiated. When we turn to the traditions of these islands we naturally ask ourselves whether we may trace the influence of the Asian ideas we have been considering.

English eagle traditions, like the bird itself, have fared ill. It is

[1]Later Egyptian texts show that the eagle replaced the falcon. Horapollo (ii.56) refers to the eagle as the symbol of the king.

more than 150 years since golden eagles bred in England though they
are well established in Scotland, after a period of rather precarious
survival, and have recently nested again in Ireland, having been
absent for some thirty years. Seven centuries ago Giraldus Cambrensis
found eagles in Ireland "as numerous as kites in other countries." The
last white-tailed eagles nested on a Shetland cliff recently enough for
the site of the eyrie to be pointed out to me by a man who had seen
the birds frequenting it.

In an Anglo-Saxon curse the eagle and the wolf are mentioned.
The wolf, like the eagle, is a creature of magical significance in
Eurasia, and to some extent also in North America.

> *Under the wolf's paw*
> *Under the eagle's feather.*
> *Under the eagle's claw*
> *Ever may you wither.*

Much earlier, when the legendary Milesians invaded Ireland, their
leader, Amergin, chanted as he set foot on the shore:

> *I am the wind on the sea;*
> *I am a wave of the ocean;*
> *I am the bull of seven battles;*
> *I am the eagle on the rock.*[1]

The full meaning of this incantation is hidden from us but perhaps we
catch an echo of the songs sung by prehistoric sorcerers dressed in
horns and hides, or bird masks and feather cloaks, who believed themselves endowed with the powers of the creatures they simulated. As
he invoked the powers of nature, Amergin called for the help of the
local mother goddess. Those who fared to new lands across the sea
might bring strange gods but they dared not offend the local goddess
of the soil. When the Maori landed in New Zealand their chieftain
uttered just such an incantation as Amergin's song. It must be
emphasized, however, that in the most ancient western traditions,
especially those of the Celtic lands, the raven and crow have far greater
significance than the eagle.

[1]According to the Welsh tale *Kat Godeu*, the Battle of Godeu, Taliessin sang a somewhat
similar song. Alfred Nutt believed the Irish version to be the older.

In Scottish tales we hear of a giant's soul taking refuge in an eagle, and of a king's son transformed into one of these birds.[1] It would appear that here we have vestiges of a belief which, among the Buriats, still takes the form of maintaining that the first shaman was the son of an eagle and a woman. The Welsh legend that King Arthur lingers in a mountain cave guarded by eagles may owe something to this type of tradition, but it is also in line with various tales of by-gone rulers who will reappear some day. These legends seem to be derived from the Sumerian myth of a god kept captive in a mountain, who revives each year—a concept which was basic to many fertility rituals, such as the Eleusinian mysteries. It might seem strange that King Arthur's epiphanies should be expected to be in the shape of a raven, chough or puffin, but not as an eagle. The explanation may lie in the superior importance of corvine birds in Celtic areas—probably even before the arrival of the Celts. Tales of the eagle guarding the cave dwelling of the superseded, but still living, raven king may be veiled references to the subordination of a culture in which the raven was pre-eminent by an eastern culture reverencing the eagle.

Support for this view comes from the analysis of the Irish myths. They may be divided into two types according to the prominence in them of the stag or the bull. The stag traditions seem to belong to a northern type of culture, the bull traditions to be derived from the Mediterranean region. From Palaeolithic times deer have had a highly important place in the art of most ancient northerly Eurasian cultures, and there are plenty of legends, such as those of Finland and Hungary, showing that the stag was considered a magical beast. Stag songs are still sung at the winter solstice celebrations of various peoples, and in a very ancient Hungarian song the raven and the stag appear together:

> *A big, black cloud gets up over there,*
> *A black raven cleans its feathers in it;*
> *Where a fast river has its spring,*
> *A round, small sward lies.*
> *A stag with a miraculous head grazes on it . . .*

[1] There are various Irish stories based on the concept of the external soul which tell of a series of animals, such as the salmon, the ram and the eagle, helping a hero to fetch an egg from inside a duck at the bottom of the sea in order to kill a giant (Aa 302). This motif, The Giant without a Heart, is extremely ancient and is found among all Indo-European peoples. It seems to have affinities with the widespread Grateful Animals (Aa 550, 553, 554) and the Oldest Animal (A 1904) motifs, which can be traced to early Indian sources.

The song discloses that it conveys hidden meanings:

> *My hiding place is an old law*
> *Holla! I hide in songs.*

Thus there is some reason to regard the stag and the raven as belonging to the ancient Arctic culture, whereas the bull and the eagle seem to be the symbols of later, intrusive southern civilisations. It has already been suggested that the raven, the most conspicuous bird around Palaeolithic man's rock shelters and hunting grounds, may be represented in the Death of the Bird-man scene at Lascaux (p. 14).

Near Snowdon, eagles were regarded as oracles, their cries were held to predict calamity, and their appearance over the plains to foretell death. We need not suppose that this belief was due to Greek and Roman traditions, conspicuous as the ominous eagle is in them. It was common knowledge among warlike peoples, as, no doubt, in Stone Age communities, that "where the carcase is, there will the eagles be gathered together." It is an easy step to the belief that these birds foreshadow or even bring about tragedy. But the eagle, being often associated with the sun and royalty, more usually presaged important or auspicious events, such as the birth of founders of dynasties or conquerors. As with so many ominous birds it could have an ambivalent character. The mental procedure involved in the generation of such traditions is easily discernible. If the presence of a bird, or other object, is lucky, its departure is unlucky. The object itself may thus reverse its status or oscillate between being propitious and ill-omened. So Cassius declares:

> *On our former ensign*
> *Two mighty eagles fell; and there they percht,*
> *Gorging and feeding from our soldiers' hands;*
> *Who to Philippi here consorted us;*
> *This morning are they fled away and gone;*
> *And in their stead do ravens, crows and kites,*
> *Fly o'er our heads and downward look on us,*
> *As we were sickly prey.*
>
> *Julius Caesar*, V.i.81

The eagle is no exception to the rule that ominous birds are very frequently associated with the weather. When it was stormy in Wales people used to say, "The eagles are breeding whirlwinds on Snowdon." There is a reference in an old Welsh tale to eagles and other birds of prey creating whirlwinds by flapping their wings. Eagles, particularly the golden eagle, to which many eagle traditions properly belong, are much more conspicuous in calm, clear weather than when it is stormy, so it is contrary to experience to associate eagles with bad weather. The Welsh traditions are versions of eastern myths founded on beliefs and rituals associating birds of prey with the mountains in which storms were seen to gather. Mention has already been made of some of these traditions of immense storm-birds in Hittite, Indian, Persian, Arabian, Siberian and North American mythology. To give one further example; the Chukchee of north-east Siberia believe that to kill an eagle will cause a tempest.

The eagle storm-bird was associated with Zeus and the lightning. The bird's right wing was buried in fields and vineyards to ward off hailstorms—a tradition so similar to that concerning owls that we may suspect the beliefs to have been related (p. 124).

Probably some Asian ideas concerning eagles reached our islands independently of classical literature. The monstrous creature in the Irish tale, with iron beak and tail of fire, which came to Ilbrec's house and shook itself so vigorously that the weapons fell from their racks on the heads of the inmates, seems to have come from where birds of fire and iron dwell, on Russian and Mongolian steppes. When we read in a Scottish tale of a lad, thrown over a cliff, who falls into an eagle's eyrie, eats the young and then escapes by attaching himself by means of his cravat and braces to the bird's talons, we are reminded of Sindbad's escape from the Roc's nest. An eagle in another of these tales, is, according to the recorder of the story, J. F. Campbell, "peculiarly eastern; he is a genius in another shape." Through monastic influence, originating in Egypt and travelling by way of southern Gaul, oriental motifs entered Irish art and literature. It is significant that Irish martyrologies record the deaths of Egyptian, Byzantine and Armenian monks in Ireland. But eastern motifs, literary and artistic, were reaching these islands before the exploits of Sindbad were known here.

In Christian times the Bible has been the vehicle by which much eagle lore has spread throughout the world, especially in the west, but few eagle traditions derived from it have become folklore. The sanctions of association with a great religion have been insufficient to naturalise among European villagers literary lore inspired by the Bible. Very little of it has become oral tradition, in spite of the popularity of the symbolic eagle with preachers in the past. The compendium of misinformation concerning the eagle elaborated by commentators on the Bible for homiletic purposes is conveniently summarised in editions of Cruden's Concordance, still used by clergy preparing sermons:

EAGLE: Is a bird of prey, whereof there is frequent mention in scripture. It is declared in *Lev.* 11. 13 to be unclean, as are all other birds of its species. . . The hawk and vulture may also be reckoned as different species of eagles. It is said that when an eagle sees its young so well grown, as to venture upon flying, it hovers over their nest, flutters with its wings, and excites them to imitate it, and take their flight; and when it sees them weary or fearful it takes them on its back, and carries them so that the fowlers cannot hurt the young without piercing the body of the old one. In allusion to this it is said, *Exod.* 19.4: That God delivered his people out of Egypt and bore them upon Eagles' wings . . . It is of great courage, so as to set on harts and great beasts. And has no less subtilty in taking them; for having filled its wings with sand and dust, it sitteth on their horns, and by its wings, shaketh it in their eyes, whereby they become an easy prey . . . It goeth forth to prey about noon when men are gone home out of the fields.

It hath a little eye, but a very quick sight, and discerns its prey afar off, and beholds the sun with open eyes. Such of her young as through weakness of sight cannot behold the sun, it rejects as unnatural. It liveth long, nor dieth of age or sickness, say some, but of hunger, for by age its bill grows so crooked that it cannot feed . . . It is said that it preserves its nest from poison by having therein a precious stone, named Aeitos, (without which it is thought the eagle cannot lay her eggs, and which some use to prevent abortion, and helps delivery in women by tying it above or below the navel) and keepeth it clean by the frequent use of the herb maidenhair . . . Its feathers or quills are said to consume other quills that lie near them. Between the eagle and the dragon there is constant enmity, the eagle seeking to kill it, and the dragon breaks all the eagle's eggs it can find . . . Being exceedingly hot and dry, it soon waxeth angry, nor keepeth, but shuns society with others . . . The kings of Babylon and Egypt are also compared to an eagle.

This passage epitomises the continuous tradition of Christian homiletic literature beginning with the Bible and the Physiologus of the first century, which contained stories from the animal-books of the Egyptian priesthood and quotations from scriptural and Talmudic sources. Wedded to material from Aristotle, Aelian, Pliny and other ancient writers, it was passed on, with embroideries, by Albertus Magnus, Gesner, Aldrovandus, Bartholomew and other compilers of pandects and encyclopaedias until, at last, it reached, and renewed its youth on, the Elizabethan stage. The eagles adorning church lecterns have a long, strange and splendid lineage.

In contrast with these literary traditions is the folk-tale describing the wren's cleverness in outwitting the eagle in the competition to decide who should be King of Birds—a type of the widespread Election of an Animal King motif. It has been recorded from practically every part of Europe and variants occur elsewhere, as in North America among the Ojibwas (Aa 220, 221; B 241, 251, 252). There are Scottish Gaelic and Irish versions. In some of the latter, the eagle assaults the wren so that it loses part of its tail or has to fly low ever afterwards. This detail is of interest as it occurs in a fifteenth century German manuscript poem and apparently in no other literary source. Variants in which the birds compete again to determine which of them can descend lowest and in which the wren wins once more by creeping down a mouse-hole are found from Holland to Poland and Roumania. The version in which the owl acts as watchman at the entrance to the hole occurs throughout approximately the same area, and also in Denmark, Jutland, Wendland, Lithuania and Little Russia, but not in Poland.

The oldest complete literary version is in Neckam's treatise *De naturis rerum* (i.78. ed. T. Wright, p. 122 f.) written about 1180 A.D. In this tale, as in some versions recorded from the vernacular more recently, the wren conceals itself under the eagle's wing rather than on its back or tail. The legend is much older. Plutarch (*Mor.* 806e), after describing some outstanding personalities concludes: "Such then, are the men to whom young statesmen should attach themselves and cling closely, not snatching glory away from them, like Aesop's wren who was carried up on the eagle's shoulders, then suddenly flew out and got ahead of him" The eagle-wren competition is not in any surviving collection of Aesop's fables, but there is a fable attributed to Aesop bearing some similarity to those we have been considering: When the birds wished to select a king, the peacock claimed to be chosen because of his great beauty. When the choice fell on him the jackdaw spoke up and said: When you are king and the eagle starts to chase us, how will you be able to help us? A similar tale comes from Armenia, but in it, the birds' spokesman is the dove.

Fully a quarter of Aesop's fables can be traced with greater or less certainty to ancient Indian sources—in particular, to the humorous beast stories in the Jatakas which were brought to Ceylon in the third century B.C. Several of Aesop's fables with birds as the principal actors are identical with Jataka tales; for example, "The Wolf and the Crane" and "The Fox and the Crow." In Jataka 270 we are told that the various creatures elected a king. Men chose a handsome man, the quadrupeds chose the lion and the fishes the *ananda* fish, so the birds also selected one of their kind. The outcome was a dispute between the owl and the crow and the ultimate choice of the swan as king.[1]

The Election of the Bird King motif is also found in another Indian source, the Avadanas, compiled in China. The owl is elected, being a good night watchman, but following the parrot's objection that he could not keep awake by day, the parrot is chosen. There are also versions from Siberia. In one the mammals select the lion and the birds the eagle. The crane was also honoured by being selected, whereupon a quarrel developed between it and the quail. The crane struck it and broke its backbone, so that it always had to fly low thereafter. Another version explains that this is why the crane carries the quail on its back on migration.[2]

Thus the components of the story, the King-choice motif, the dispute among the birds, the election of the eagle and the carrying of one bird on the back of another, are all found in Asia. There the wren

[1]In Madagascar there is a story of the rejection of the owl and hawk, and the election of the shrike *Dicrurus forficatus* as king. This appears to be a modification of an Indian tale.

[2]There may be some connexion between this type of story and another dealing with quarrels among the animals. In some of these tales the cause of strife is interference with the wren's nest. This is in line with the widespread belief that to tamper with this bird's nest is unlucky (p. 152).

is mainly a secretive denizen of high mountain ranges, so that its absence from the tale, and almost entirely from Asian folklore, is not surprising. We must therefore assume that it took its place in the King-choice story when it came to Europe, well before the time of Plutarch. When an ornithological fable grows by accretion and substitution, the bird adopted into it has often already attained some status in folk belief, so the wren had probably achieved mythological status in Europe when the motif arrived. If we adopt a plausible emendation to a passage in the pseudo-Aristotelian tenth book of the *History of Animals*—which contains stories with an oriental flavour, such as the tale of the cinnamon bird with its nest of spice—the eagle and the wren were regarded as enemies. Pliny (viii.25) is quite explicit on their antagonism. Suetonius says that the wren predicted Caesar's death and was torn in pieces while it was carrying away a laurel branch. In Syrian designs the eagle is shown bearing a wreath. The same motif appears very occasionally in archaic Greek art. The eagle and the woodpecker were also traditionally at enmity. The woodpecker was said to break the eagle's eggs. We may have a reminiscence of this conflict in *The Parlyament of Byrdes* (Harl. Misc. v.507):

> The Specke. *Then in his hole, says the wood-specke*
> *I wolde the hawk had broke his necke.*

Does all this indicate a conflict between beliefs established in Europe and intruding Asian ideas?

This suggestion might seem to involve attaching undue importance to the legend of the rivalry between the eagle and the wren, but for the fact that in most European languages, including Roumanian, Lithuanian and Polish, the wren's name implies royalty. Irish, Scottish Gaelic, Welsh, Manx and Breton are exceptional, as also are English and Icelandic, though in England the goldcrest is called the "kinglet." In the familiar Irish wren song the wren is "king of all birds" and there is a Scottish Gaelic quatrain in which the wren proclaims himself king. Yet one could hardly discover any bird whose appearance and behaviour less suggest a claim to royal honours. There must be some mythological explanation of this strange situation. The view that the wren became king because of its victory over the eagle in the altitude contest, or, in other words, that it was enthroned after the story was elaborated, and in consequence of it, will not bear scrutiny. It is

FIG. 76. Woodcut from Olaus Magnus, 1555, *Historia de gentibus septentrionalibus,* showing owls, bats and a goatsucker. Bats were long classified as birds.

much more probable that, as suggested, the wren was incorporated into the story because of its already important status in Europe.[1] Some writers have supposed that the royal title originally belonged to the goldcrest, because of its head adornment and its name, implying kingship in some languages, such as modern Greek, but the wren was king—βασιλεύς—in classical Greek and it is incredible that all over Europe a complete transference of myth and ritual could have occurred without leaving definite traces. For 2500 years, and probably much longer, the wren has been king, if only in name, in Europe.[1]

In contrast, the eagle has no common name in the main Indo-European languages. This would be consistent with the bird's having acquired eminence in the ancient Asian civilisations and its fame having reached Europe, motif after motif, from further east. Even this brief survey has shown that Babylonian, Egyptian, Hebrew, Scythian and Indian contributions can be identified.

[1]According to a Breton legend Christ gathered the birds for the flight competition and the robin won by flying up from the eagle's back. There is a similar modern Greek fable. Both are comparatively recent variants.

There is little or no evidence that the eagle attained divine or royal status in Europe apart from Asian influence. In Greece, where the eagle was closely associated with Zeus, Asian ideas affected art and thought in many ways. As we have seen (p. 61), swan beliefs probably reached Greece from the north but the lineage of the eagle is eastern. On the other hand, there is no indication of any kind that the eagle's rival on European soil, the wren, was ever respected in Asia. One bird was king in Asia, the other in Europe, and the Election of the Bird King legend records the conflict between the two. The wren is driven underground in spite of its subtlety. It becomes a pretender to the throne, a demoted king, and as we shall see in the next chapter, it has its day once a year when it is acclaimed as king but sacrificed—as divine kings were sacrificed long ago. Each bird represented, it seems, one of the two fundamental principles consciously or subconsciously recognised by mankind for untold ages. The eagle is king of the heavens, the representative and symbol of the sun and powers of the sky, the wren belongs to the earth, creeping into holes and crevices in or near the ground. According to Argive tradition Trochilos, the wren, was the son of Triptolemos, the inventor of the plough, and therefore, presumably connected with the earth, as was Keleos, his brother, who, while in the cave of Zeus was turned into a green wood-pecker, a bird associated with fertility and the plough (p. 104). The wren was believed to have oracular, and probably supernatural, powers (p. 142). It may well have been regarded as possessing qualities rather similar to those of the snake which also creeps into holes and is closely in touch with chthonic forces. In folklore the eagle and the owl are alike enemies of the wren and the snake (Fig. 76, p. 138). Thus in the rivalry between the eagle and the wren we seem to have evidence of the supersession by solar beliefs from Asia of chthonic magico-religious ideas lingering in Europe.

Recapitulating and expanding suggestions already made, the eagle or anserine bird in early symbols nearly always represents sky powers, often the sun, but sometimes, especially in the case of the eagle, storm powers, thunder or lightning (Fig. 74, p. 127), the fish and snake represent darkness, earth and water, the chthonic forces. Often the latter are sexual symbols. Their ambivalence is thus explained, for sex involves attraction and repulsion. The elaborate courtship displays of birds are known to have evolved through the conflict of these drives. Human sexual and social activities have a similar foundation.

Mythology and psychology give constant evidence of this. Here is the key to the interpretation of many legends, the thread which may guide us through the labyrinth of ancient traditions. Fights with the dragon or serpent, whether the hero be Etana or St. George, are seen to have a deep psychological significance as well as a cosmic meaning. We are able to interpret the significance of the descent of the priestess into the cave at Eleusis, and the representations of Mithras killing the bull in the cave with the snake below and the raven above (Fig. 50, p. 75). We glimpse the meaning of the conflict between chthonic-lunar and solar ideas which runs through mythology and the associated division of communities into matriarchal or patriarchal. We see that underlying festivals, such as the Celtic Lugnasad on 1 August, and New Year celebrations in general, was the desire to establish equilibrium between the two great contrasting principles—represented in Chinese thought as the Yin and the Yang. All this is symbolised by the sky-bird and the chthonic creeping creature. As Shelley wrote in *The Revolt of Islam*,

When the Snake and Eagle meet—the world's foundations tremble

CHAPTER 9

THE WREN HUNT AND PROCESSION

THE Wren Hunt is among the most elaborate bird rituals surviving in Europe and is best preserved in the British Isles, though the casual observer of some of the present-day jollifications might not be greatly impressed. In an Irish village on St. Stephen's Day (26 December) he might see a tumultuous party of lads dressed in ludicrous garments. such as pyjama jackets and women's blouses, some with faces blackened, going from house to house, stopping here and there to sing a few doggerel lines and to collect a coin from the householders (Plate 26, p. 145). He could not be blamed for failing to realise that he was beholding a ritual of great antiquity. Moreover, if he were to seek for references to the custom in early literature, such as the Greek and Latin classics, he would find no mention of it. Thus the historical method which has been used in our investigation of the folklore of such birds as the goose and woodpecker cannot be applied. Fortunately, as our study of diver folklore showed, when the historical approach fails we may have recourse to another technique—the geographical— and this can be adopted in studying the Wren Hunt. We must therefore first consider the distribution of this ritual.

ENGLAND

Contrary to general belief the Hunting of the Wren was an English custom.

Cornwall. Everyone possessing a gun used to go out on St. Stephen's Day and shoot so indiscriminately that it was dangerous to walk the lanes. The origin of the practice was said to be that a bird awakened St. Stephen's guards as he was about to escape. This is one of the Irish explanations of the Wren Hunt, so this battue may have evolved from the Hunt. There is a Cornish rhyme:

Hunt a robin or a wren,
Never prosper boy or man.

This might seem to suggest that the intrusion and dominance of a belief that it is unlucky to kill wrens had deflected the hunters to the pursuit of other birds, but inconsistent ideas of this kind are common in folklore, especially in regard to sacrificial animals which may be killed only at one season of the year.

Devonshire. The observances in this county are mentioned later (p. 148).

Dorsetshire. The custom persisted, notably at Iwerne Minster, until the middle of the nineteenth century.

Sussex. In 1891 Borrer wrote: "In my young days it was a regular institution to hunt it at Christmas time, when numbers of boys, on both sides of the hedges, amused themselves by beating the hedges and throwing at the wren whenever it showed itself, with knobbed sticks about 18 inches long called 'libbets'." In spite of this persecution it was considered unlucky to touch a wren's nest in some parts of Sussex.

Surrey. According to Hazlitt the wren was hunted in this county.

Essex. At Christmas-tide boys used to kill wrens and carry them about in furze bushes from house to house singing a verse similar to that commonly sung by Irish Wren-boys:

The wren, the wren, the king of all birds,
On St. Stephen's Day was caught in the furze.

It is unlikely that in Essex wrens were usually caught in furze bushes, whereas in Ireland they are often chased where this shrub flourishes. The rhyme, but probably not the custom, may have been introduced from Ireland. It is of interest that when this wren song was transplanted from Ireland to Newfoundland it was adapted to its new surroundings by the substitution of "firs" for "furze."

Suffolk. The Wren Hunt took place on St. Valentine's Day.

Gloucestershire. The Wren Song has been collected but there is no record of its having accompanied the ritual.

Oxfordshire. The Wren Hunt and Wren Song are recorded.

Buckinghamshire. For a period at the middle of last century, the wren was chased at Eton by the schoolboys. This was called "toodling." It has been suggested that the custom was introduced by an Irish boy.

More probably it came from Wales. In Pembrokeshire at Twelfth Night, the season at which Wren-hunting and "sowling" took place there was a custom called "tooling." A man would enquire, "Did I leave my saw (or some other tool) behind your beer barrel?" and so scrounge a drink. "Toodling" may be a corruption of "tooling."

Nottinghamshire. Swann, writing in 1913, states that to his knowledge, the wren was hunted along the hedgerows "within recent times" by boys armed with stones.

Warwickshire. "Shacking the wren" as it was called, might be carried on at any time during the winter.

Derbyshire. Hunting wrens on Sunday was called "jenty" (i.e. Jenny) hunting.

Lancashire. There is a reference to the Wren Hunt in this county but I have been unable to trace any well authenticated record.

Westmorland. Indiscriminate shooting of birds occurred on St. Stephen's Day.

Cumberland. On St. Stephen's Day men and lads shot birds.

North of England. In this region, over an unspecified area, St. Stephen's Day was called "Wrenning Day."

Thus there are traces of a Bird Hunt throughout much of England, but the Wren Hunt was evidently most firmly established in the south and west.

SCOTLAND

As we might expect from the decreasing evidence of the Wren Hunt as we go northwards, there is no reason to believe that it was customary in Scotland. There is one recorded instance. At Kirkmaiden in Galloway boys used to go out on New Year's morning to catch wrens. When one was caught its legs and neck were decorated with ribbons and it was then released. The ceremony was called "The Deckan' o' the Wren." A man who had taken part in it gave an account in the 'nineties. The custom may have been imported from the Isle of Man, for the Galloway Scots called there a great deal on smuggling expeditions. This seems more probable than that this isolated observance was a survival of a custom established in early times.

A Wren Song, apparently in the dialect of the south-west was included in the second edition of David Herd's *Ancient and Modern Scottish Songs*, which first appeared in 1776, but as a related version had been published in England 32 years earlier in *Tommy Thumb's Pretty Song Book* the ditty may have been borrowed from it.

There were Scottish New Year shooting forays similar to those in Cornwall and northern England. It was customary on New Year's Day for men and boys to sally forth "gun in hand before daybreak in search of some bird or wild animal, no matter how small, that they may draw blood and thus make sure of one year's good fortune." This notion—that blood must be shed on New Year's Day—was widely accepted and many a Scots housewife used to choose the first day of the year for killing a fowl. Thus it can be assumed that the slaughter of birds and beasts around the New Year had sacrificial implications.

FRANCE

Leaving aside for later consideration wren ceremonial in Ireland and the Isle of Man, where it still survives, and Wales, where it did so until recently, we turn to France, where the celebrations were sometimes elaborate. Sonnini, whose book *Travels in Upper and Lower Egypt* was translated into English in 1800, wrote: "While I was at Le Ciotat (near Marseilles in France) the particulars of a singular ceremony were related to me, which takes place every year at the beginning of Nivose (the latter end of December): a numerous body of men, armed with swords and pistols, set off in search of a small bird which the ancients call Troglodytes . . . the common wren . . . When they have found it (a thing not difficult because they always take care to have one ready), it is suspended on the middle of a pole, which two men carry on their shoulders, as if it were a heavy burthen. This whimsical procession parades around the town; the bird is weighed in a great pair of scales, and the company sits down to table and makes merry. The name they give to the Troglodytes is not less curious than the kind of festival to which it gives occasion. They call it at Le Ciotat, the Pole-cat or *Père de la bécasse* (father of the woodcock), supposed by them to be engendered by the polecat, which is a great destroyer of birds, but which certainly produces none."

At Carcassonne the Wren Boys of the Rue Saint Jean assembled on a date near the end of the year, and went out of the town to beat bushes in search of wrens. The first to kill one was proclaimed King and carried the wren back to town on a pole. On the evening of the last day of the year the King proceeded through the streets with all

Plate 25. Indian painting by a Mughal artist (*c.* A.D. 1610-1625) representing the mythical Roc attacking a herd of elephants while being itself attacked by the Phoenix. Several mythological and artistic traditions have contributed to this design. Cf. p. 128. (*British Museum*)

Plate 26. a. Wren Boys' procession, Athea, Limerick, 1946. The collection is being taken. Cf. p. 155. (*Kevin Danaher*)

b. Wren Boy musicians. Two are playing the *bodhrán*, a local traditional form of drum. Cf. p. 155. (*Kevin Danaher*)

who had joined the hunt, carrying torches and accompanied by a drum and fife band, stopping at some of the houses to chalk on the doors *vive le roi* and the number of the New Year. Early on Twelfth Day the King, arrayed in a blue mantle, wearing a crown, and carrying a sceptre, went to High Mass at the parish church of St. Vincent, preceded by a man carrying a wren fastened to the top of a pole decorated with a wreath of olive leaves, oak or mistletoe cut from an oak. Later, accompanied by his retinue, he visited the bishop, the mayor, the magistrates and other notable citizens, collecting money to defray the expenses of the banquet which took place in the evening and concluded with a dance. The ceremony was abolished at the Revolution, revived at the Restoration and again suppressed after 1830.[1]

At Entraigues the hunt took place on Christmas Eve. When a bird had been caught it was presented to the priest and released from the church pulpit with a rose coloured ribbon attached to it after the midnight Mass. Women helped to chase the wren at Mirabeau, and if they succeeded in capturing one, and the men failed, they had the right to chase the men and blacken their faces with mud and soot. Bonwick, writing in 1894, remarked without giving further details, that in France the wren was hunted and killed "devotionally" on Twelfth Day and afterwards solemnly buried in the churchyard.

The wren appeared in other types of ceremonial in western France, especially as a token form of tribute in connexion with the fêtes called Bachelleries. They were customarily held in May but latterly might be somewhat earlier or later. These celebrations were a jubilant spring rite encouraging the close association of young unmarried people of both sexes. Perhaps their origin may have been in pagan orgiastic ceremonies—in spirit they seem to have had much in common with the spring festivals of young people in ancient China—but they became closely integrated with local social and religious customs. During feudal times the gentry took them under their patronage and participated in some quaint ceremonies, which suggest that the relationship of the seigneurie to the peasantry in pre-revolutionary France was not so aloof as we are sometimes wont to assume. For example, a document of 24 September, 1590, forwarded by the Seigneur

[1]There are discrepancies as to the date on which the proceedings began. Sébillot states that the foray was on 31 December and the ceremonial visit to the mayor on 6 January. Other authorities describe the hunt as occurring on the first Sunday of December and the procession on Twelfth Day.

de Sanzay to Henry IV, provided that in consideration of their dues to the Seigneur being remitted, the newly-married should set up a May-pole every May Day in front of his chateau and dance around it.

Associated with the Bachelleries was a form of football similar to the Lincolnshire Haxey Hood game. It was so rough that it was proscribed in 1369, though it persisted in one district until 1857. Men on horseback also tilted at a dummy—a survival of the tournament—and in at least one municipality, a Queen as well as a King of the fête was elected. Perhaps traditions of this kind have had some influence on the present pleasant custom of electing Queens representing local industries. As I have seen it in northern France, it is a much jollier, less commercialised and exhibitionist procedure than at English seaside resorts.

In these ceremonies the wren nearly always figured as a form of tribute. The Abbey of St. Germain des Près at Naintré preserves a document of 1663 in which the prior undertakes to give thirty pots of wine each year to the "bacheliers," provided that they bring him a living wren (Pourveu que les dits bacheliers apportent au dit prieur le roy Bertault en vye). It is stipulated that unless the wren has nine feathers in its tail the prior owes the young people nothing. Also the prior undertakes to pay a certain sum of money if a wren is brought to him at Christmas or New Year's Day. It is also stated that they must present a pair of white gloves to him—a custom reminiscent of that obtaining at English Courts of Assize when there are no criminal cases. The priory of Chateau-Ponsac in Creuse required a wren, captured by an unarmed hunting party, to be produced as tribute on New Year's Day. The captor became King of the Fête. He used to go in procession with fife and drum accompaniment to the church, and during High Mass present the bird to the prior, the young people affirming at the same time that they had obtained the wren by legitimate hunting methods and not by means of a gun or a bow and arrow. This latter requirement, together with the traditional use of clubs or other archaic weapons, suggests the antiquity of the Wren Hunt. Newly-married couples at Villiers (Cher) had to visit the steward of the estate on the next Trinity Sunday after the wedding, bearing on their shoulders the large wooden receptacle in which grapes were crushed, with a wren inside. In Limousin a man was named *roi de la tirevessie*. He had to remove his clothes and jump into the water. He then took a wren on his wrist and proceeded to the town where he plucked it, scattering the feathers in the air. Finally it was presented to the representative of the seigneur. Near Tulle in Upper Limousin, the wren was borne in a wagon. On one side sat couples married less than seven years, on the other, couples with longer experience of matrimony. Afterwards, these couples competed in a tug of war. Sometimes the tribute consisted of other birds than the wren. According to a document of 1690, the King of the Bachelleries came with fifes playing to present two chickens and a pair of white gloves to the Seigneur de Cheneché. Another document of 1393 stipulated that two harriers were to be presented.

As at Marseilles, these wren ceremonies were often conducted in such a manner as to suggest that the bird was immensely large and ponderous. At Mardillon, near Chatillon-sur-Indre, the wren was brought to the seigneur tied with strong new ropes in a wagon drawn by four black oxen. Michelet states that in "une seigneurie de France" —he believes in Lorraine—the peasants paid tribute in the form of a serin placed in a carriage drawn by four horses, and that in Franconia, a token tribute of a wren or grasshopper was paid. The atmosphere of burlesque which pervades wren ritual should not be dismissed as tomfoolery. All the indications are that at one time the ceremonies were of great significance, but that when they lost their meaning, people modified them to "save face" while continuing ritual which had not quite lost its numinous import. Why were the nobility and high officials of church and municipality involved in these apparently farcical proceedings? Always, in one form or another, the wren is ceremonially presented or exhibited to those of higher rank. This is most naturally explained on the hypothesis that wren ceremonial represents the vestiges of a cult honoured by folk whose observances were tolerated by their superiors. If so, the ritual represents an early, submerged stratum of culture.

The degradation of the ceremonial into burlesque must also be interpreted psychologically. At solemn ceremonies all over the world there is often a grotesque component of levity, as in the boisterous behaviour at Irish wakes, and the mockery of the bride at Chinese weddings. So, today, many a superstitious custom is performed with a laugh—a way of protecting oneself from ridicule while ensuring that "chance," "fate," or "gremlins" are not offended.

The element of burlesque is as evident in wren songs as in the ritual. Here is a somewhat free translation of the Breton song recorded by Luzel:

THE DEATH OF THE WREN

One day I went for a walk, and then
What should I catch but a spunky wee wren

I held him fast; he couldn't get out,
Penned in the cow-house he quickly got stout.

When he'd grown fat and had put on weight,
Up came the butcher to settle his fate.

When he arrived and the lads he led,
The din they made would have wakened the dead.

Off he skedaddled to save his life,
When the butcher brandished his carving knife.

Four sturdy waggons with steel-shod wheels
Rolled off to Nantes stuffed with his quills.

When they departed they left enough stuff
Four feather beds to pack with his fluff.

This song was sung on 11 November, 1863, St. Martin's Day, but it is uncertain whether it had any special connexion with Martinmas.[1]

In Devonshire until the first half of the nineteenth century, villagers carried a wren suspended on a pole borne on the shoulders of two men, as in some regions of France. Pretending to hoist their heavy burden into a wagon they sang:

[1] The Breton song, "Plumer le roitelet" follows the cumulative sequence of the well-known "Plumer l'alouette." It recounts the dismemberment of the wren and was used as a game during long winter evenings. Those who omitted words or made mistakes had to pay a forfeit. This emphasis on word-perfection, characteristic of the repetition of ancient tales, has played an important part in preserving folklore. Another Breton song, "Dépecer le merle" is of this ancient and widespread type. A fragment of another Breton song refers to the Wren Hunt:

I went off to hunt in the woods,
Never, never, shall I get there!
A little wren I managed to catch,
Never there, there, there, never shall I get there.

The song "Les noces du Roitelet" is commented on in the next chapter.

I've shot a wren, says Rabbin to Bobbin;
Hoist! Hoist! says Richard to Robin . . .
I'll take a leg, says Rabbin to Bobbin, etc.

So it goes on with various characters represented as heaving different portions of the wren into the cart, the sense being, not that the bird is dismembered, but that all the participants help to hoist the carcass.

This song occurs in various versions. In Oxfordshire it describes the discussion by the party of how to deal with the shot wren. "We'll borrow feyther's cart—We must hire a wagon—How shall us get her in?—We must have some ropes" and so on. The Manx song refers to the securing of the wren with iron bars as well as ropes. The Yorkshire variant has diverged from the presumed original. Its theme is a bird's nest and the wren is not mentioned. The question and answer occur: "How shall we get home? We'll hire a cab, etc." Thus the song has lost its point—the conveyance serves, not to carry the wren but to take the hunters home. In a Gloucestershire version three men are hired to carry the bird, six to cook it, and "all the town" are invited to partake. Other variants have been collected in Scotland and even in the Orkneys, the wren is dismembered, and, as in Brittany, its feathers used to stuff a bed. Apparently, the theme was carried north of the Tweed without any ritual being associated with it.

Thus these wren songs indicate the homogeneity of French and English wren traditions, and support other indications that there was a relationship between the rites observed in France and south-west England.

WALES

In a version from Carmarthenshire it is emphasized that the Hunt must be conducted in the old way rather than the new. The wren is to be killed with bow and arrow rather than with cannon and guns, to be cut up with hatchets and cleavers rather than with knives and forks, and to be boiled in cauldrons and pans rather than kettles and pots. The reference to firearms indicates that the song took its present form after their introduction, but the theme must be older and the emphasis on the use of ancient implements, as in France, illustrates the forces of conservatism at work to maintain traditions passed on from much earlier times. The mention of knives and forks in the Manx variant shows that this part of the song cannot be earlier than the eighteenth century, for these were not in general use until after 1726.

In Wales, the Wren Hunt was particularly associated with Twelfth Night, but the date of the celebration varied. Owen, writing at the end of last century, remarked that he had a dim recollection of participating in the Hunt on St. Stephen's Day, but Peate states that it took place in readiness for the procession on Twelfth Day. Edward Lhuyd (*ob.* 1709), one of the earliest authorities, refers to the procession in Pembrokeshire on Twelfth Night, and as other writers endorse this, there can be no doubt of its accuracy. In the 'sixties, however, the Wren Procession took place in Cardiff on St. Stephen's Day, but this was due to Irish influence—an example of the reanimation and modification of a ceremony through influence from a related cultural stream separated from it long before. Sir W. Goscombe John wrote in 1929: "I remember as a child groups of young roughs—they were generally Irish, I think, going round the Canton district of Cardiff on Boxing Day with a holly-tree decked with ribbons and a dead *wran* with a bottle of spirits attached. The song they sang included the well-known lines, 'St. Stephen's Day was caught in the furze'." Such an importation increases the probability that the Galloway observance was introduced from elsewhere. In Pembrokeshire, at Epiphany, a boy came round with coloured paper streamers in his hat and a wren in a cage. He sang:

> *Come and make your offering*
> *To the smallest, yet the king,*

and let the bird go.

At Llanidloes, and doubtless elsewhere, the bird was pursued with sticks along a hedge and was often killed accidentally. If a wren could not be secured, another bird was substituted. The bird was usually carried in a receptacle such as a be-ribboned stable lantern, but often in a fairly elaborate "Wren House." This might be made of wood, with doors and windows (Plate 27, p. 160). (A hollow turnip was sometimes used in Ireland). In the Tenby neighbourhood the body of the wren was placed in a Wren House with a square of glass at either end, and sometimes the box might be surmounted by a hoop or circle. (The bird was sometimes carried between crossed hoops in Ireland). This structure was called "Noah's Ark" and it was borne by four men on poles fixed to the corners—as elsewhere, burlesquing the size and weight of the bird. Meanwhile the women went "sowling." Sikes also describes the procession in Pembrokeshire with the wren in a paper box borne by four men supporting four poles. The song exaggerating the size of the equipment needed was sung, and the occasion honoured by "sowling" and "tooling." Lhuyd remarks: "They are accustomed in Pembrokeshire, etc. to carry a wren in a bier on Twelfth Night; from a young man to his sweetheart, that is two or three bear it in a bier (covered) with ribbons; and sing carols. They also go to other houses where there are no sweethearts and there will be beer, etc. And a beer from the county they call Cutty Wran." According to Owen the homes of couples married during the year were visited in the Christmas holidays by a party bearing a wren, or a sparrow if a wren was not available, on a miniature bier. They were serenaded with Welsh doggerel:

> Here is the wren,
> If he is still alive,
> Or a sparrow
> To be roasted.

The husband would regale the young men with beer. When the bird was carried in a Wren House it was usually alive. We are told by Davies that "Every young lady, and even old ladies, used to compete in presenting the grandest ribbon to the wren." If no invitation was forthcoming, a curse was pronounced: "Come wind, blow and overthrow this house." The procession was accompanied by performers on various instruments.

The choice of newly-wed couples for visitation contrasts with the formal visits paid to church and other dignitaries in France, and the less formal visits to the "big houses" in Ireland. It suggests that wren ceremonies were more closely integrated into the whole social structure in France than in the British Isles. No doubt the newly-weds were chosen partly as having attained a temporary distinction in the community, partly because of the ancient and widespread tradition of "guying" the newly-wed, and also because it was thought that in their domestic bliss they should be open-handed, but dimly in the background may have been the notion that sexuality should have some place in festivities at the turn of the year. As we have noted, the newly-wed participated in wren ritual in France and at Carcassonne the bird was carried in a bunch of mistletoe—a plant with erotic, pre-Christian associations.

The Wren Hunt persisted in Wales, as elsewhere, in spite of the widespread tradition that the bird should not be molested. "Whoever robs a wren's nest shall never enjoy good health in his life" says a well-known Welsh couplet, and according to a Cardiganshire saying, to destroy the nest was to forfeit eternal salvation. Tegid describes the dire penalties which he was told as a child would be visited on those who harmed the bird, and Owen states that it was sacred, save at one time of the year.

Isle of Man

The Wren Procession still survives in an attenuated form in the Isle of Man (Plate 28, p. 161). A party of boys goes around on St. Stephen's Day, mainly in the towns, gabbling the Wren Song prestissimo as a pretext for collecting coppers. No bird, nor anything to represent one, is carried. The procedure illustrates the principle that the solemn rites of the forefathers may in due course become the recreations of their descendants' children. In Ireland the Wren Boys include young men. (It should be remembered that the use of "boy" in Ireland is cognate with "girl" in England, indicating unmarried status rather than immaturity). In the Isle of Man the participants are always children, though apparently the last degradation of male ritual has not been reached—the performance of the ceremonies by little girls.

Waldron, describing the Manx proceedings in 1736, said: "Having caught the wren they kill her, and lay her on a bier with the utmost solemnity, bringing her to the parish church and burying her with a whimsical kind of solemnity, singing dirges over her in the Manx language, which they call her knell, after which Christmas begins." Down to the eighteenth century the Hunting of the Wren took place in the small hours of Christmas Day. After prayers in the church at midnight, preceded by the ringing of the bells, the lads went out in search of a victim.

Another early account in *Kelly's Manx Dictionary*, is worth quoting in full: "On St. Stephen's Day the inhabitants of this district (Baaltin=Baldwin) assemble to hunt the little wren, which, when caught and killed, they fasten to the top of a long pole and carry about in procession with drums beating and colours flying, and distribute for money the feathers of the bird, which are esteemed by the purchasers to be a charm against all evils for the ensuing year. So far is common with the practice of other parts of the island; but in Baaltin the body of the naked wren is deposited with much ceremony in Kilammon (The site of the modern chapel of St. Luke; built 1836), and the evening concludes with a variety of games in the open ground which adjoins. While some think this to be an emblem of the change from human sacrifices to that of beasts, in the offerings of Baal, others think, with apparently more reason, that it is a superstitious memorial of the death of the saint."

The second explanation is a typical interpretation. The first has an element of truth in it, in spite of the unsound folk-etymology on which it is based. As the prefix *kil* signifies "church" there was apparently an earlier church on this site, and as Christian places of worship were frequently built on the site of pagan sanctuaries, the wren burial, may, perhaps, have been localised there for a long time.

Other explanations are attributable to the urge folk feel to account somehow for a custom, the significance of which they have forgotten. Waldron quotes a legend about an enchantress Tehi who rode a milk-white palfrey and led men to destruction in a river, afterwards flying off in the form of a bat.[1] In descriptions published later, we are told that the siren transformed herself into a wren. MacTaggart, in the *Scottish Gallovidian Dictionary,* stated that Manx fishermen believed that a sea sprite, attended by storms, haunted the herring shoals and was seen flying away in the form of a wren. So seamen liked to have a dead wren in their boats to ward off evil. Train's version is more sophisticated: "In former times a fairy of uncommon beauty exerted such undue influence over the male population, that she, at various times, induced by her sweet voice, numbers to follow her footsteps, till by degrees she led them into the sea, where they perished. This barbarous exercise of power had continued for a great length of time, till it was apprehended that the island would be exhausted of its defenders; when a knight-errant sprang up, who discovered some means of countervailing the charms used by this siren, and even laid a plot for her destruction, which she only escaped at the moment of extreme hazard by taking the form of a wren. But, though she evaded instant annihilation, a spell was cast

---

[1]As an illustration of the contrary connotations an animal, or other object, may acquire, it may be mentioned that while the bat is of evil omen in many parts of the world yet it is a symbol of good luck in China, this being explained as due to the same syllable signifying "bat" and "happiness" in Chinese. In South Shropshire it was regarded as a duty to kill bats which were considered evil creatures while in the northern part of the county people carefully refrained from harming them.

upon her, by which she was compelled to reanimate the same form every succeeding New Year's Day until she should perish by a human hand." This seems to be a rationalisation bringing the Tehi legend into conjunction with the knight-errant motif to explain superstitions about the wren.

Train states that there was no special day for pursuing the wren, but that on St. Stephen's Day it was carried around suspended by the legs from twin hoops decorated with evergreens and ribbons. (The hoops with evergreens are sometimes still carried). Townley, in 1790, noted that the bird was attached to a long pole, together with a handkerchief as a banner. Dyer describes the wren as affixed to a pole with wings outstretched, while Clague says that it was fastened to a stick borne between two boys "tied with ribbons for a sign of their good going (success)." He mentions that the feathers were kept in a purse, and that the carcase might be brought on board one of the boats of the herring fleet to bring good luck. Bullock says that the feathers were treasured "with religious care" as talismans against shipwreck throughout the coming year, but Train noted that the bird was buried by the sea or on waste land. It was said of the wren's captor that he would be "the great man of the day at that time" and would have good luck throughout the year. It will be noted that these ceremonies were similar in many respects to those which took place in southern France.

The author of "A Sailor Boy's Experience", which appeared in 1867, remarks that in the neighbourhood of Hamilton in Scotland sailors used to catch and pluck a wren before setting out on a voyage, divining from the way the feathers fell whether the herring fishery would be successful or not. Probably they acquired these notions from Manx fishermen.

IRELAND

The Wren Hunt survives more vigorously in Ireland than elsewhere. Throughout most of Munster, Leinster and Connacht the Wren Boys appear on St. Stephen's Day, but it is very remarkable that, as shown by the answers to a questionnaire kindly distributed at my suggestion by the Irish Folklore Commission, wren ritual is virtually absent from an area almost coextensive with the province of Ulster (Fig. 77).[1]

[1] Mr. J. C. Beckett of Queen's University, Belfast, tells me that Wren Boys used to appear at Ballinderry, Co. Antrim.

FIG. 77. Map of Ireland showing distribution of wren ritual. The ritual is observed at present, or was observed until recently, in all districts S. of the line and is absent N. of it. (After a map provided by the Irish Folklore Commission).

Parties average four to ten members, though there may be as few as two or as many as twenty. The wren is hunted with sticks along the hedges, but sometimes, a day or two beforehand, a bird is caught roosting in its nest, usually in the cottage eaves. In some areas the procedure has become so commercialised that the Boys do their round on bicycles or even motor cars, to the displeasure of those from whom they solicit offerings, for in the past, there seems often to have been an understanding that the Wren Boys should appear only in the locality where they lived. They are usually lads aged 10–14, but here and there men up the age of 30 take part.

In many areas the wren is borne on a bush, such as ivy, adorned with ribbons, on a pole or on sticks shaped like a cross; in others it is carried in some small container such as a hollow turnip, a match box with a glass cover so that the corpse can be shown to "Doubting Thomases." Sometimes more than one wren is carried—occasionally up to a dozen. Where the killing of the wren is disapproved the Boys carry a potato with feathers stuck into it to resemble a wren, or some other object, such as a celluloid budgerigar. Now and then, when a wren cannot be obtained, or would be objected to for some reason, a robin or some other small bird is substituted.

The verses about the wren are usually recited or sung in English, though there are wren songs in Irish. Other ballads or songs may be

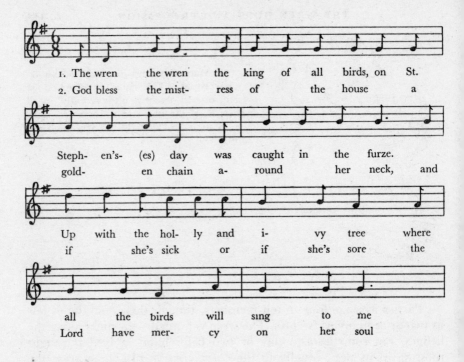

1. The wren the wren the king of all birds, on St.
2. God bless the mist- ress of the house a

Steph- en's- (es) day was caught in the furze.
gold- en chain a- round her neck, and

Up with the hol- ly and i- vy tree where
if she's sick or if she's sore the

all the birds will sing to me
Lord have mer- cy on her soul

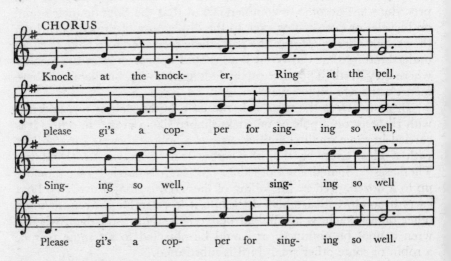

CHORUS

Knock at the knock- er, Ring at the bell,

please gi's a cop- per for sing- ing so well,

Sing- ing so well, sing- ing so well

Please gi's a cop- per for sing- ing so well.

FIG. 78. The Song of the wren boys as sung in Cork city in 1946. Words and music transcribed by Mrs. J. O'Kelly.

sung according to the district and the occasion. At some of the houses
the Wren Boys dance. They are usually welcomed and given refresh-
ments. The proceeds are either divided at the end of the day, or, more
generally, pooled for a dance or a "spree" that night (Fig. 78, p. 156).

The carcase of the wren is often thrown away in the evening, but
in a few localities it is buried at or near an inhospitable house, though
there is one Co. Clare record of its being interred, as a mark of honour,
at the house where the Boys had been best treated during the day.

The Wren hunt and the Folk Play in Ireland

In some places wren ritual is combined with forms of the traditional Folk Play, well known in England. The Boys are dressed in the
usual grotesque manner. In a few places a man and a woman, the
latter often a man in disguise, act the part of Fools in the Procession.
In other places the bladder of a pig or cow, slaughtered for meat at that
time of year, is inflated and mounted on a stick. The bearer playfully
strikes onlookers with it. Only rarely do women or girls take part. At
Adrigole, Co. Cork, in the 'nineties Wren Boys, who were usually
young men over twenty years of age, disguised themselves in goat-
skins with the horns on the wearer's head. There are a few other
records of horns and goat-skins being worn. An account from Co.
Kerry describes a wooden horse with two Wren Boys under it, capering
about and performing various antics. In Roscommon, the Wren Boys'
leader was dressed in straw and one of the party wore feminine attire.

The most elaborate Irish wren ritual on record concerns the
activities at Dingle, Co. Kerry. Up to 35 men took part, some carrying
wooden swords, others wielding a Fool's bladder on a stick, wearing
suits of straw or disguised as women. These were called *oinsigh*—
women fools. The party carried banners and poles, the bearers being
decked with ribbons in the same style as the Mummers of the Folk
Plays. The "Captain" wore an old style green uniform and carried a
sword.[1] The Wren Man, who carried the dead wren in a holly bush
fastened to a pole, also wore a special costume. A mock battle was
staged between those bearing swords, the Fools and the strawboys
with bladders.

Such performances are probably derived from ancient Dionysiac
ceremonial which embodied death-and-resurrection rites characteristic

[1]Elsewhere he wore a three-cornered hat with a bird's wing.

of the ancient civilisations of the Middle East. The most complete rituals survive in the Balkans. At the conclusion of the Spring Carnival in Thrace a procession goes through the streets of Malko-Tirnovsko. The principal personages are a man, called the Kuker, and a woman called the Kukerica. Both make lascivious gestures. The man's face is blackened with soot, he carries a club and wears a goatskin. The "woman" is a man in petticoats, also with blackened face. In the procession are other youths arrayed as girls, and masked women dressed as men. A King, Judge and other officials are represented, and those they condemn in the mock court are beaten. Contributions are solicited from bystanders by men wielding clubs. Towards evening the Kuker ploughs a few furrows and sows some corn. The man who plays this part is regarded as committing a deadly sin. All join in a boisterous carousal at night.

In other localities the celebrations vary. A man may be dragged over the newly-ploughed land, and in some places elaborate masks representing the horned heads of animals or the head of a bird are worn. These bird masks worn ritually here and in Austria, remind us of the beaked participants in Palaeolithic rites (p. 19).

The extent to which these observances are accompanied by pantomimic obscenities varies. There may be a procession of masked men clad in goatskins and "policemen" brandishing swords. Two boys are dressed as brides and there is a woman called *Babo* (unmarried mother) who carries a cradle with a swaddled puppet representing an illegitimate baby. One of the girls is pursued by a skin-clad man and a mock marriage is enacted; but the bridegroom—the baby speedily grown to maturity—is slain by a second goat-skin clad man. He is then represented as restored to life and the marriage is supposed to be consummated. Thus the Play concludes, but the brides are yoked to a plough which they drag widdershins around the village while the spectators shout: "May wheat be ten piastres the bushel! Amen, O God, that the poor may eat!"

Dionysiac ritual established itself widely throughout Europe but, as is customary with archaic rituals, elements tended here and there to become separated and to evolve independently or in association with other fragments of the original pattern. The Sword Dance, for example, survives in parts of central Europe, such as Austria, and in northern England it is associated with the Folk Play on Plough Monday. The ritual of dragging around the plough may occur independently of

Play or Dance. The Morris Dance and the Play are more strongly represented in southern England, though the Play seems to be unknown in Norfolk and Suffolk. Thus we see how, in Britain, the tradition branched and different elements received emphasis according to circumstances in different areas. Away from the Sword Dance area in England the Folk Play was dislocated from the fertility rites of spring and became attached to the Christmas festival. So, in all probability, it became associated with the Wren Procession in Ireland through there being no appropriate spring festival to which it could become attached.

In Ireland the Folk Play is recorded throughout Ulster except in Cavan, Monaghan, and perhaps Fermanagh; also in Louth, Wexford and, according to Mr. V. R. E. Dobbs, a remote area on the Kilkenny-Carlow border. Here, the Wren Boys performed the Play. In versions from Donegal and Tyrone there appears a character called The Wren, and in the latter area he demands "a trate" as do the Wren Boys in their song. Thus in southern Ireland where the Wren Hunt prevails the Wren Boys might perform the Play, but in the north, where the Hunt is unknown, the Wren only makes a courtesy appearance.

According to Green the Folk Play in north-east Ulster has closer affinities with the Play in the north-west of England than with southern England. This writer is " strongly of the opinion that there was an original Irish *ludus*, preserved in Ulster and parts of Leinster, by fitting on to it an imported English text. Elsewhere it has degenerated into the simple Wrenboy processions of Saint Stephen's Day." This conclusion cannot be accepted, for even where, as in Donegal, the characters Jack Straw and the man-woman survive in the Play, linking it with primitive versions, there are no versions in Irish. Our survey of the Wren Hunt shows that it has a history independent of Dionysiac ritual, and in Ireland its association with it appears to be adventitious. There are many indications that the Folk Play arrived from England comparatively recently. It is tempting to believe that the masquerading in straw or skins is a relic of a form of the Play brought to Ireland in ancient times, and to suppose that the Mummers, masked and disguised like Wren Boys, who attend weddings in Kilkenny provide a link with the fertility observances in primitive Plays, but more probably these customs are the outcome of the deep-set impulse to introduce an element of the grotesque into ceremonies. Steevens mentions that court Fools wore calf-skin coats, and remarks: "The custom is still preserved in Ireland; and the fool in any of the legends which the mummers act at Christmas always appears in a calf's skin or cow's skin." Although apparently archaic practices which are not recorded from England occur in Irish performances of the Play, yet even in Donegal, where the characters Jack Straw and the man-woman survive in it, there are no versions in Irish.

Some German authorities have mentioned the existence of the Wren Hunt in Iceland, but it never occurred there.

EXPLANATION OF THE WREN HUNT

As with the explanations given for eating goose at Michaelmas, so with the accounts concerning the origin of wren ritual—their multiplicity and inconsistency show that we are dealing with very ancient ceremonial the origin of which has been forgotten. It is said that a wren, hopping on a drum, awakened the Danes and so prevented the Irish from surprising them, and that King William's army was about to be attacked when a wren awakened a drummer by hopping on his drum and so enabled him to sound the call to arms in time. Another version is that wrens alarmed Cromwell's forces when the Irish were stealthily advancing on them. Such explanations, it will be noted, are consistent with the Wren Hunt occurring in the predominantly Roman Catholic area of Ireland and not among the intrusive, mainly Protestant people in Ulster. Yet another explanation is that when St. Stephen was making his escape, a wren alighted on his gaoler's face and awakened him. It is also said that when our Lord was hiding in the garden a wren betrayed Him with its loud ticking notes. Children who hunted tits near Valenciennes gave a somewhat similar explanation of the custom. We find the wren on bad terms with an Irish saint in the legend of St. Moling, which provides the earliest literary reference to the Wren Hunt and yet another explanation of its origin. The saint cursed the wren because it ate his pet fly: "He that marred for me the poor pet that used to be making music for me, let his dwelling be for ever in empty houses, with a wet drip therein continually. And let children and young persons be destroying him."[1] The

---

[1] If a small gold object found in a ring-fort represents a wren, as some archaeologists believe, this would be valuable evidence of the importance of the bird in Ireland in early times (Plate 27, p. 160).

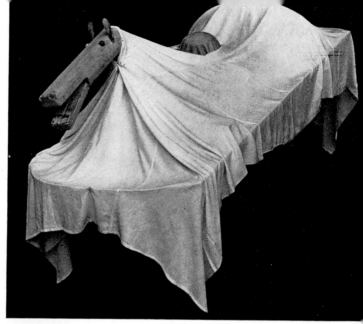

Plate 27 a. Hobby-horse or *Láir Bhán* (White Mare) used by Wren Boys on St. Stephen's Day in the Tralee district, Co. Kerry. The movable lower jaw was worked with a string by the operator concealed in the sheet. Similar or related contrivances are used in other countries of Europe and Asia, including Indonesia. Cf. p. 157. (*National Museum of Ireland*)

b. Gold ornament, said to represent a wren, found during excavations at a ring-fort, Garryduff, C. Cork (*c.* 6th century A.D.) Cf. p. 160. (*M. J. O'Kelly and Cork Public Museum*)

 Actual size of ornament.

c. Decorated Wren House in which the wren was carried in procession in Wales. Cf. p. 150. (*National Museum of Wales, Welsh Folk Museum*)

Plate 28. Manx Wren Boys in Ramsey, 1904. (*G. B. Cowen and Manx Museum*)

enmity between the wren and Christian saints suggests that this bird, like the woodpecker, was displaced from high magical status by Christianity. In Irish hagiology the wren is referred to as *magus avium* and in Cormac's Glossary it is described as a Druid bird which makes predictions. Details of the oracles drawn from the behaviour of the wren have survived. Writers refer to the bird as having been "domesticated," but it is not tameable in this sense, though perhaps it was kept for periods in a cage for magico-religious reasons as geese were kept in enclosures by the Britons of Caesar's time. The appearance of the wren in the folktales of Celtic regions supports the one-time importance of the bird in ancient belief. The story of "The Wren and the Stonechat" is known only from Ireland and Gaelic-speaking Scotland. The Scottish tale of Conan Corr, the Wren, and his Twelve Sons, which describes their unsuccessful efforts to pull up a carrot, reflects the interest in the characteristic which has always attracted people's attention—its small size. The delight of folk in imagining the downtrodden scoring over the proud—as in Cinderella—appears not only in the flight competition motif, but also in "The Wren and the Bear" in Grimm's tales.

The Origin of the Wren Hunt

The problem of how wren ritual arose may be approached in two ways. We may draw inferences from the character of the ceremonial and its presumed magico-religious affinities, or we may learn something of its past history from its distribution. In regard to the first of these, it is a natural inference that the Hunt, taking place, as it does, about the winter solstice, belongs to the great category of rites which have as their object the banishment of evil influences at a seasonal crisis. We might classify it with, for example, the pursuit of a man in a cow-hide on St. Kilda at Hogmanay (New Year's Eve), or the chasing away of dogs from Breadalbane households on New Year's Day. But there is no definite evidence that the wren was ever a scapegoat in the Old Testament sense of a sin-bearer driven from the community, nor treated as were the two sparrows offered according to Mosaic law by a cleansed leper (Lev. xiv.4). However, there is much to suggest that the Wren Hunt was sacrificial. The bird was reverenced but killed at one season only, the feathers were regarded as talismans, the body was sometimes buried with respect, the chief human actor was regarded as in some sense a king, and the bird itself was given a royal title. Ritual of somewhat similar pattern was enacted in some other areas in connexion with mammals and birds. In the Isle of Man the procedure involved in killing "St. Catherine's Hen" resembled in a number of respects the Hunting of the Wren.

It has been suggested that a parallel to the Wren Hunt is to be found in Sumerian mythology. The winged storm-god Zu, coveted the sovereignty of Enlil, the earth-god, who with Anu, the heaven-god and Ea, the water-god formed a divine triad. One morning, at sunrise, when Enlil was seating himself on his throne and arranging his crown on his head, Zu snatched the destiny-tablet of the gods and flew off to his mountain where he went into hiding. The gods were greatly distressed and Anu called for a champion who would fight Zu on their behalf. The god Adad was chosen, but refused to fight, and so with several other gods. The remainder of the myth is missing, but apparently one of the gods succeeded in retrieving the tablet. The theory has been advanced, based on the designs on seals, that a ritual was enacted at the New Year, in the course of which, a figure representing Zu was ceremonially chased, but the text of the myth, read at the New Year festival, does not mention this procedure. None the less, cylinder seals show a bird in flight, apparently damaging trees or herbage and pursued with a weapon by a god. We have a scene in which the bird is carried on a mace like a dead game bird by one god, while another bears what are evidently specimens of the destroyed vegetation. Another shows a bird-man—that is a figure dressed to appear birdlike—before a god in a scene of judgment (Figs. 79 and 80, p. 163). (Figures partly resembling birds are sometimes demons). It is difficult to believe that these scenes are unconnected with the myth of Zu. However they are interpreted, they suggest mythology and probably ritual, associated with the New Year, in which a bird is chased, killed, and carried in procession. The bird may have been regarded as a scapegoat. Possibly the dying down of the vegetation in winter was attributed to it, or rather to that of which it was a symbol, and its destruction was regarded as giving magical aid to the powers of fertility associated with the New Year. If so, the ceremonial represented may be the prototype of the Wren Hunt.

Zu was a storm god, associated with the dusty underworld where the dead wear feathers and wings like birds, and the Zu myth is a version of a common theme—the temporary triumph of the forces of

FIG. 79. Babylonian cylinder seal (Dynasty of Akkad) apparently representing the Zu bird damaging vegetation and being chased by gods. (After Frankfort, 1939).

FIG. 80. Babylonian cylinder seal (Dynasty of Akkad). The Zu bird is being carried suspended from a mace while what may be a specimen of the damaged vegetation is brought before the god Ea. (After Frankfort, 1939).

disorder. This is in keeping with our interpretation of the seals. The twelve days from Christmas to Epiphany within which wren ceremonies usually occur appear to be an ancient intercalary period equating the lunar to the solar year. Wren ceremonies, therefore, come within the category of observances held at this time involving a temporary reversal of law and custom—as, for example, the appointment of a Lord of Misrule or Boy Bishop. As we have seen, the wren and the Wren Man were regarded for a brief period as kings and the wren is treated with mingled honour and despite like a sacrificial victim; indeed, like a divine king.

If, as was suggested earlier, the eagle-wren competition for king-ship carries reminiscences of the supersession of chthonic by solar religion, through the diffusion of Asian ideas to Europe, the status of the wren in myth and ritual is explicable. Zu represented the under-world—and no bird might more readily be conceived to embody subterranean, chthonic powers than the crevice-frequenting wren. But there is insufficient evidence to establish a direct connexion between the Zu myth and the Wren Hunt.

A review of the evidence, suggests strongly that wren ritual came to Britain by the prehistoric route from the Gulf of Lions up the west coast of France—a route by which Mycenaean influences reached Britain.[1] Here we have an illustration of how Asian cultural elements could be carried to our shores. Although there are no traces of the Wren Hunt except in western Europe, it is possible that in Greek swallow ritual and the Portuguese cuckoo procession (pp. 183 and 204), we have vestiges of rites derived from a common ancient source.

Why should the Wren Hunt be absent from Ulster but present throughout the rest of Ireland? If it could be shown that some cultural influence affected Ulster in ancient times, which did not extend to the rest of the country to any appreciable extent, we might find a hint as to the culture with which wren ritual was associated.

The megalithic culture in western Europe consisted of two phases, represented by Passage Graves and Gallery Graves. There is a broad correlation between the distribution of Gallery graves and the Wren Hunt, if we omit the Mediterranean islands where wren ritual is unknown. The Mediterranean graves differ considerably from Irish types, though in Sardinia, Malta, and the Iberian peninsula, there are Neolithic types which seem to have provided the inspiration for develop-ments in Ireland north of the central plain. The most significant fact is that a special type of Gallery Grave, the Horned Cairn (now some-times included in a larger category, the Court Cairn) with two entrance walls forming a kind of vestibule for the performance of ritual, is mainly confined to Ulster and South-west Scotland, areas from which the Wren Hunt is absent. The Horned Cairn area extends some dis-tance into Connacht, but this overlap with the Wren Hunt region may

[1]Comparisons of Greek and Irish myths made by Krappe indicate that some of the latter have affinities with archaic Mediterranean traditions. Christiansen has also shown that some folk-tales probably came to Ireland from the Iberian peninsular. Mahr has pointed out that designs on stone monuments at Lough Crewe have affinities with this region.

well be due to the northward encroachment of the ritual throughout the centuries.[1] The Wren Cult can thus be plausibly connected with the Gallery Grave folk whose monuments are distinct from those of the builders of Horned Cairns.

Any explanation of the peculiar distribution of the Wren Hunt in Ireland must take account of the unlikelihood that, where such a practice was well established, it could have been extirpated without trace. We must assume, therefore, that it was never established in Ulster. If it could be shown that the people who built Horned Cairns settled in Ireland later than the builders of other types of megalithic grave, this would weaken the argument against Horned Cairn builders being Wren people. But the folk who built the Horned Cairns were Neolithic and the other types of megalithic tombs are later. The main period of construction of Passage Graves was after the Gallery Grave period. Thus there is evidence that Ulster was occupied by people who did not practise the Wren Cult. Their culture proved resistant, at least in some respects, to that of the builders of other types of grave than the Horned Cairn—folk who came with their Wren Cult by the trade route through France from the Mediterranean.

If we are correct in connecting the Wren Cult with the builders of a particular type or types of Gallery Grave, this suggests more uniformity of ceremonial than has seemed probable hitherto. Some archaeologists have assumed that the megalithic structures represent the worship of strictly localised divinities, because the ceremonial equipment varies greatly even within groups of monuments, and others have supposed the megalith builders to have been an alien, ruling aristocracy, cult missionaries or even merchants in trading posts. Of course any generalisation concerning structures which varied greatly and were built over a great period of time is liable to be wide of the mark, but the distribution of the Wren cult is only explicable in terms of a form of culture in Southern Ireland differing in certain respects from that in the North. In the previous chapter we noted some indications that early northerly traditions persisted in Ulster.

---

[1] The St. Martin's Eve ceremony of pouring the blood of some animal or bird, such as the goose, at the corners of the house has been studied by Mr. O'Sullivan of the Irish Folklore Commission. It is absent from Ulster also and from a considerable area of S.W. Ireland. Legend traces its origin to an incident in which St. Martin reproved people for grinding corn on a day when no wheel should turn. He was ground to pieces in the mill. Parallels are to be found in the mythology of the ancient Middle East. A number of birds, including the kingfisher and hen harrier, are associated with St. Martin in France.

The Black Pig's Dyke, following approximately the old southern boundary of Ulster, testifies to a cultural division which has persisted into our own time.

We may conclude that the Wren Cult reached the British Isles during the Bronze Age and was carried by megalith builders whose cultural inspiration came from the Mediterranean region. Probably these folk cherished mainly solar magico-religious beliefs. The Wren Hunt represents New Year ceremonial having as its purpose the defeat of the dark earth-powers and identification with the hoped-for triumph of light and life.

CHAPTER 10

FIRE-BIRDS

The Robin & the Wren

ONLY in Britain, and particularly in England, is the robin a universal favourite, though it is prominent in the folklore of north-western France and rather less so, of Germany. It has pet names in several north European countries. Modern beliefs about the bird cannot be traced to Greek or Latin sources and even its name in classical Greek is not certainly known. The association between the robin and the wren in folklore, the reciprocity of their traditions, and the general approximation of the areas in which the two birds were, and are, honoured, suggest that both came into prominence in the same cultural milieu.

All over the British Isles disaster is said to follow the ill-treatment of the robin. In Bucks it was believed that he who broke a robin's leg or wing would fracture his own leg or arm. The consequence of breaking the eggs would be the breakage of something belonging to the culprit. Similarly on Dartmoor it was said that taking a robin's nest was bound to be followed by the smashing of one's own crockery. In Wales a person who stole the eggs was in danger of becoming a victim of witches or of the devil. Irish folk were convinced that if anyone killed a robin a swelling would appear on his right hand, and in Suffolk a schoolboy's bad writing was explained as due to a robin having died as he held it. Similar beliefs were held in Germany and Czecho-Slovakia. Of swallows, too, it was said in England:

> *And if in any's hand she chance to die,*
> *'Tis counted ominous, I know not why.*

The hand of a person who killed a robin would always shake. A West Riding miner is recorded as having said: "My father killed a robin and had terrible bad luck after it. He had at that time a pig which was ready for pigging: she had a litter of seven and they all died. When the pig was killed the two hams went bad! Presently three of the family had a fever, and my father himself died of it!" The long arm of coincidence need not be invoked to explain these disasters. Probably the pigs were suffering from trichinosis and the illness of the farmer and his family was due, not to the dead robin but to living round worms.

In Yorkshire and Germany alike there were traditions that the cows of the man who killed a robin would give bloody milk, and the Tyrolese believed that epilepsy would follow interfering with the nest. As recently as 1944 a Herefordshire man declared that a cat which ate a robin would lose a limb—though it is correctly believed in the countryside that, as a rule, cats will not eat robins.

The robin is coupled with the wren in a great many admonitory rhymes, such as:

Devon. *Kill a robin or a wren,*
Never prosper, boy or man.

Essex. *The robin and the redbreast,*
The robin and the wren,
If ye tak' out of the nest
Ye'll never thrive again.

Herefordshire. *The robin and the wren*
Are God Almighty's cock and hen;
The swallow and the swift
Are God Almighty's gifts.

Lancashire. *The robin and the wren*
Are God's cock and hen,
The spink and the sparrow
Are the de'il's bow and arrow.

When Welsh boys carried around a wren at the New Year they sang with delightful inconsistency:

Cursed is the man
Who kills a robin or a wren.

There was also a saying,

Tom Tit and Jenny Wren
Were God Almighty's cock and hen.

Two of my neighbours, one a distinguished graduate, were surprised to be told that robin and wren are not male and female of one species. "Tom Tit" is a local name for the wren still used in East Anglia. An old belief that the wren is the tit's paramour may be due to confusion between the two names. A ballad quoted by Herd and Chambers was based on these matrimonial—or, perhaps, etymological, complications. In it the robin admits to the wren that he gave a ring to the "ox-ee." The theme of the bird wedding is widespread in European folk songs. There is also a Japanese version (B 282ff; Type 224).

In the East Riding, the companions of a lad known to have robbed a robin's nest would gather around him, pointing their forefingers, hissing and booing. Then they sang:

> *Robin takker, robin takker,*
> *Sin, sin, sin.*

The friendly regard for the robin has not prevented its being widely considered a bird of ill omen. In Leicestershire and Rutland it was thought unlucky for one to enter a house, though elsewhere this event was considered propitious. According to Scottish sayings a wren around a house brings luck. In Suffolk an intruding robin was an omen of death, and it was believed in Wales that a robin singing on the threshold presaged illness or death. At Hurstpierpoint School there is a tradition that if a robin sings on the altar of the chapel one of the boys will die. By a coincidence this sequence actually occurred some years ago—but robins not infrequently enter churches and occasionally nest in them. A robin tapping on a window was widely regarded as a portent of disaster, and all over England there are people who are apt to feel frightened when any bird, mistaking its reflection for a rival, flutters at a window pane. The death of T. E. Lawrence in a motor cycle accident was connected by a friend he had been visiting with the tapping of a bird on the window. The superstition is due to fear inspired by an unnatural happening interpreted as having personal relevance. In Bucks the plaintive piping of a robin was thought to foretell death, and in other parts of the country it was considered ominous for a sick person to hear the bird singing. Perhaps the apparently sad cadences of the robin's autumnal song encouraged such ideas.

Since killing a robin presaged misfortune, it is not surprising that

caging the bird was to invite disaster. A would-be poet, J. H. Pott,
writing in 1780, warned his readers:

> *For ever from his threshold fly,*
> *Who, void of honour, once shall try,*
> *With base inhospitable bread,*
> *To bar the freedom of his guest;*
> *O rather seek the peasant's shed,*
> *For he will give thee wasted bread,*
> *And fear some new calamity*
> *Should any there spread snares for thee.*

Blake's lines on the same theme are well known.

The robin has long been regarded as a weather prophet but
popular beliefs disagree. Aldrovandus stated that it predicted rain,
and a robin "shrieking" on a hedge was said to foretell bad weather.
In East Anglia the rhyme runs:

> *If the robin sings in the bush,*
> *Then the weather will be coarse;*
> *If the robin sings on the barn,*
> *Then the weather will be warm.*

As a boy in Ulster I was told that a robin singing on high branches
foretold fine weather. This is also believed in Northumberland, a
region from which emigrants went to Ulster during the Plantations.
Perhaps these beliefs are due to the song being uttered from higher
perches during the breeding season than in autumn and winter when
the bird is not so ardent and the weather is more inclement. In
Scotland, if a robin frequented the immediate neighbourhood of a
house in autumn, the inhabitants expected an early or severe winter,
while in south-east Ireland a redbreast entering a house foretold snow
or frost. No doubt these notions arose from *ex post facto* interpretations
of the movements of robins seeking food in hard times. The principal
significance of this weather-lore may lie in its indicating that in popular
belief the bird once had mysterious powers. As we have noted, influence over the weather is apt to be the last aspect of the power attributed
to it which a bird relinquishes—as it is sometimes the first magico-
religious capacity with which it is credited.

Birds already regarded as possessing supernatural powers often acquire an accretion of superstitions as a consequence of the numinous feelings they arouse. Examples of this are provided by the ballad of Cock Robin and the legend concerning the bird's solicitude for the dead. The nursery rhyme and the tale of *The Babes in the Wood* both associate the robin with funeral rites, though they belong more to literature than to oral lore, and therefore will not be discussed in detail here. The notion of birds impersonating human beings, which is the motif of the rhyme, is not far removed psychologically from the impersonation of birds and beasts by men, which has had a continuous history from the Palaeolithic to the present day. This has already been sufficiently commented upon, so far as visual art is concerned, but it may be noted that in *The Birds* of Aristophanes (*editio princeps* 1486), a play in which the drama has not yet emancipated itself from ritual, we have a literary example, analogous to some visual representations, of a transitional form between the magico-religious and the secular (Plate 29, p. 176).[1] In some respects the burlesques of "The Birds' Mass" by mediaeval goliardic wandering scholars recall the spirit of Aristophanes' play. The most elaborate example of "The Birds' Mass" is *La Messe des Oisiaus* by Jean de Condé (*c.* 1275-1340) sung in honour of Venus. This was an outcome of the bird debate, a literary device which had a considerable vogue in such works as *The Owl and the Nightingale* written 1189-1217 by Nicholas or John of Guildford. Both are developments of the Court of Love literature. The theme is given a religious turn by Skelton in *The Harmony of Birds* and Lydgate in *The Devotion of the Fowls*. In Skelton's *Phyllyp Sparrowe*, written before the end of 1508 the birds invited to the sparrow's funeral come,

> *With dolorous songs funeral,*
> *Some to sing and some to say,*
> *Some to weep and some to pray,*

reminding us of the birds "sighing and sobbing" for poor Cock Robin. Skelton tells us,

> *Robin Redbreast*
> *He shall be priest,*
> *The requiem Mass to say.*

[1] Cf. also "Speeches of Birds" (Mantik-uṭṭair) by the Persian poet Farid ud-din 'Aṭṭar *ob.* 1230).

The swallow hallows the hearse, the popinjay and mavis respectively read the Gospel and Epistle, and so forth. Herrick's *To the Lark* continues the motif:

> *Sweet singing lark*
> *Be thou the clerk*
> *And know thy when*
> *To say, Amen.*

In *The Marriage of Cock Robin and Jenny Wren* we have :

> *Then on her finger fair*
> *Cock Robin put the ring;*
> *'You're married now' says Parson Rook;*
> *While the Lark amen did sing.*

Herrick in *The Wassaile* represents the cock and hen as saying Amen. Skelton and Drayton both refer to the wren as "Our Lady's hen."

There is, however, another tradition of bird officiants at ceremonies, apparently very ancient, which has a definite bearing on the origin of the ballad concerning the death of Cock Robin. An old German rhyme runs as follows:

> *Who is dead? Breadless.*
> *When will he be buried?*
> *On the evening of the day after tomorrow*
> *With spades and with shovels.*
> *The cuckoo is the gravedigger,*
> *The stork is the bell-ringer,*
> *The lapwing is the clerk,*
> *With all his sisters and brothers.*

Another version from Latvia was sent to me by my friend Mr. John Millers:

> *One herdsman died, the others cried.*
> *The Pig dug the grave on a high hill;*
> *The Tit carried the news to his parents;*
> *The Goat mounted to heaven to ask forgiveness;*
> *The Woodpecker carved a cross on a fir tree;*

The Cuckoo tolled in a crooked birch;
The Fly preached the sermon:
All the birds said the funeral prayers;
Their words mingled in the tiny twigs.

In a rhyme current some eighty years ago in Languedoc, four ravens ring the knell, the cat carries the coffin and the partridge wears mourning.

To account for the similarities and differences in these rhymes one must postulate some early form or forms which, variously modified, established themselves in widely separated regions.

Although the earliest printed version of *The Death and Burial of Cock Robin* dates from about 1744, there is what might be an illustration of it in a fifteenth century stained glass window at Buckland Rectory, Gloucester (Fig. 81, p. 174). However, apart from the design consisting of a robin-like bird transfixed by an arrow, there is no evidence for or against its being connected with the nursery rhyme.

We may infer that *The Death and Burial of Cock Robin* probably took its present shape in the hands of a ballad-maker who used a framework of traditional material.

The earliest literary reference to the robin's care for the dead is in Lupton's *Notable Things*, which appeared in 1579: "A Robbyn read breast, fynding the dead body of a man or woman, wyll couer the face of the same with Mosse. And as some holdes opinion, he wyll couer also the whole body." The manner in which this is phrased suggests that the author is here quoting oral lore and not relying, as he usually did, on written sources. In *The Owle* Drayton wrote:

Covering with moss the dead's unclosed eye,
The little redbreast teacheth charity.

When Shakespeare wrote Cymbeline about a year later, his reference to the robin "with charitable bill" covering the dead may have been inspired by Drayton's lines rather than by Lupton's comment. Herrick's robin which brought leaves and moss to cover the sleeping Amarillis may well carry a reminiscence of Drayton's bird. Although the earliest copy of *The Children in the Wood* dates from late in the seventeenth century there is a reference of 1595 to it (Fig. 82, p. 175). Of the dead children we are told:

No burial this pretty pair
From any man receives,
Till robin redbreast piously
Did cover them with leaves.

The robin's role as "The Sexton of the Wood" in the anonymous
Pleasant History of Cawood the Rook (1640) is in the tradition of bird
officiants which has already been discussed.

None of the continental references to the covering of corpses by the
robin is early enough to preclude the tradition having been derived
from English sources but in Brittany it is a popular belief that the robin
sings sorrowfully near a body until it is buried.

It is easy to reconstruct how the idea of the robin acting as sexton
arose. The bird is very inquisitive, perching around and singing near
any strange object. It also carries leaves and moss to its nest in woods
where any dead body lying on the ground is likely to be that of a
murderer's victim. Such observations had only to be linked with the
tradition of birds officiating at funerals to provide a theme to stimulate
poetic imagination for several generations.

Although these themes, the robin's death and its ministry to the
dead, are probably the best known lore they must both be considered
rather late and adventitious accretions attached to what Donne called
"the household bird." It is more likely that the robin's boldness in

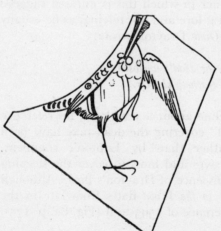

FIG. 81. Glass painting in Buckland
Rectory, Gloucestershire. The bird is
represented with the markings of a
robin and is shown pierced by an
arrow. (After Woodforde, 1944).

FIG. 82. Woodcut from the Roxburghe Ballads showing robins strewing leaves on the bodies of the babes.

Britain, as compared with its behaviour on the continent, brought it into popular favour than that superstitious regard for it rendered it "tame," though, of course, immunity from human persecution over a long period may cause bold birds to become even more fearless. The character which caught people's attention was the red breast. From at least as early as the time of Neanderthal man, who placed red ochre or haematite with his dead, to the present day, the colour red, associated as it is with blood, has been connected with life-giving powers. A sick Australian aborigine is rubbed with a mixture of red ochre and fat, and a Chinese bride is arrayed in brilliant red. But red has another association which has given rise to an immense range of symbolism. It is the colour of fire. Ever since man learned to use fire—and this dates from not later than the time of Peking man—it has been to him a good servant but a bad master. It gives light and heat, but on the wings of the thunderstorm death and destruction may be borne. Those practitioners of esoteric arts, the metal workers of the Bronze and Iron Ages, knew how to make fire do their bidding, but the power they had enslaved might run amok and reduce a village to ashes.

It was to this mysterious, equivocal power that the robin's red breast showed that it was allied, and hence there are strange, primitive elements in the bird's folklore. In Scotland it used to be said, that it was a sin to kill a robin because "he had a drop of God's blood in his veins," while in Brittany, according to Souvestre, writing in 1838: "On assure que le bon Dieu l'appelle dans son paradis pour lui suçer le sang, lorsqu'il s'en trouve incommodé." The Bretons say that robins which have been to fetch fire can speak Latin and sing:

> Cusse, cusse, cusse, cusse,
> Istine spiritum sanctum tuum,
> Il y a dix bons dieux.

Such ideas suggest that pagan notions about the bird have been incompletely Christianised.

We might have expected the robin to acquire its reputation as a fire bird by virtue of its glowing breast, yet although this badge has undoubtedly contributed to its being associated with fire, folklore indicates that its fire associations may have been transferred from the wren. In some traditions either the robin or the wren may take the place of the other. Thus Rolland states that in France, "on Candlemas Day a cock robin is killed, spitted on a hazel twig and placed before the fire. Immediately it is in position this improvised spit begins to turn." Lupton wrote: "It is much to be marvelled at the little bird called a Wren, being fastened to a stick of hazel newly gathered, doth turn about and roast itself." There may be a reference to this custom in the Waterford Wren Song:

> On Christmas Day I turned the spit,
> I burned my fingers, I feel it yet:
> Between my finger and my thumb
> I eat the roast meat every crumb.

Perhaps the game of "Robin's alight," played in Cornwall, is derived from some such practice. The players, sitting by the fire, pass a whirling, burning stick from one to another. The person holding the

Plate 29. a. Oinochoè depicting actors
or dancers representing birds. Black
on red panel (*c.* late 6th century B.C.).
This is probably anterior to the
state-recognised performance of
comedy. Cf. p. 171. (*British Museum*)

b. Apulian *lekythos* depicting the
Judgment of Paris (3rd quarter of
4th century B.C.). Hera holds in
her left hand a sceptre terminating
in a lotos bud on top of which is a
cuckoo with wings outspread. Cf. p.
207. (*British Museum*)

Plate 30. Attic red-figured *kratér* depicting the Death of Prokris (*c.* 440 B.C.). As she draws her last breath a soul-bird escapes into the air. Cf. pp. 22, 49 (*British Museum*)

stick when the flame expires pays a forfeit. A similar game was played in Scotland.

In Guernsey there was a widely accepted belief that the robin brought fire to the island from across the sea. According to another legend the wren fetched water from the mainland—a notion so gratuitous that we may suspect the perversion of an earlier tradition. There are many similar tales of a bird or other creature bringing fire to islands in the South Seas and elsewhere. Elements in these stories reveal that the legends probably embody historical fact to the extent that they record the carrying of fire from island to island by early voyagers. These Guernsey stories tell us that the legends rather than the birds travelled across the sea.

On the continent the fire-fetcher is the wren rather than the robin, though there is a Breton legend that the robin went to get a fire-brand from hell. In Jutland and Champagne the story of the eagle-wren rivalry ends with a reference to the wren's scorched appearance being due to its having flown too near the sun. From Normandy comes the tale that the wren offered to bring fire for man but had its feathers burnt off in the attempt. The owl was the only bird which did not offer feathers to clothe the poor wren, so ever since the owl has been ostracised by the other birds. A Breton legend explains that the eagle, king of birds, condemned the owl to lurk in a hole by day because of its uncharitable behaviour. It will be noted that, as in some of the flight competition legends, the owl and the wren are at enmity. A related French story explains the robin's ruddy breast as due to its having hurried so quickly to aid the burning wren that it became scorched. In another Norman version the wren volunteers after the lark refuses to fetch fire, and the bat is condemned for not providing any feathers for the naked wren. According to a legend from Lorient, the robin helps to bring fire by snatching it from the blazing wren and passing it to the lark, who brings it to earth. The robin's singed breast witnesses to its heroism on this occasion. In another Lorient legend, also recorded from Haute-Bretagne, the wren fetches fire, not from heaven but from hell, and is scorched while escaping through the key-hole. There is a French tradition that if a wren's nest is destroyed, the bird will set the house or barn on fire, and in Wales it was said that if you killed a robin your house would be burned down.

The hero of the Welsh version of the fire-fetching legend is the robin, but instead of bringing fire or water to men, he flies with water to quench hell's flames: "Far, far away is a land of woe, darkness, spirits of evil and fire. Day by day does the little bird bear in his bill a drop of water to quench the flame. So near to the burning stream does he fly, that his dear little feathers are scorched, and hence he is called Bronrhuddyn (*i.e.* breast burned or breast scorched). To serve little children the robin dares approach the infernal pit. No good child will hurt the devoted benefactor of man. The robin returns from the land of fire, and therefore he feels the cold of winter far more than his brother birds. He suffers in the brumal blast: hungry he chirps before your door. Oh! my child, then in gratitude throw a few crumbs to poor Redbreast." The sentimentalisation of the story indicates that it has been modified from an older version and the description of hell shows Christian influence.

Thus, now the wren, now the robin, figures in these tales, and it might seem that the explanation is to be found in the rhymes recording them to be cock and hen of the same species. But primitive people are usually excellent naturalists, expert in identifying birds, so it is unlikely that the confusion of the two species was due to inaccurate observation. If not, it may well have arisen, like many other strange conceptions, as a rationalisation to meet subconscious emotional demands. These confusions, substitutions of one bird for another, and the identification of robin and wren as male and female of the same species, can best be explained as due to the fusion of two cultural traditions—one in which wren ritual was prominent, and another, localised particularly in northern France and Britain, in which the robin received special honour. On this hypothesis the Breton song, "Les noces du roitelet" and our own nursery rhyme, "The Marriage of Cock Robin and Jenny Wren" proclaim the marriage, not merely of two birds but of two streams of culture. Again, if the "robin" tradition were particularly strong in Britain and the "wren" tradition identified, as we have shown (p. 166), with a cultural invasion from the Mediterranean, we would have an explanation why, in the Channel Islands lying between Britain and the continent, the role of fire-bringer was transferred from the wren to the robin. Here, the wren, though without status as fire-bringer, is not completely ousted but is honoured, somewhat incongruously, as a water-carrier. A compromise has been effected. Both are culture-heroes (Plate 31, p. 192).

The robin may have acquired its reputation as a fire-bringer from the wren, but the wren cannot have inspired the motif. It possesses

hardly any of the attributes which proclaim the connexion of a bird
with fire. Although it is somewhat ruddy, like the weasel, squirrel
and fox which were hunted in a ritual way at Midsummer, its appearance and habits do not suggest an association with fire. Neither the
robin nor the wren flies up to heaven like the swallow, nor does either
make thunder like the woodpecker and snipe. Undoubtedly the fire-
bird conception is extremely ancient and the legend has been transferred from one species to another throughout millennia, the myth
accommodating itself to the local fauna as it travelled (Plate 19,
p. 112).

These and other fire myths can be grouped regionally according
to their special characteristics—an indication that there has been
cultural diffusion over wide areas. Thus in South America the fire-
bringer is frequently an amphibian—explicable when we remember
that a number of species of toad and frog have red markings. The
myths of the origin of fire from the toes of a goddess are too fantastic
to have arisen independently in the Marquesas and New Zealand.
Similarly, the appearance of the dog in the fire-myths of New Guinea
and Melanesia is most plausibly explained as reminiscent of the time
when men with a knowledge of fire-making, accompanied by their
dogs, reached these islands. Moreover, the association between the
fire-bird and the flood in various parts of the world can hardly be due
to independent invention. The lineage of our west European fire-
birds can be traced to very remote times and distant places.

The Swallow

As fire-bringers the robin and wren have a reputation only in
western Europe. In eastern Europe and Asia fire is fetched by the
swallow or, sometimes, another bird. The Walloons seem to be the
most westerly folk who credit the swallow with this achievement,
though in Germany there is a tradition that it protects the house from
fire and storms. It shares honours with the wren, for it is said that
when the swallow was fetching fire from heaven a hole was burnt in
its tail, but the wren seized the fire and brought it to earth at the cost
of losing its own feathers. The story ends with the owl refusing to
supply any of its own plumage and thereby earning the detestation of
other birds. Thus the swallow, like the robin in northern French
stories, might be styled an auxiliary fire bird—a hint that in this tale a

compromise has been reached in regard to the prominence to be given to two birds, each with a claim to be the hero, one eastern, the other western. We may have a reminiscence of their rivalry in the legend that, after the altitude competition, the eagle set the swallow to guard the wren.

Further east the swallow does not share its glory. In one Lettish story the devil throws a firebrand at it as it flies off with fire—hence its red markings and forked tail. In another, the sparrow, who guards fire for the devil, chases the swallow as it carries fire to man and plucks some feathers from its tail. In yet another we are told that the swallow fetched heavenly fire after the Deluge when all fires had been extinguished. A strange story, which occurs in several variants, describes how the spider brought fire while the devil slept. The swallow escaped with it, leaving some feathers in the devil's claws.[1] The Buriats of southern Siberia attribute the swallow's forked tail to the injury inflicted by an arrow shot by Tengri, the sky-being, as the bird carried fire to man. In Turkey Jews say that the swallow brought water to quench the fire consuming the temple in Jerusalem—a story resembling the Welsh robin legend. The valiant bird has remained blackened, as if by smoke, ever since. We seem to have an echo of the same theme in a story from Ceylon which tells of the swallow-tailed flycatcher fetching fire from heaven. The crow dipped its wings in water and extinguished the flames. Hence these birds are always at enmity. There are rather similar legends in North America among tribes such as the Tsimshians of British Columbia and the Pawnees whose cultures bear traces of influence from Eurasia. In Australia and the Admiralty Islands also there are tales of bird fire-bringers.

The swallow has high qualifications as fire-fetcher—it flies high and has red markings as well as smokey blue plumage. The robin has only its red breast and the wren slightly rufous plumage to suggest affinities with fire. It seems probable that if, as appears likely on general grounds, the conception of a bird fire-bringer diffused into Europe from elsewhere, the swallow was the original culture hero and in the course of time the robin and the wren became its surrogates.

[1]This tale has points of resemblance with others in the French Congo and among the Loango in which a spider and a bird fetch fire from heaven. A woodpecker is also involved. The similarities suggest cultural contacts. However, the Californian legend concerning the man and woman who survived the flood may be independent. Their descendants, the Spider and Snake Indians, secured fire, the former by means of gossamer balloons and the latter with a ladder.

Popular sentiment protects the swallow from disturbance throu
most of Eurasia and North Africa.

The swallow is also connected with water and fertility. 1
associations are not as contrary as they might seem, for, as Dun
has pointed out, there is a close connexion between fire- and vegeta-
tion-rites. In ancient times Isis was said to have taken the form of a
swallow. Elliot Smith maintained that the antipathy between the
dragon and this bird in Chinese mythology could be traced to Egyptian
ideas. In the east the dragon is, basically, a fertility symbol. The
Chinese say that it is fond of roasted swallows. Anyone who has made
a meal of swallows should avoid crossing water as the dragon lurking
in the deep might be tempted to attack. Chinese threw swallows into
water to attract the attention of the divine powers when they prayed
for rain, and to this day the birds are considered lucky and propitious.
Nesting ledges are provided on houses, even in the narrow, thronged
streets of Canton, and throughout most of China there is a strong
feeling against taking the eggs. An offering to the Genie of the households used to be made on the day of the arrival of the swallows to
secure the fertility of the women, and one of the Odes describes how
Heaven decreed that the swallow should come down and give birth to
the Shang dynasty—referring to the egg swallowed by their ancestress
which brought about her pregnancy. The most modern form of the
Chinese character for "sacrifice" corresponds to "spirit" plus "swallow
on its nest."

In England it is widely believed that it is lucky for swallows or
martins to build under the eaves:

> The martin and the swallow
> Are God Almighty's birds to hollow (hallow).

By a decree of 1496 storks and swallows were protected in Milan.
Not only in this country but also in France and Italy swallows flying
low are said to foretell rain. Similar beliefs were held by Greeks and
Romans. The birds hunt their prey near the ground or water in dull
weather when there are few thermals to carry insects into the air.

In *The Art of Love* Ovid remarked,

> The gentle swallow no one seeks to take,
> But in what place she will her nest may make;

FIG. 83. Greek vase painting showing a man and two boys greeting the first swallow in spring. (After Reinach, S. 1899. Répertoire des vases peints).

and Aelian stated that the bird was sacred to the household gods. Perhaps Gerard Legh in his *Accedence of Armorie* (1562) was expressing an elaboration of this tradition when he wrote: "Wheresoever he breedeth, the goodman of the house is not there made cockolde, what day soever he be married on." But such beliefs were not universally held. In the Irish saying that the swallow is the devil's bird and the Scottish tradition that it has "a drap o' the de'ils blood in its veins" we have further examples of the ambivalence of bird beliefs. However, some confusion with the swift—the devil-bird—may have occurred. In classical times, and more recently in parts of France, Germany and England the swallow was sometimes regarded as of evil omen. In general, however, it was a propitious species among the Greeks. On a black-figured vase, now in the Vatican, a man and two boys are seen welcoming the first swallow. A boy says, "Look, there's a swallow;" the man cries, "By Herakles, so there is:" the other boy shouts, "There she goes," and then "Spring has come." (Fig. 83). Athenaeus (360c) quotes the song with which the Rhodians welcomed the swallow, and still in spring Greek and Macedonian children go through the streets carrying a wooden swallow, singing and soliciting gifts (Plate 24, p. 125). The joyous spirit of these ballads is exemplified in lines from a Macedonian swallow song:

> *March is come, he is welcome;*
> *The blossoms burst forth, the land is filled with scent.*
> *Out with fleas and bugs, in with health and joy.*

The ritual is so similar to the procedure of the Wren Boys that it is tempting to believe that here, and in the related Crow Song ceremonial, we have traces of the cultural influence from the East which developed into the Hunting of the Wren in western Europe.

The traditions of the swallow's stone and the swallow's herb need not be discussed in detail. So far as Britain is concerned they belong rather to literary lore than folklore. Pliny, Albertus Magnus, Avicenna and other scholars speak of the stone to be found in the belly of a young bird at or before the August full moon. It was considered effective in warding off epilepsy. In Normandy and Brittany such stones were credited with power to cure blindness. One of the prescriptions for obtaining them is very similar to that already mentioned for securing springwort. In France and Germany it was said that the magpie knew the secret of the springwort. Magpie concoctions were prescribed for epilepsy. Doubtless all these traditions concerning the stone and the herb are ultimately derived from eastern legends. As the swallow's herb, celandine, was used by the bird, according to Pliny (viii, 27), to restore the sight of its young, it appears that these tales are related to beliefs concerning the eagle's stone as well as the swallow stone and the woodpecker's herb (p. 106). The Elizabethan dramatists, having a taste for curious items of unnatural history, liked to mention such things. Chester, in *Love's Martyr*, refers to,

> *The artificiall nest-composing swallow*
> *His yong ones being hurt within the eies*
> *He helps them with the herb calcedonies.*

Swallows were used medicinally in China and England. Lei Hiao (420-477 A.D.) gives the following recipe: "To use dragon's bone, first boil some aromatic herbs. Wash the bone twice in hot water, then reduce it to powder and place it in bags of thin stuff. Take two young swallows and, after removing their entrails, stuff the bags into the swallows and hang them over a spring. After one night take the bags out of the swallows, remove the powder and mix it with a preparation for strengthening the kidneys. The effect of such a medicine is as if it were divine." Cyranides recommended swallow medicine for epilepsy and Willughby, in the *Ornithology* (1678) tells how to cure this disease with a concoction of 100 swallows, one ounce castor oil and white wine. A rather similar prescription appears in Mistress Jane Hussey's Still-room Book (1692):

How to make my Aunt Markam's swallow-water.
"Take 40 or 50 swallows when they are ready to fly, bruise them to pieces in a mortar, feathers and all together you should put them alive in to the mortar. Add to them one ounce of castorum in pouder, put all these in a still with white wine vinegar. Distill it as any other water . . . You may give two or three spoonfuls at a time with sugar." This barbarous concoction "is very good for the passion of the heart, for the passion of the mother, for the falling sickness, for sudden sounding fitts . . . for the dead palsie, for apoplexies, lethargies and any other distemper of the head. It comforteth the brains . . . "

Belief in swallows as remedies for epilepsy goes back to the notions of classical writers who associated the bird with frenzied or unintelligible speech because of its rapid twittering, as in the myth of Philomela and elsewhere (*Lycophron*, 1460; Aesch. *Ag.* 1050; Aristoph. *Ran.* 93). Euripides (*Alcmena* fr. 91) commented on the bird's fondness for ivy—a mythical notion due to its being the plant associated with the rites of Dionysos. We are reminded of the history of the belief that the eggs of owls and storks cured drunkenness (p. 117). By association the swallow was caught up into the same circle of beliefs. Pliny remarked (xxx, 51), on the authority of King Orus of Assyria, that swallows are potent against inebriation and the bites of mad dogs (xxxviii (10) 43, xxix, 26).

This discussion shows how the swallow's most striking characteristics have given rise to different groups of associations. Its migration and liking for feeding over water account for its connexion with spring observances and fertility, its red breast is the characteristic which links it with fire traditions, its twittering suggested its prescription for affections whose symptoms are incoherence or frenzy. So, as with so many other birds prominent in folklore, by false but in their way plausible inferences, fantastic associations arose and were transmitted for centuries because men are apt to cling to ancient beliefs until, or even after, they are demonstrably untrue. But irrational notions sometimes serve a useful purpose, enabling people to live more integrated lives than they would be able to do without them. It may seem ridiculous that the swallow's chattering should ever have been regarded as indicating how the bird could be used medicinally, but we should not forget that underlying the mistaken inferences involved, was the sound belief, which led eventually to progress in medicine, that, could men discover clues by which to identify the appropriate minerals, plants and animals, their healing virtues could be exploited.

CHAPTER II

SONG-BIRDS AND TOADS

Nightingale, Yellowhammer, Lark, Stonechat & Wheatear

I T is often impossible to draw a hard and fast line between oral and literary lore because one is apt to graduate into the other, though, as we have already remarked, folklore can become literary lore more readily than literary lore folklore. Thus the wren has rich folklore associations but never acquired literary eminence, whereas the nightingale owes its fame to poets rather than peasants.

Country traditions concerning the nightingale are very meagre and deal mainly with the date of its arrival. For instance,

> *On the third of April*
> *Come in the cuckoo and the nightingale.*

In Germany there are similar rhymes:

> *Tiburtius kommt mit Ruf und Schall,*
> *Er bringt den Kukuk und die Nachtigal.*

"Saint Tiburtius (14 April) arrives with song and call; he brings the cuckoo and the nightingale." As the date mentioned in the English jingle is Old Style the two migrants are reputed to arrive on the same date. The main nightingale invasion of England is from the end of the third week of April until the end of the third week of May, so the early dating in the English rhyme suggests that, not only the bird, but also this scrap of folklore is a migrant from over the water. The nightingale was called "barley-bird" in East Anglia because its song was first heard when the barley was being sown, but the same nickname has been given in various parts of England to the grey and yellow wagtails, wryneck, greenfinch, siskin and common gull. In *Aenigmata* Aldhelm referred to the nightingale's return in spring as symbolising Christ's resurrection. This seventh century poem thus contains the first allusion to the bird in our poetry.

Primitive people are not interested aesthetically in bird songs. Few natives would pause in wielding their paddles to listen to a bird as Bates records his canoemen doing when the quadrille wren sang. A bird's supposed magical power or its significance as an omen is that which raises its status for folk of the lower levels of culture. Legends about bird songs, as distinct from bird calls, are the product of sophisticated society. The beauty of the songs of the robin and wren has added nothing to the eminence of these birds in folklore.

Although Alcuin mentioned the nightingale's continual songfulness as illustrating how worship should perpetually ascend to Almighty God, the nightingale's song has not always rendered it beloved. The listener, especially in southern Europe, kept awake by the birds' filibustering chorus, sometimes longs for such interludes of silence as are said to have embellished Macaulay's conversation after his return from India. A poet of the Greek anthology protested,

> *Leaf-loving nightingales, loquacious sex,*
> *Sleep quietly, I beg, and cease your din.*

More recently, Girton girls have complained that the nightingales interfered with their studies. The motif of the birds which keep silent at the behest of a saint or other distinguished person is centuries old. The Persian historian Tabari said of David, the type of the sweet singer, that "when he went about to chant the praises of the Most High, the birds of heaven came, and settling about his head, hearkened to him." The idea may be a development of the Orpheus theme.

The tale of St. Cainnic who bid the noisy birds of El Inish hold their peace, and similar themes in Celtic hagiology may have been influenced by eastern legends. The Monk and Bird motif apparently reached the continent from Ireland at the end of the twelfth century. It seems more likely that to it, rather than direct eastern influence, is due the legend of St. Francis preaching to the birds (Plate 32, p. 193). There is a story of Edward the Confessor which relates how, annoyed by the songs which interrupted his devotions, he prayed that nightingales might never be heard at Havering atte Bower in Essex. In Holland a similar story is told of St. Oda and the magpies. There is

also a saying that since a hermit cursed the nightingales at St. Leonards
they have never returned to the proscribed area. The belief that the
female is more garrulous than the male among birds and men may have
given additional point and piquancy to these stories.

The somewhat patchy distribution of the nightingale in England
and its restricted range—the area south of a line from the Humber
to the Severn—lent additional plausibility to stories accounting for
the absence of the bird from some localities and for myths such as
that it is only found where cowslips are common and (at Doncaster)
in places where hops are grown.

Apart from such trifles there is practically no English oral nightingale lore, and the bird would hardly deserve mention here were it
not for its eminence in literary traditions. These illustrate certain
aspects of the evolution and transmission of beliefs about birds in
England, such as the already-mentioned reluctance of country people
to accept literary bird lore into folklore. Poets have been glad to use
bird images, as Shakespeare used the eagle and the owl, because they
were already saturated with symbolical meaning, but they have seldom
succeeded in endowing a bird or other animal with sufficient emotional
significance for it to become a popular symbol. Thus, in spite of the
effective use of the cormorant as an illustration of greed by Shakespeare
and as a similitude of the devil by Milton, folklore has practically
nothing to say about it.

Among the curious literary conceits concerning the nightingale is
the notion that it sings with its breast against a thorn. This has never
become folklore. The first reference in English literature is in Thomas
Lodge's *Scillaes Metamorphosis* (1589):

> *A Nightingal gan sing; but woe the lucke;*
> *The branch so neare her breast, while she did quicke her*
> *To turne her head, on sodaine gan to pricke her.*

Giles Fletcher, who published his love poems in 1593, unites this
conceit with another which became popular with poets:

> *So Philomel, perched on an aspen sprig,*
> *Weeps all the night her lost virginity,*
> *And sings her sad tale to the merry twig,*
> *That dances at such joyful mystery.*

Ne ever lets sweet rest invade her eye
But leaning on a thorn her dainty chest
For fear soft sleep should steal into her breast
Expresses in her song grief not to be expressed.

A year later, in *The Rape of Lucrece*, Shakespeare referred to "Philomel that singst of ravishment,"

And whiles against a thorn thou bear'st thy part
To keep thy sharp woes waking.

The author of *The Passionate Pilgrim*, at one time believed to be Shakespeare but now considered to be Richard Barnefield, wrote:

Everything did banish moan,
Save the nightingale alone.
She, poor bird, as all forlorn,
Lean'd her breast up-till a thorn
And there sung the dolefull'st ditty,
That to hear it was great pity.
'Fie, fie, fie,' how would she say,
'Tereu, tereu!' by and by.

Referring to the nightingale Andrew Marvell remarked in *Upon Appleton House:*

The thorn, lest it should hurt her, draws
Within the skin its shrunken claws.

Pomfret, writing towards the end of the eighteenth century declared:

The first music of the grove we owe
To mourning Philomel's harmonious woe;
And while her grief in charming notes express'd,
A thorny bramble pricks her tender breast.

There are references to the legend in Sir Thomas Browne's *Vulgar Errors* (III, xxviii) and a sermon of Thomas Adams, who died in 1653, but the earliest allusion known is in a work by Aneau published in Paris in 1571:

Au printemps doux et gracieux,
Le rossignol à pleine voix

Bonne louange au dieu des dieux,
Tant qu'il faict retentir les boys,
Peur du serpent il chante fort,
Toute nuict et met sa poitrine
Contre quelque poignante espine
Qui le réveille quand il dort.

English writers familiar with this passage may have introduced the legend to our literature. This version of it was known to Sir Thomas Browne for he doubted "whether the nightingal's sitting with her breast against a thorn be any more than that she placeth some prickle on the outside of her nest, or roosteth in thorny and prickly places, where serpents may least approach her." However, in England, in contrast with some continental habitats, the woods and coppices frequented by the nightingale usually contain no great quantity of thorny shrubs and the connexion between thorns and nightingales would more naturally arise further south.

In French oral folklore there appears to be no mention of the nightingale which keeps herself awake with a thorn. From whence, then, did the idea come? Ingersoll says that "there has arisen in Persia a literature of the nightingale, or 'bulbul,' springing from a pathetic legend, if it is not simply poetic fancy—that as the bird pours its song in a continuous strain of melody it is pressing its breast against a rose-thorn to ease its heart's pain." His suggestion that Fletcher might have picked up the notion while he was Queen Elizabeth's envoy at Moscow in 1588 seems mistaken in view of Lodge's use of this conceit in 1589, the year in which, after contemptuous treatment by the Russians, Fletcher returned to England. So far as I am aware the Persian nightingale is not said to use a thorn to maintain wakefulness but the piercing of the nightingale by a rose thorn is so prominent in Iranian poetry that very probably from this source the motif reached European literature. Thus Hafiz, as translated by Gertrude Bell wrote:

The nightingale with drops of his heart's blood
Had nourished the red rose, then came a wind,
And catching at the boughs in envious mood,
A hundred thorns about his heart entwined.

Divan, XIV

and,

Upon a branch of the straight cypress-tree
Once more the patient nightingale doth rest:
"Oh Rose!" he cries, "evil be turned from thee!
I sing thee all men's thanks; thou blossomest
And hope springs up in every joyless heart—
Let not the nightingale lament apart,
Nor with thy proud thorns wound his faithful breast."

Divan, XXXII

In the songs of the troubadours a frequent theme is love-making beneath a thorn. A famous *alba* begins:

In a leafy orchard, underneath a thorn
the lady clasps her lover in her arms
until the watchman cries he's seen the dawn.
O God! Oh God! How quickly dawn comes round.

A little later in the poem we hear of the birds beginning to sing. Such associations may have prepared the way for the theme of the thorn-pierced nightingale.

Lydgate linked the rose and Christ's passion in *A Song of the Nightingale*. It has been suggested to me by Professor T. Harrison that this reference, together with the Breton legends ascribing the robin's red breast to the bird's efforts to remove Christ's crown of thorns, may have contributed to establish the association between the bird, thorn and love, but the motif seems to have entered English literature as a developed legend, most probably from Iran through French literature.

The notion that the nightingale's song is melancholy appears in many Greek and English writers, though in the *Phaedo* (85a) Socrates alludes to it and other birds singing for joy. To Chaucer and Coleridge it was "the merry nightingale" and Izaak Walton said that the bird "breathes such sweet lowd music out of her little instrumentall throat that it might make mankind to think miracles are not ceased." The sadness which English poets detected in the nightingale's song was due to the influence of the myth of Philomela and Procne. It relates that Tereus cut out the tongue of his wife Procne lest she should disclose that he had violated her sister Philomela. Tereus was transformed into a hoopoe, Philomela into a nightingale and Procne into a swallow. The legend explains the swallow's quasi-human twittering, but through the errors of Apollodorus and Ovid Philomela and not Procne was said to have been mutilated, and so Shakespeare wrote in *Titus Andronicus* (II.iii.43), "Philomel must lose her tongue today." Graves explains the origin of the tale in his characteristic way as due to a misunderstanding of a painting in a temple at Daulis showing a priestess in a trance, with the laurel leaf by which she induced the ecstasy protruding from her mouth, but he quotes no evidence that such a representation ever existed. D'Arcy Thompson's suggestion is more plausible—that the myth carries veiled allusions to the worship of Adonis at the vernal equinox, in which flute-playing was prominent. We have already noted (p. 57) that Daulis, where Tereus ruled, and after which the nightingale was given its now superseded name *Daulis luscinia,* may have been the centre of a bird cult. Even in recent times an archaic spring festival was celebrated there.

According to folk tales told in Finland, France, Germany and England, there was a time when the nightingale and the blindworm had only one eye apiece (A2341.5). The French version relates that one day, when the blindworm was asleep, the nightingale stole its eye in order to make a presentable appearance at the wren's wedding. (This suggests that the legend is later than other folklore about the marriage of the wren.) When the reptile discovered its loss it vowed to catch the nightingale asleep and recover its eye. Ever since the nightingale has sung night and day in order to stay awake. According to another tale the blindworm used to possess excellent eyes but the nightingale, who was sightless, borrowed them to attend a fairy wedding. It refused to return them but by way of compensation sings night and day to the blindworm. If Shakespeare had known these stories he would hardly have made the mistake of suggesting that the nightingale does not sing by day "when every goose is cackling" (*M. of V.* V.i.105) but he must have been acquainted with some related traditions, for Juliet says, "Some say the lark and loathed toad change eyes" (*R. & J.* III.v.31). Shakespeare's toad was "ugly and venomous" though according to literary lore quoted by such writers as Vincent of Beauvais and Gesner, and popularised by Tudor writers, it bore in its head a precious stone (*A.Y.L.I.* II.i.13) which, when fashioned into a ring gave "forewarning against venom." (Fig. 84). This legend, was derived from the East. In Malaya snakes are still believed to carry a magical stone in their heads or mouths. Sometimes they fight each other for it. This *bezoar,* which is mentioned by Hafiz (xxxvii) is held

Plate 31 a. Christmas card showing a robin and two wrens with a doll half-buried in snow—a fanciful elaboration of robin and wren folklore. Cf. p. 173. (*Collection of George Buday*)

b. Madonna and Bird (14th century). Riom. Eglise du Marthuret. Cf. p. 21. (*Photo-Edition G. d' O. Olliergues, Puy-de-Dôme, France*)

Plate 32. The Call to the Birds (14th century MS). This type of representation was originally inspired by Revelation XIX, 17, but became modified through the influence of tales and pictures of Saint Francis preaching to the birds. Gaily coloured and elegantly shaped birds have supplanted the birds of prey shown in earlier Franciscan and Apocalyptic pictures. The soberly coloured wren may be placed with the brightly hued species at the top of the tree because of its reputation as King of Birds. It takes the place of its rival, the eagle, which appears in the earlier pictures. Cf. p. 187. (*British Museum*)

to be an antidote against snake bite. The legend has a counterpart in Chinese mythology.

The witches in Macbeth (IV.i.6) had good reason to add a toad with its "sweltered venom" to their "charmed pot" for the amphibian exudes the poisons bufotalin and bufogin from glands scattered over its body when it is roughly seized. (A dog which catches a toad drops it quickly and foams at the mouth). This tradition is derived from Latin sources such as Pliny (xvii. 12) and Aelian. Apuleius mentions that a buried toad emanates poison. The notion was passed on to horticulturists by Thomas Hyll in the *Art of Gardening* (1593) as a device by which they could rid their gardens of pests. Lupton remarks that a toad buried in an earthenware pot in a field will drive birds away and prevent tempests. Boccaccio, whose *Decameron* owes not a little to Apuleius, tells a story of a man and his sweetheart who die after rubbing their teeth and gums with sage leaves. A toad was found at the roots of the plant whose poisonous breath had infected it. Lupton retells the story. Such traditions illustrate the tendency of plagiarists to exaggerate the sensational. In the fable of the barnacle goose we shall find other examples.

The toad is associated with other birds besides the lark. Scottish boys used to sing:

> *Half a paddock, half a toad,*
> *Half a yellow yorling:*
> *Drinks a drap o' the de'il's bluid*
> *Every May morning.*

"Yellow yorling" is the name for the yellowhammer in Scotland and also in parts of the North of Ireland. Turner, in 1544, wrote "yowlryng" and there are a number of North of England variants. Scottish children used to hang any yellowhammers they could find. They took each nestling, attached one end of a thread round its neck and looped the other, with a small stone tied to it, around a beam. When the stone was struck the wretched bird was jerked into the air. This barbarous custom was called "spangie-hewit"—apparently from "spang" meaning to fly off with elasticity, and the Anglo-Saxon *heafod*—head. It may have been derived from a ritual which was at one time more widespread. In his work on Czecho-Slovak superstitions Grohmann says, "It is believed that the yellowhammer procures three

FIG. 84. Woodcut from the Hortus
Sanitatis showing a man obtaining the
toad stone from a toad's head.

drops of the devil's blood on the 1st of May, for which reason it is
persecuted by the peasantry."

In Scotland the swallow (p. 182), stonechat and magpie, like the
pied wagtail in Ireland, are also reputed to have a drop of the devil's
blood.[1] Scots folk said that the stonechat's eggs were incubated by a
toad. Toads were also believed to hatch out the chicks of wheatears,
and on this account, the birds were killed. Similar ideas were already
prevalent in the thirteenth century for Albertus Magnus (XXIII. 112)
remarked that though uneducated folk mistakenly believe that a toad
incubates the eggs of the (crested?) lark in fact moderate heat from the
sun hatches them. Aldrovandus rejected the story as ridiculous. The
legend that quails mate with toads probably arose because of a superficial resemblance between the two creatures. This tradition does
not seem to be connected with that of the incubating toad.

The naturalistic explanation of the fable—that it arose from the
finding of a toad on or near a bird's nest—is not very plausible, although
toads have been known, very occasionally, to squat in nests. The

[1]The association between the sprightly wagtail and the devil seems so gratuitous that
one suspects some mythological connexion. Perhaps we have a clue in the activities of the
bird in Siberian creation myths. Pied plumage has diabolic associations.

incubating toad may have been generated from the fancies of mediaeval scholars. Neckam, who was born at St. Albans in 1157, wrote (I, 75): "When the cock is nearing old age, it sometimes lays an egg which is hatched by a toad, and from it emerges a basilisk." Vincent of Beauvais (*Spec. Nat.*, XXI, 24) quoting "writings of the ancients" tells a similar tale, remarking that the egg is hatched by a serpent or a toad. Bartholomew gives this legend, quoting the Venerable Bede as his authority, but I have searched Bede's works without finding the reference. The basilisk, as the name for some kind of serpent, came into literature in the Septuagint translation of Isaiah lxix, 5, which, rendered into English, reads: "They break the eggs of adders and weave the spider's web: he who would eat of their eggs, having crushed the wind-egg, finds in it a basilisk." Jerome translated this into the equivalent of: "They break the eggs of adders and weave spider-webs: he who eats of their eggs will die, and what has been warmed (incubated) will break forth into a basilisk." Aelian (III, 31) had commented that the basilisk dies in convulsions on hearing the crowing of a cock.

Probably certainty as to the evolution of the incubating toad tradition is unattainable. The most plausible surmise would appear to be that early folklore about toads hatching eggs came into literature through more than one channel and thus received elaboration. It is difficult to believe that Scottish children derived their ideas about toads from the fancies of mediaeval scholars.

The remarkable "scribbling" on the yellowhammer's eggs, which inspired the names "writing lark" (Notts., Yorks., Northants.), "writing master" (Salop), "écrivain," (Brittany), and "Schryver" (Brabant), gave rise to the belief that they were "gouted with the taint o' the de'il's blood." Probably it was supposed that the markings were cabbalistic signs. If so, this may be a clue to the yellowhammer's diabolical reputation. Perhaps the stonechat and the wheatear became associated with the devil because their calls, suggestive of pebbles being knocked together, heard by timorous people in desolate places, may have aroused apprehension of unseen, evil presences moving close at hand. In County Kerry the wheatear's Irish name is equivalent to "the cunning old man under a stone." The fancied resemblance of the yellowhammer's phrase to human speech may similarly have contributed to the bird's evil repute, for, as we have noted in connexion with several species, quasi-human bird utterances are commonly regarded as uncanny and devilish; because the devil is conceived as the personification of evil and a being with partly human and partly animal characteristics, birds which seem to partake of two natures are associated with it. In Scotland the yellowhammer sings, "Whetil te, whetil te, whee! Harry my nest, and the de'il tak ye," and the bird is called "De'il, de'il, de'il take ye!"

The malediction which the yellow yorling utters has not prevented its persecution. Boys used to play "periwinkie" with its eggs, whacking blindfold at them with a stick. In Denmark a sufferer from jaundice is advised to eat three yellowhammers, including feathers and bones. This is probably a jocular suggestion inspired by mediaeval beliefs that birds with yellow markings (such as the yellow-eyed stone curlew) were effective medicinally against this malady. The sinister significance of the colour yellow still survives in the use of a yellow flag as a signal of quarantine.

The impression remains that these considerations do not fully explain the incubating toad and devil's blood beliefs and the connexion between them. We may regard the devil's blood tradition as simply a way of stating that a creature is ominous but exactly how these various birds got their evil reputation remains obscure.

CHAPTER 12

THE HARBINGER OF SPRING

The Cuckoo

THE cuckoo shares with the swallow the prestige of being an ambassador of spring, and like it, is expected on traditional dates throughout Europe:

S. France	21 March	
N. France	1 April	
Germany	14 „	SS. Valerian and Tiburtius
England (Sussex)	14 „	
England (W. Riding)	21 „	
Norway	1 May	SS. Philip and James

Locally in the English counties the cuckoo is commonly said to arrive on the date of a fair, if one happens to be held about the appropriate time. In Hertfordshire, as a countrywoman assures me, it comes to Sawbridgeworth Fair. There is a Herefordshire saying that "the cuckoo comes to Orleton Fair (23 April) to buy a horse and goes to Brom (Brompton Bryan) to sell him." Gilbert White noted 7 and 26 April as the earliest and latest dates for hearing the first cuckoo at Selborne. On the Scottish border 1 and 2 April were April Fool or Gowk days, when, among other tricks played on simple folk, they were sent on fool's errands carrying a missive inscribed with the couplet:

> *The first and second of April*
> *Hound the gowk another mile.*

Before the change in the calendar these dates were 12 and 13 April according to our reckoning so that April Fool's Day corresponded fairly accurately with the date of the gowk's arrival.

The thirteenth century English song "Sumer is icumen in," and the Song of St. Guthlac in the *Codex Exoniensis* in which the cuckoo announces the year, show that in earlier times, as today, the cuckoo was the welcome harbinger of spring. A mediaeval scribe paused to scribble in Irish on the margin of the manuscript he was copying:

> *The cuckoo in his mantle grey*
> *Cries on all day through lush tree tops,*
> *And verily—God shield me still!*
> *Well speeds my quill beneath the copse.*

In old German law the beginning of spring was expressed by the phrase, "When the cuckoo calls." and Macedonian peasants still rise early during the first three days of March to listen to the birds. He who first hears the cuckoo is counted lucky. There are Siberian tribes which date their spring ceremonies by its call. A long succession of English poets, including Shakespeare and Spenser, have honoured the cuckoo as the "messenger of spring." Flowers which bloom when the cuckoo is calling, such as the cuckoo pint *Arum maculatum* and cuckoo flower *Cardamine pratensis*, are named after it; also the "cuckoo spit" froth which conceals the froghopper in its wingless stage. Ray pointed out that the then current belief that it dropped from heaven was mistaken. That the froth is due to the cuckoo's promiscuous expectoration does not seem to be an ancient tradition but Devon boys believed that the insects developed into birds—an example of a misunderstood name generating folklore.

A host of rhymes annotate the months according to the cuckoo's activities. The Norfolk version runs:

> *In April come he will;*
> *In May he sings all day;*
> *In June he changes his tune;*
> *In July he prepares to fly;*
> *In August, go he must.*

In Sussex the rhyme is completed with:

> *If he stay until September,*
> *'Tis as much as the oldest man can remember;*

and in Suffolk:

> *In September, you'll allus remember;*
> *In October, 'ull never get over.*

The Devon jingle is more picturesque but less accurate than the usual version:

> *In March the guku beginth to sarch;*
> *In Aperal, he beginth to tell;*
> *In May, he beginth to lay;*
> *In June, he alterth 'is tune;*
> *In July, away a dith vly.*

In the West of Scotland and Guernsey it is related that the cuckoo flies on perceiving the ripening barley, and continental legends say that it departs on hearing the sickles in the corn.

Before the cuckoo lays her egg she picks up an egg from the host's nest, holds it in her bill as she sits and flies off some distance to eat it. Country rhymes show that something of this was known long before British ornithologists studied the bird's behaviour.

In Northamptonshire the cuckoo is called "Suck-egg." According to the Scots song,

> *The cuckoo's a fine bird, he sings as he flies;*
> *He brings us good tidings, he tells us no lies.*
> *He sucks little birds' eggs to make his voice clear,*
> *And when he sings "cuckoo" the summer is near.*

The Sussex version ends with,

> *She picks up the dirt in the spring of the year,*
> *And eats little birds' eggs to make her voice clear.*

In Devon it is said that the cuckoo "comes to eat up the dirt," and continental sayings of a similar nature show that the meaning is that the bird arrives when the land is drying up after the winter. Germans say that the cuckoo cannot call until he has eaten a bird's egg and a Spanish proverb declares, "I am like the cuckoo which cannot sing until I have my stomach full." Another continental tradition is that the cuckoo stammers late in the year because of an egg in its throat. If rustic wiseacres are inaccurate in discriminating the sex of singing birds their blunders are no worse than those of Milton and Keats.

All over the world the calling of various species of cuckoo is associated with rain and the birds are often called "rain-crow" or its equivalent—due, no doubt, to their loud, reiterative notes coinciding with the rainy season. In the East Riding the cuckoo's frequent calling is regarded as a sign of rain and Matthew Arnold wrote in *Thyrsis*:

> *So have I heard the cuckoo's parting cry,*
> *From the wet field, through the vext garden-trees,*
> *Come with the volleying rain and hissing breeze.*

In Scotland the rhyme is still current:

> *On the 9th of April*
> *The gowk comes over the hill,*
> *In a shower of rain*
> *And on the — of June*
> *He turns his tune again.*

From being associated with changes in the weather the cuckoo acquired a reputation as forecaster of the weather and other events. Hesiod advised the farmer to plough when the cuckoo called from the oaks, but more recent tradition attributes to it foresight concerning the whole season:

> *When the cuckoo comes to the bare thorn,*
> *Sell your cow and buy your corn;*
> *But when she comes to the full bit,*
> *Sell your corn and buy your sheep.*

There are Irish and Welsh rhymes to the same effect.

The next step in the chain of association was to assume that a bird so knowledgeable about future events must be able to forecast tides in the affairs of men. Pliny (*Nat. Hist.* xxx. 25) remarked that a person hearing the cuckoo has only to gather earth from around his right foot to obtain a potent flea repellant. Perhaps it was from this or closely related beliefs that ritual for divining one's future spouse arose. In north-east Scotland the custom was to turn around three times on one's left heel and then search in the hollow for a hair. It would be the same colour as the hair of one's future wife or husband. In the west of Scotland one looked for a hair on the sole of one's left foot, but in Ireland on the right foot. In Westphalia seeing the first swallow was the signal to search for this significant hair. Gay, in his "Shepherd's Week" puts into the mouth of a girl who had heard the first cuckoo these words:

> Upon a rising bank I sat adown,
> And doff'd my Shoe, and by my troth I swear,
> Therein I spied this yellow frizzled Hair,
> As like to Lubberkin's in curl and hue,
> As if upon his comely Pate it grew.
> With my sharp heel I three times mark the ground,
> And turn me thrice, around, around, around—

May some astute yokel have exploited the belief by secreting some of his hair in the shoe of his beloved? The tradition can be traced in print at least as far back as 1685 in an edition of "Mother Bunch's Closet" in which we read: "The first time you hear the cuckoo sing look under your left shoe and you will find hair of the colour of your wife or husband without the help of the devil."

It is said that in Denmark a cuckoo was carried at weddings—presumably as a fertility talisman—as a goose was carried in China. In the Harz mountains one was placed in the bride-chamber and a cuckoo dance was performed at North Friesland weddings. In Czecho-Slovakia its calls predict the number of children which will be born to a married couple—a somewhat extravagant belief. At Whitsuntide in south-east Russia folk danced around a pole surmounted by a cuckoo. Practically throughout western Europe the bird is more or less playfully consulted concerning future events. Yorkshire and Guernsey children recite a rhyme asking the cuckoo to foretell by the number of its calls how long they have to live. This belief goes back at least to the 13th century, for it is mentioned in Le Roman du Renart, and is, or was, widespread in Europe. In England and on the continent, as, for example, in Portugal, it was believed that a girl could discover how long she would remain unmarried by counting the calls of the first cuckoo. No wonder the Danes say that the cuckoo does not build a nest because it is kept too busy answering the questions of young and old.

So percipient a bird may predict evil as well as blessedness; and in the magical world of portents your luck may turn on what might seem a trivial detail. In Scotland and Norway it is unlucky to hear the cuckoo before breakfast, but the Scots say that good fortune awaits you if you hear it while walking:

> *Gang and hear the gowk yell,*
> *Sit and see the swallow flee,*
> *See the foal before its mother's 'ee*
> *'T will be a thriving year wi' thee.*

In the Hebrides it bodes ill to hear the cuckoo while hungry. Welsh folk used to say that a child born the first day the cuckoo calls would be lucky all his life, but in the Principality and also in Somerset, a cuckoo heard after midsummer may be a portent of death. To be gazing on the ground on hearing the first cuckoo was believed in Midlothian, Berwickshire and Cornwall to be a warning of an untimely fate.

As the cuckoo does not build a nest it was considered a lazy bird and if you had anything to do with it you might become tarred with the same brush, for in the primitive realm of magic contagion spreads in subtle and unaccountable ways. Thus there is a German tradition that if you do not wash your face after seeing the first cuckoo, you will become very sunburnt and freckled during the year. Newcastle folk execrated the slothful cuckoo:

> *Cuckoo, scabb'd gowk,*
> *Mickle said, little wrought,*

while, according to Herefordshire, Norfolk and Sussex rustics, to hear the first cuckoo in bed portended illness or even death. In France, those who hear the first cuckoo fasting will be slothful during the year, or may suffer numbed limbs. In Somerset boys used to run their fastest on hearing the cuckoo to ward off laziness, and in Saxony, it was said that you must roll over on the grass after hearing the first cuckoo.

Although the lack of the domesticities in the life of the cuckoo might be supposed to have given rise to the cuckoo-cuckold tradition, it is a literary conceit rather than folklore. In the *Asinaria* of Plautus a wife, finding her husband *in flagrante delicto* shouts, "What? is the cuckoo still lying there? Get up, gallant, and go home." It has been supposed that the bird's name was thus used as an epithet because of its parasitic reputation, but the connotation seems to be slothfulness rather than adultery. Pliny (*Nat. Hist.* xviii.66), commenting on lazy vine dressers, remarked, "They were anciently called cuckoos, that is slothful, because they did not prune their vines until that bird began to sing, which is later than the proper time." D'Arcy Thompson commented that it was in Latin rather than Greek, and in Early English and Elizabethan rather than Middle English, that the cuckoo's cry was "unpleasing to a married ear" but Aristophanes' *Kokku* suggests "cuckold" as well as "cuckoo." The evidence in Latin writings, consisting of the reference in Plautus and a phrase in Juvenal (vi. 275) is very slight. "Cuckold" apparently came into English from the Old French "cucuald" as "cukeweld" and "cokeweld" (Cf. *Owle and Nightingale; Piers Plowman,* iv. 10) in the thirteenth century when the cuckoo was called "cuccu" as in the song of that date. To those unaware of its French antecedents the word would not suggest any obvious association with the bird. In France "cuckoo courts" and other ceremonies were held in which husbands deceived by their wives appeared. The epithet "The Cuckold King" for Mark, King of Cornwall, in the Arthurian romances harks back to French literary usage. In German, but not in English, there is an association between the word for cuckoo—*Gauch* or *Kuckuck*, and an adulteress. Dr. Johnson seems to have been using his imagination, or unreliable sources, when he explained: "The Cuckow is said to suck the eggs of other birds and lay her own to be hatched in their place; from which practice it was usual to alarm a husband at the approach of an adulterer by calling 'Cuckoo' which by mistake was applied to the husband." Although Chaucer, probably influenced by French ideas, had hard things to say of the cuckoo (*Parlement of Fowles*) the Tudor playwrights must bear most of the opprobrium for degrading the status of the harbinger of spring to what Green called him in *A Quip for an Upstart Courtier* "The Cuckold's Quirister."

A sense of how precariously human life is poised between happiness and tragedy pervades the outlook of simple folk, and is reflected in the ambivalence with which imagination endows the objects of its interest. So the prophet of spring, resurgent life and wedded bliss may presage death, disaster or, in the literary tradition, infidelity. In Norfolk it was said that if a cuckoo flew overhead or alighted on a rotten branch it was an omen of death, and if a crow and a cuckoo settled on a house where a hawk was already perched there would be three deaths. Fortunately such an ill-assorted trio would not be seen on a roof-top once in a blue moon. On St. Kilda, where the cuckoo seldom comes, it was believed to presage calamity and some disaster was apt to occur which could be correlated with the bird's unwelcome visit. The abnormal is often interpreted as foretelling catastrophe. Thus, when a cormorant perched on Boston Stump it was held to foreshadow death, and many found confirmation of their belief when a ship was wrecked with the loss of 300 lives.

The point of the compass at which the cuckoo calls may be considered fraught with significance. In Cornwall a cuckoo heard on one's right was lucky, and in Ireland a cuckoo on one's left was unlucky. Irish folk thought that the direction in which you heard the first cuckoo indicated where you would live during the year and a rhyme declared:

> A white lamb on my right hand,
> So will good come to me,
> But not the little false cuckoo
> On the first day of the year.

According to a German tradition, if the first cuckoo were heard in the north, the year would be disastrous, if in the south, it would be a good butter year.

Apart from the "heel and hair" procedure—the practice of turning a coin in one's pocket when the first cuckoo is heard—and one or two other playful customs, there is no ritual associated with the bird in Britain but it figures in a remarkable ceremony in Pragança, near Cadaval, in Portugal. According to Rodney Gallop "a battue is held and a cuckoo trapped, installed in a cart with an old woman on either side, the one spinning and the other winding the wool, and brought in state into the village with an escort of 300 horsemen." Gallop comments on the striking resemblance between this custom and the Wren Hunt. Unfortunately, the description given is hardly adequate to permit of detailed comparison between the two ceremonies, but they, and the Greek swallow ritual, involve the capture of a bird and a parade with it. The ceremonial, taking place near the vernal equinox and involving cart- and spinning-wheels as well as a cavalcade, suggests sun-worship, as the wheel and the horse were important solar symbols.[1] The Wren Hunt, Cuckoo Parade, and the Greek Crow and Swallow Ceremonial may all have had their origin in the same primitive complex of ideas. The seasonal bird-hunt and parade appear to be absent from other parts of the world apart from the ritual which was enacted in Babylonia (p. 162).

If more were known of another Portuguese custom it might throw light on the significance of the Cuckoo Parade and other bird ceremonies. At Formilaçao a person named "Cuckoo" releases a sparrow and finches, shouting "There goes a cuckoo for . . . parish." It would seem that the small birds may be surrogates for a cuckoo scapegoat and that the custom may have very ancient antecedents. We have already referred to the Hebrew custom at the cleansing of a leper when one of two birds was killed and the other allowed to fly away (*Lev.* xiv.7,53), presumably to carry the leprosy with it. The rhetorician Dio Chrysostom (*Orat.* liii) refers to the Greek practice of anointing swallows caught in the house and allowing them to escape, apparently with the intention to remove bad luck. The Malays have a very similar custom. When the Huzuls of the Carpathians saw the first swallow of the season they said, "Swallow, swallow, take my freckles and give me rosy cheeks." In order to "make the curse fly away" from a childless woman the Battas of Sumatra set a swallow free. While the similarities in these bird scapegoat ceremonies are so great as to suggest that they may be related to one another, the ideas on which they are based have little in common with the Cuckoo Parade and Wren Hunt.

There is a possibility that a ceremony related to the Cuckoo Parade was once observed in Britain and that we have vague reminiscences of it in the boys' prank, "Hunt the Gowk" played in Scotland and the north of England. In this connexion Lewis Spence has called attention to the old Scottish extravaganza *King Berdok* in which it is related that the King of Babylon wooed Mayiola, "the golk of Mary-

---

[1] There is a Breton belief that when the cuckoo is first heard a menhir turns thrice but in spite of the evidence associating megalithic monuments with solar worship it would be precarious to use this as evidence that the cuckoo was a solar bird. The wryneck or 'cuckoo's mate" was associated with the sun in Greek beliefs.

land," for seven years. At length he carried her home in a creel. When he arrived there was only an owl's nest inside. He went to seek her again but was pursued by her father and his supporters. Maryland is the abode of ghosts and spirits, the domain of the fairies, and Mayiola may carry a suggestion of the month of May. In Scotland the cuckoo was called *eun-sidhe*, bird of the fairies. It was believed that in winter it retired to the tumuli associated with the "good people." The fairies have many characteristics similar to those of people earlier than the Iron Age.

In Asia the cuckoo is, or was, honoured over a wide area. It may have symbolised the sun hidden by clouds in Vedic religion. Certainly it was regarded as prophetic and gifted with supernatural wisdom. A cuckoo perches on the head-dress of Numinchen shamans in Manchuria, and after a Gilyak cremation, a wooden model of a cuckoo is placed above the effigy representing the dead man. Among the Ainu the cuckoo is believed to bewitch people and he who dares to imitate its note risks enchantment.

According to the Chronicle of Prokosz a cuckoo god used to be worshipped in Poland at a temple erected to the god Zywie on a hill named after him: "There during the first days of May, very many people came together and prayed devoutly for continued health and prosperity to him whom they used to think the giver of life. Moreover, those people especially sacrificed there who had heard the first notes of the cuckoo, having a superstitious belief that they would live for as many years as the bird repeated its call. For they used to think that this great ruler of the world was transfigured into a cuckoo to proclaim to them the events of life. Hence to kill the cuckoo was regarded as a crime, and on him who did so the magistrates would inflict capital punishment."

If this account were reliable, it would be valuable evidence of bird-worship in Europe but some good authorities consider it spurious. Probably it is much later than the tenth century to which it was alleged to belong. However, A. B. Cook thought that it was for the most part genuine and showed that confirmation was available for some of the details. Thus a fifteenth century authority who obtained the names of old Slavic divinities from folk songs refers to Zywye as "god of life." However, if cuckoo worship had been firmly established it is unlikely that so little evidence should have survived. Perhaps a local cuckoo cult existed here and there in Europe as, in modern times, in Bombay, where a species of cuckoo was worshipped by high-class Hindu women for a month called "The Festival of Cuckoos."

A comment by Aristophanes in *The Birds* has been cited as evidence of the exalted status of the cuckoo in antiquity:

> *In Sidon and Egypt the cuckoo was king*
> *They wait to this hour for the cuckoo to sing—*
> *And when he begins, be it later or early,*
> *They reckon it lawful to gather their barley.*

The comic poet was no authority on Egyptian ritual. He confused the cuckoo and the hoopoe. The hoopoe utters a note somewhat resembling the cuckoo's and was, and still is a sacred bird in Egypt. Confusion of the two species is hinted at in the Czech legend that the hoopoe borrowed the cuckoo's crown to wear at a wedding but never returned it. So the cuckoo calls "Kluku! Kluku! You knave! You knave!" and the hoopoe replies "Jdu! Jdu! I'm coming! I'm coming."

The nearest the cuckoo came to apotheosis in Europe seems to have been in its association with Zeus, for the Greek god wooed Hera in the guise of a storm-driven cuckoo on Mount Kokkygia in Argos. So Hera (Juno) is depicted with a cuckoo on her sceptre (Plate 29, p. 176). Perhaps the exploits of Zeus as an amorous bird may be traced back to Minoan beliefs in the appearance of divinities as birds. Gilbert Murray, commenting on Hera's cuckoo, remarks that with isolated exceptions the attribute is original and the god is added. As we noted earlier (p. 123), this argument has to be used with caution and there is no proof that Hera was originally a cuckoo. But that she was of the kin of eastern Mother Goddesses can hardly be questioned and the stories of her lover appearing as an eagle, vulture, swan, hoopoe, cuckoo or woodpecker may be veiled reminiscences of the fusion of the sun-worshipping Hellenes from the north with the Helladic people they found in Greece. As the associate of the goddess the cuckoo may well have been substituted for the hoopoe in Greece.

Aristotle (H.A. 563b 24) mentioned and rejected the fable that the cuckoo turns into a hawk in winter. This notion was current until recent times in Britain and is rendered plausible by the resemblance between the cuckoo and the sparrowhawk, but more than mistaken identification seems to have been involved. In fable the hoopoe also changes into a hawk and both birds were solar symbols in Egypt, so the idea of a cuckoo-hawk metamorphosis is apparently derived from eastern sources and is not, as the unsophisticated might suppose, due to the uncritical observations of English yokels. The history of this scrap of folklore warns us against assuming that strange notions arose "naturally" where they are found and that the explanation of them is straightforward.

On the other hand it should not be assumed too readily that because a belief is odd or an observance strange it must have had an archaic origin. It has been argued, for example, that the myth of "The Pent Cuckoo" and the existence of so-called "cuckoo-pens," especially on the Berkshire Downs and Chiltern hills, are evidence of ancient ritual in the course of which the cuckoo, believed to personify the spring, was captured and imprisoned in order to maintain spring fertility as long as possible. The story, which appeared with a number of other facetious tales in "The Merry Tales of the Wise Men of Gotham" in 1630, is as follows:

> On a time the men of Gotham would have pinned in the cuckoo, whereby shee should sing all the yeare, and in the midst of the town they made a hedge round in compasse, and they had got a cuckoo and had put her into it, and said Sing here all the yeare, and thou shalt lack neither meat nor drinke. The Cuckoo as soone as she perceived her selfe incompassed within the hedge flew away. A vengeance on her said they. We made not our hedge high enough.

This fable belongs to a group of similar stories in which well-meaning people do absurd things, as, for example, mistaking the moon's reflection in a pond for a cheese and trying to rake it out. Other stories about penning the cuckoo were localised in Northumberland and Somerset. They are merry tales, not traditional myths. Primitive people do many strange things for ritualistic reasons but to attempt to pen the cuckoo behind a hedge would seem even more ludicrous to them than to more sophisticated people. As J. E. Field has shown, the term "cuckoo pen" is probably an etymological corruption, "pen" meaning a summit, as in Pen y ghent, and "cuck" being derived from a root signifying "to scold" as, for example, in "cucking stool," used for ducking women suspected of witchcraft. There is a possibility that there may be more than Field suggests in these tales. Mr. Lethbridge tells me that he "was brought up on the story of the old woman who lets out the cuckoos to bring in the spring." He suggests that, if this is real folklore, the "old woman" may be the Cailleach, goddess of winter. If the cuckoo were known to be liberated after the Portuguese ceremony already mentioned we would have support for this suggestion —but all this is speculative.

Throughout Europe, and also in Asia, as among the Ainu, there are tales of people being transformed into cuckoos. In many of these the cuckoo utters words of human speech—an indication that its pseudo-human call is largely responsible for the evolution of these legends. Albanians say the bird is a beautiful lady seeking her dead brother and calling, "Ku, ku?—Where are you?" According to a version current in Czecho-Slovakia the cuckoo is a woman who hid herself when Christ approached lest she should have to give him a loaf. When He had passed she leaned out of a window calling "Guc-kuck"—"Look, look" and was turned into a cuckoo. In Germany the story is that a baker or miller's boy robbed the poor of their dough and when God blessed the oven's contents he broke off pieces, shouting "Gukuk"—so he became a cuckoo and is called *Beckerknecht*. Grimm cites a related story which has affinities with a legend related of the woodpecker and the owl (A 1958.0.1; Type 751A) (pp. 97 and 98). "Christ was passing a baker's shop when He smelt the new bread and sent his disciples to ask for a loaf. The baker refused but the baker's wife and six daughters were standing apart and secretly gave it. For this they were set in the sky as the Seven Stars, while the baker became the cuckoo (baker's man), and so long as he sings in spring, from St. Tiburtius' Day (14 April) to St. John's (24 June) the Seven Stars are visible in heaven." Perhaps the motif may originally have belonged to the cuckoo and been transferred to other birds. The grey, dusty appearance of the cuckoo's plumage would readily suggest association with the miller, just as the mealy leaves of a form of the garden auricula gave rise to its old-fashioned name "Dusty Miller." More-over, the cuckoo is linked with milling in barbarous tales which appear to contain reminiscences of primitive practices. In the Baltic area, and also in Roumania, it figures in stories of cannibalism. A wicked stepmother kills a step-child and serves the cooked flesh to her husband —a motif similar to that in the tale of Philomela and Procne (Aa 720). She conceals the heart and bones in some hiding-place, such as a hollow tree. The remains of the murdered child come to life as a cuckoo and eventually the bird kills the wicked woman—in one Esthonian version by dropping on her a hot stone from the baking oven, in another, with a mill stone. In these tales the cuckoo is a transformed innocent while in the legends in which our Lord appears he is a punished malefactor. Perhaps this indicates that in those regions of Europe where paganism lingered, the Baltic and the Balkans, reverence for the cuckoo as a bird connected with the life-giving powers of spring persisted, so that the notion of it as a metamorphosed malefactor was not acceptable. This view is not contradicted by an Esthonian variant in which the Christian element is obviously a later interpolation. After the child has been murdered, Christ comes to the cottage asking for a drink, which the father gives Him. He tells the father that in spring the children will appear as two living creatures from the East gable of the house—where the stepmother had hidden the remains. In due course they emerge as a cuckoo and a swallow. It will be remembered that in the story of the metamorphosis of a woman into a woodpecker as a punishment for refusing to give bread to Christ and his apostles, she was called Gertrude. The cuckoo was associated with Freya, the spring goddess of fertility, whose functions St. Gertrude inherited. All three birds which figure in the "miller's daughter" motif have pre-Christian pagan associations. Thus we perceive how the impact of Christianity modified traditions. No doubt analogous modifications have occurred wherever two culture streams met.

Cuckoo folklore shows that once a bird has attracted attention and acquired emotional significance, beliefs may accumulate around it and generate others. In spite of the folk mind's conservatism it is apt to alter the heritage passed on to it by adding here, subtracting there, and elaborating underlying imagery or latent associations. Even etymological confusion may give rise to myths and legends. Although in ancient times the cuckoo seems to have been associated with the life-giving powers resurgent in spring there is no conclusive European evidence that it was regarded as divine. Current British folklore concerning the bird seems to be the outcome of fairly recent processes of association stimulated by a romanticism which is alien to the primitive mind.

CHAPTER 13

WINGED SOULS

IN the *Daily Sketch* of 8 November 1954 there appeared the following:

SILENCE BROKEN BY A MOTHER'S SONG

A song rose in the silence of the Cenotaph yesterday. A mother sang it as the Queen, the Duke of Edinburgh and thousands of people observed the two minutes' pause at the Remembrance Day service. It was sung by 58-year-old Mrs. Winifred Robins whose only son, David, was killed in a minesweeper in 1941 . . . "It was David's favourite song," she told me. "It was the first thing I taught David as a child. I'm sure he wouldn't have minded me singing it with the Queen and all those people listening."

Mrs. Robins looked up at the sea-gulls wheeling in the overcast sky. "David told me they had the spirits of dead seamen," she said. "I like to think he was right."

Thus, at a great national religious ceremony we find a woman expressing her belief, or half-belief, in the transmigration of souls—a doctrine far older than Christianity. The incident illustrates vividly how ancient notions, living a ghostly, underground existence, may survive for centuries after they have ceased to be philosophically acceptable or theologically orthodox. But, it may be asked, is this generalisation, with its implications, justified? May not these beliefs about sea-gulls be dismissed as the fancies of a sentimental sailor-lad or his ship-mates inspired by the dangers of war-time and akin to such legends as that of "The Angel of Mons" in the first world war? Need we seek further for an explanation of the belief in sea-birds as embodying the spirits of the dead than in the imagination of distraught men who, luckier than their companions in surviving the torpedo or mine, watched the white birds wheeling over the scene of the disaster?

Yes, we must. These beliefs are not due to the myth-making activities of minds under the strain of modern war. Their geographical distribution is extensive and they can be traced far back in time.

Michael Fairless in *The Roadmender* describes a trip he made in a fishing smack: 'Then Daddy Whidden spoke, "A follerin' bürrd," he said. I got up and looked across the blue field we were ploughing into white furrows. Far away a tiny sail scarred the great solitude, and astern came a gull flying close to the water's breast.

Daddy Whidden waved his pipe towards it.

"A follerin' bürrd," he said again; and again I waited; questions were not grateful to him.

"There be a corpse there sure enough, a corpse driftin' and shiftin' on the floor of the sea. There be those as can't rest, and her'll be mun, her'll be mun, and the sperrit of her with the bürrd."

The clumsy boom swung across and we changed our course, and the water ran from us in smooth reaches on either side: the bird flew steadily on.

"What will the spirit do?" I said. The old man looked at me gravely.

"Her'll rest in the Lard's gude time, in the Lard's gude time— but now her'l just be follerin' on with the bürrd."

The gull was flying close to us now, and a cold wind swept the sunny sea. I shivered. Daddy looked at me curiously.

"There be reason enough to be cawld if us did but knaw it but I 'mos used to 'em, poor sawls." He shaded his keen old blue eyes, and looked away across the water.'

This might be regarded as fanciful had we not confirmation of it from other parts of the coast. In *English Idyls* P. H. Emerson wrote: "I found that on certain parts of the east coast many of the old fishermen believe that they turn into gulls when they die. It was with great difficulty that I found out that this strange belief in a post-mortem transformation existed at all, but once having learned it, I found to my astonishment that the belief was common, but was spoken of with much reserve. I have never seen any mention of such a superstition existing in our day, and should feel obliged to any critic who could throw light upon it. I asked one fisherman if he did not dislike their being shot on this account. He replied philosophically, 'No! they hev been dead oncet, they hev been on earth oncet, and we hev got quite enough old men now.'

'And the children,' I asked, 'what becomes of them?'

'I believe all the young uns what die are kitties (kittiwakes), they don't come to gulls. They have not to be so artful', he added sententiously.

'And the women?'

'The women,' he replied, 'don't come back no more, they have seen trouble enough; but the old women torturise the young 'uns.'

These extraordinary statements are recorded here verbatim as they were written down in my notebook. I found that all these opinions were held by many of the fishermen."

This account occurs as a note to a tale about a fisherman seeking his dead brother who had foretold that he would return as a gannet after death and be recognisable by his "black armsleeves." In stories of metamorphosis, colours are often retained when shape is altered.

Similar beliefs were held, and probably persist, in other places around our coast. The notion that gulls embody the spirits of drowned persons is said to linger among Irish fishermen. According to Mr. T. C. Lethbridge Cornish fishermen believed it when he was a boy. In West Sutherland it was held that the souls of the departed inhabited seagulls and that consequently killing them would bring bad luck. The inhabitants of St. Kilda cherished a similar superstition.

As the quotations show, the belief in the transmigration of souls was not associated with a single species. It was applied to gulls in general, sometimes to kittiwakes in particular, and even to gannets. The Irish belief that swans should not be disturbed because they embody the spirits of the dead belongs to a rather different tradition (p. 48). Other coasts are haunted by different soul-birds. In Brittany fishermen say that the spirits of skippers who treated their crews harshly are condemned to flutter for ever over the sea as storm petrels. According to other traditions they are the souls of drowned mariners seeking the prayers of the living, or they are devil-birds, flitting over the corpses of the lost. The names bestowed on the storm petrel in France and Britain—*oiseau du diable, satanite, satanique,* Witch and Waterwitch, indicate its sinister reputation. In the West Indies the name *diablotin* for some species of petrel still survives from the days of French domination. When I was crossing the Sea of Marmara in a French ship shearwaters were pointed out to me as "âmes damnées." Doubtless it was to these birds that Dallaway referred in his book

Constantinople, Ancient and Modern which appeared in 1797. Speaking of the Bosporus he said: "Scarcely a minute passes but flocks of aquatic birds, resembling swallows, may be observed flying in a lengthened train from one sea to the other. As they are never known to rest, they are called Halcyons, and by the French 'âmes damnées.' They are superstitiously regarded by all the inhabitants." Tristram speaks of greater and Manx shearwaters in the eastern Mediterranean "skimming along the coasts in long lines of many hundreds" and says that because of their restless habits and sombre plumage Moslems believe them to be "tenanted by the souls of the condemned."

Far out in the ocean where the albatrosses glided in the wake of sailing ships similar beliefs were transferred to them:

> *At length did cross an Albatross*
> *Through the fog it came;*
> *As if it had been a Christian soul,*
> *We hailed it in God's name.*
> *God save thee, ancient Mariner!*
> *From the fiends that plague thee thus!*
> *Why look'st thou so? With my cross-bow*
> *I shot the Albatross.*
> *And I had done an hellish thing,*
> *And it would work 'em woe:*
> *For all averred, I had killed the bird*
> *That made the breeze to blow.*

The incident on which Coleridge, at Wordsworth's suggestion, based his poem occurs in Shelvocke's *Voyage* (1726). Seamen are said to have believed that albatrosses sailing around a ship brought bad weather and that killing them was unlucky, but this belief was not as widespread as has been supposed, for sailors used to slay these birds to make tobacco pouches from the webbing of their feet.

The albatrosses belong to the same Order as the shearwaters and petrels. How easy it was for beliefs concerning some species of the family to be transferred to others, or even to gulls, is shown by the history of the word Mollymawk. It is a corruption of the Dutch Mallemuck, compounded of "mal" (foolish) and "mok" (gull) and was apparently first applied to the fulmar. Ray, in his *Synopsis methodica Avium* (1713) adopted the term but in modern times it has been written Mollymawk and applied particularly to the smaller species of albatross. Sailors sometimes use it of various brownish sea-birds, the giant petrel, skuas and even immature gulls. In Yorkshire the fulmar and glaucous gull were called Mollemoke or Mollemawk. Practically all these birds are considered weather-prophets—usually forecasting storm.

Literary sources for most of our British bird folklore become very meagre or fail altogether in the seventeenth and sixteenth centuries. It is not to be wondered at that references to marine soul-birds are hard to find considering how few writers interested themselves in such matters. Occasional allusions to weather-forecasting birds occur, as, for example in Purchas' *Voyages* (iv, 1317). Here we are told of "the calcamar"—"as bigge as turtle-doves." "The men of the countrie say, that they lay their egges in the sea, and there they hatch and breed their young; they flie not, but with their wings and feet they swimme very swiftly, and they foreshow great calmes and showres, and in calme weather they are so many along the shippes that the mariners cannot tell what to doe, they are even the very spite it selfe, and melancholy." This seems to be the halcyon fable transferred to some marine species on the coast of Brazil. It shows that, as we might expect, seamen carried their traditions with them to other continents.

Although sea-gull soul-birds are difficult to discover as we pursue our search into the Middle and Dark Ages we find a strand of tradition which seems to have sprung from the same source as the beliefs we have been discussing. There are versions of St. Brendan's Voyage in Latin, French, English, Saxon, Flemish, Irish, Welsh, Breton and Scottish Gaelic. It is still related by Irish shanachies. Although the earliest extant version, the *Navigatio Brendani*, dates from the eleventh century the tale may be assumed to be older. Carney traces its origin to an allegory composed in a Christian community of the seventh or eighth century. In the course of their strange travels the saint and his companions arrive at a beautiful island. There, beside a well stands a tree covered with white birds whose singing is like a heavenly choir. One of them explains to Brendan: "One time we were every one of us angels, but when our master Lucifer fell from heaven for his high pride we fell along with him, some higher and some lower. And because our offence was but a little one our Lord has put us here without pain in great joy and merriment to serve what way we can upon this tree."

The story, as it has reached us, is a sophisticated, composite literary product and by no means a transcription of oral folklore. Various strands of tradition may be detected or suspected in it, including Scandinavian elements and borrowings from the Irish legend of the Voyage of Maeldune. Strong Christian influences are apparent, as also are eastern traditions, especially in the incident of landing on a great fish or whale, which is derived from Arabian sources. The essence of the episode with which we are concerned is the finding by mariners on an island of white birds which retain their human voices from the time when they were men.

Can an earlier tradition containing all or most of these elements be found? We have such a tale in the legend of the Birds of Diomede. The Greek hero of the siege of Troy who was able to overcome all mortals who came against him, and even to defy the gods, landed at last on the Islands of Diomede, the *Isole dei Tremiti* off the coast of Apulia, and there mysteriously disappeared, or was buried. Out of compassion his companions were turned into birds. The descriptions given by Vergil (*Aen.* xi. 271 *sq.*), Ovid (*Met.* xiv. 497 *sq.*) Pliny (x. (44) 61) and others leave no doubt that the birds were Mediterranean shearwaters (*Procellaria diomedea*). Gesner identified them, and Aldrovandus, who received a specimen from the Augustinian friars there, figures a specimen (*Ornith.* (1637) iii, 58). Cochorella (*Thes. Antiq. Siciliae,* xiv) mentions that the birds make noises like squalling children and Gesner tells a tale of a Duke of Urbino who while a guest at the monastery heard such sounds and, drawing what seemed the obvious conclusion from them, severely rebuked the friars for their immoral behaviour.

So many superstitions about bird-human transformations are concerned with birds whose voices have a human quality that the most plausible explanation of the Birds of Diomede is that the legend of their earlier existence in human form arose through seafarers landing near the breeding colony being impressed by the moaning, wailing and squalling underground noises on an island over which shearwaters flitted restlessly in the dusk. It may be that the *Isole dei Tremiti* were regarded as haunted by human spirits long before the reputed landing of Diomede and his companions.[1] All the essential elements of the belief

[1] Many islands have been regarded as the dwelling-place of strange female beings, sirens, naiads, witches, priestesses and so forth. Perhaps the strange voices of seals as well as of their bird inhabitants may have encouraged these ideas.

which seafarers carried across the oceans and which still persists in the Mediterranean are here. Thus breezes from the Islands of Diomede may have wafted St. Brendan to the Island of Birds, and today still bear the soul-birds around our coasts.

THE SEVEN WHISTLERS AND THEIR KIN

The mysterious Seven Whistlers cannot be precisely identified, but the reader who has followed the previous discussions will appreciate that our inability to attach a scientific name to these creatures does not imply a confession of ignorance, but rather constitutes a clue to their significance as folklore. Just as the multiplicity of explanations of a custom provides evidence of its antiquity, so the variety of species called Seven Whistlers furnishes a hint that the superstition is derived from ideas more complex than those associated with a single ominous bird.

Yarrell thought that the belief was due to the impression made on people by the calling of bean geese arriving on dark nights from their northern breeding grounds, but in Portugal the aerial noises to which folk refer as the passing of the Seven Whistlers are caused by wigeon— birds which, unlike geese, utter whistling notes. They are believed to be the souls of unchristened babies. In Lancashire golden plover whistling overhead were said to be the souls of Jews who had taken part in the Crucifixion, doomed to wander for ever—an example of the fusion of the Wandering Jew legend with another tradition. These birds were called "whistlers" in North Wales and regarded as death omens. After a colliery disaster at Wigan people reminded each other that the Seven Whistlers had been heard, and in Leicestershire miners used to refuse to enter a pit after hearing the birds, believing that a calamity was imminent. In South Shropshire and Worcestershire the Seven Whistlers are said to be six birds in search of another. When they find him it will be the end of the world. Wordsworth in a Sonnet (1807) wrote of an old dalesman:

> He the seven birds hath seen that never part,
> Seen the Seven Whistlers on their nightly rounds
> And counted them.

He associates them with Gabriel's hounds. Swainson thought that golden plover inspired these ideas.

In the *Faerie Queene* (II.xii.36) Spenser alluded to

> *The rueful Strich still waiting on the beere*
> *The Whistler shril, that whoso heares doth die.*

Webster, in *The Duchess of Malfi*, wrote that

> *The Schritch-Owle and the whistler shrill*
> *Call upon our dame aloud*
> *And bid her quickly don her shroud.*

These words are uttered by Bosola who has just announced himself as the Common Bell-Man, the messenger to those shortly to be executed. Because this personage and the bird were both regarded as heralds of doom the owl and the bell became associated in literature and art (Fig. 71, p. 115).

Swann annotates "Seven Whistler": "The Whimbrel: from the clear whistling note supposed to be repeated about seven times." The call is, indeed, repetitive, though in my experience repeated less than seven times on migration, and often more than this number on the breeding grounds. However, this explanation is almost certainly merely a sophisticated modern attempt to pin a name to the Seven Whistlers. The numeral referred originally to the number of the whistlers, not the character of their utterance. Swann remarks that "whimbrel" is mentioned by Willughby in 1678 and points out that Skeat derived it from the bird's cry, resembling "whim." Skeat was no ornithologist and "whim" bears little resemblance to any of the bird's various calls. In the *Durham Household Book* of 1530, the bird is mentioned as the "whimpernel," the allusion being to its whimpering, as hounds do. Indeed some of its utterances resemble those of hounds. Willughby was probably misled by the pronunciation or spelling of his informant.

Flocks of curlews, passing over at night and uttering their plaintive, musical calls have also been regarded as the Seven Whistlers, and in the North of England their voices were said to presage someone's death. The curlew's low-pitched fluting is sufficiently near the range of the human voice to arouse in our hearts the sense of weirdness which we are apt to feel on hearing sounds which have some similarity to, but do not really belong to, the world of men. One of the most eerie of such sounds is the clanging as of a church bell in the midst of the dense South American forest—the voice of the bell bird. Buckland quotes a conversation with an old character who told him that there was always an accident after hearing "them long-billed curlews." He mentioned an occasion when, after a flock had passed, a boat over-turned and seven men were drowned. Near Sheffield, where curlews are still found on the moors, they are, or were, called "Gabriel's hounds." In Devon they are known as "Wish" or "Wisht hounds." Swainson remarks that "sometimes the cry is exactly like the yelping of a pack of hounds" and quotes Bishop Mant, but the calls of whimbrel on the nesting-grounds approximate most closely to his description:

> Shouting loud
> To warn their comrades of the way,
> Lest darkling from the line they stray,
> Wake the dull night with startling sounds;
> Well might you deem the deep-mouthed hounds
> Raised in full cry the huntsman's peal,
> Or clamoured for their evening meal.

Probably it was the resemblance between the curlew's call and the human voice or whistle which brought about the association between curlews and goblins. The word "whaup," used in Scotland and the North of Ireland of the curlew, is also the name of a goblin with a long beak which moves about under house-eaves at night. So Sir Walter Scott makes one of his characters say "there's a sort o' worricows and lang nebbit things about the land." Also there is the Highlander's prayer to be saved "from witches, warlocks, and aw lang-nebbed things."

The mystery of the Seven Whistlers might seem to be complicated further by their association with "Gabriel's hounds" but herein may lie the explanation of this belief. The term "gabble-ratchet" was used in Yorkshire and elsewhere for geese flying clamorously at night. "Gabble" is apparently a corruption of "Gabriel," and according to mediaeval glossaries, this is connected with *gabbara* or *gabares*, meaning a corpse. "Ratchet" is from the Anglo-Saxon *raecc* and Middle English *racche* or *rache*, a dog which hunts by scent and gives tongue. (From this "ratchet owl" is derived).[1] The frightening effect of these

[1] Low, in *The Domesticated Animals of England* (1846) comments: "The hounds employed in England for the chase of the wild deer were generally termed raches . . . Their voice was deep and sonorous." Cf. *Midsummer Night's Dream*, IV.i.117.

"corpse hounds" was described by Alfred Newton "The sounds are at times very marvellous, not to say impressive, when heard, as they almost invariably are, on a pitch-dark night, and it has more than once happened within the writer's knowledge that a flock of geese, giving utterance to them, has continued for some hours to circle over a town or village in such a way as to attract the attention of the most unobservant of its inhabitants, and inspire with terror those amongst them who are prone to superstition."

That birds so different as curlews and geese have been regarded as Gabriel Hounds suggests that the notions connected with one species have been transferred to another. As the sounds made by geese are so much more like the baying of hounds than the curlew's whistling there can be no doubt that, of the two, geese have the better claim to the title. Moreover, as curlews are also called "Seven Whistlers" on account of their nocturnal calls it is probable that traditions, originally belonging to "Gabriel Hounds," have been transferred to them.

Newton queried Swainson's accuracy in stating that Yorkshire folk called nightjars "gabble ratchets", but Swainson quoted Macquoid, who had remarked in *About Yorkshire* that these birds were so called in Nidderdale and were said to be the souls of unbaptised infants. However, Nelson, in *Birds of Yorkshire*, confirmed that the nightjar is known around Thirsk as "Gabble-ratch." The explanation of this name given by local folk is an example of rationalisation. They say it is derived from the fact that the bird "ratches" (hoots) on the gables of houses. But this explanation suggests an owl, as the nightjar's churring does not resemble a hoot and owls are apt to perch on houses much more frequently than nightjars. Thus, apparently, a name associated more with ominous nocturnal sounds than with any particular species, was applied locally to the nightjar. Through further etymological and ornithological confusion the name "ratchet owl" arose. The "*Hel-rakke*" or death-hound of the Danes was "a bird with a large head, staring eyes, crooked beak, sharp claws," which in olden times was believed to fly around screeching at night, foretelling deaths. The German *Leichhuhn* (corpse hen), *Grabeule* or *Todtenvogel* was a spectral creature with lazy flight—presumably owing its imaginary being to owls rather than nightjars, though in Shropshire the latter were known as "lich fowls" (corpse fowls). The voice of the nightjar has long been regarded as of evil omen, as in the *Carmen de Philomela*. In Poole's *English Parnassus* we read:

Night Jars and Ravens, with wide stretched throats,
From yews and hollies send their baleful notes.

Possibly the name "puckeridge," used in West Sussex and elsewhere, mentioned by Gilbert White, is derived from the elfin spirit
Puck. The canard that the nightjar sucks the udders of goats and
causes them to go blind can be traced as far back as Aristotle, but the
adoption of the Latin name *Caprimulgus* by Turner and its translation
into English by Merrett (1667) and Willughby may have been responsible for these fallacies in England, though, perhaps, the use of similar
names in almost every European language indicates that the belief
was current even before Aristotle's time. Mediaeval writers and
artists confused the nightjar and the night raven (Fig. 76, p. 138). The
Caprimulgidae are viewed with superstitious concern almost everywhere they occur because of their strange call-notes or songs and
nocturnal habits. In New England the whippoorwill is said to portend
death, and in the southern Alleghanies the number of times that the
bird repeats its cry is believed to indicate how many years a bachelor
will remain unmarried. Some American Indians deduce the number
of years the listener will live from its calls. These beliefs may have
been brought to the New World by European settlers and some of
them may be derived from cuckoo lore. Indians and negroes living
along the Amazon spare nightjars as they regard them as the souls of
the departed. When I visited caves in the West Indies where the
queer nightjar-like *guacharo* was nesting I was told that the strange,
raucous quasi-human groans and snarls of the birds deep in the dark
caverns had given rise to the belief among the negroes that the ghosts
of dead malefactors were confined in them.

A principle of interpretation which we have already used justifies
the inference that the association of Gabriel hounds with unbaptised
children and Jews indicates that these traditions are pre-Christian.
(The extent to which Scandinavian influence persisted in Yorkshire,
and the survival of the Anglo-Saxon terms "gabble-ratchet" and
"Gabriel hounds" suggest that we are concerned with Germanic traditions). It can hardly be doubted that the Gabriel Hounds and
Seven Whistlers legends were derived from the "Wild Hunt" belief
which has been recorded in various forms from many parts of the
world, but had special importance in Germanic regions (E501.4.4).
When the tempest rages and the wind shrieks on winter nights a

ghostly company of hunters rides across the sky, and earthly hounds give tongue in response to the spectral pack. Spirits of the dead join the tumultuous cavalcade—for according to Teutonic belief it was the fate of disembodied spirits to haunt familiar places or wander through the air. Odin often leads the throng.

The Wild Hunt tradition appears in Britain in various forms, some fragmentary. For example, the *cwn wybr*, dogs of the sky, also called *cwn annwn*, dogs of hell, of Welsh folklore, must be of the same breed as the hell hounds of German mythology.

It will be remembered that the raven is identified with Odin, so there is some force in the argument that in stories of the Wild Hunt we have the origin of the belief in the night raven. There are folk tales which tell of two ravens which follow the Hunt, and in Danish folklore we hear of the night raven preceding it. A number of different species have been identified as the night raven, but scholars have mistakenly sought an ornithological rather than a mythological explanation. They have looked for a bird which is nocturnal and has some raven-like quality, such as a hoarse voice, rather than asked themselves to what stream of folklore the tradition belongs. Albin (1738-40) concluded that the night raven was the night heron, which, indeed, is still *Nycticorax* in scientific nomenclature, but Willughby and Goldsmith identified it as the bittern. Both of them, as well as other writers, commented on the dread aroused in villagers' hearts on hearing the bittern's boom. Their conclusion was based on a simple but unsound inference—the bittern is heard at night and is feared by the superstitious, therefore it is the night raven. Bishop Hall remarked of a superstitious man, "If a Bittourn fly over his head by night, he makes his will." Harrison stated that the bird regarded as the night raven in the Isle of Ely was the cormorant. Again, the multiplicity of attempted identifications shows that the belief has become separated from its roots.[1]

[1]The bird mentioned in *Leviticus* (xi. 16) which has puzzled translators is called "night hawk" in the English versions but "night crow" in Welsh. It has been identified with the "corpse bird" (cf. Swainson) and the tawny owl. There seems to be no cogent reason to believe it to have been this particular species of owl rather than another. In *A Mirror for Magistrates* the nightingale is referred to as the night crow:

> *Sweet are the songs that merry night crow singes*

and,

> *It is a sport to heare the fine night crow*
> *Chaunt in the queere upon a pricke-song plaine.*

The Wild Hunt myth evidently became attenuated so that all that remained of it in some areas was a belief in a nocturnal bird which uttered harsh cries and presaged calamity—the night raven. So the field was clear for speculation and myth-making. Thus under "Night-crow" Batman (Bartholomew) tells us: "This kind of owl is dog-footed and covered with hair; his eyes are like the glistering ice; against death he useth a strange whoop." Did the association with dogs occur because of some lingering reminiscence of the ghostly hounds of the Wild Hunt? The Tudor poets and dramatists used the name for its emotional effect without concerning themselves too closely with ornithological exactitude. Spenser wrote in the *Faerie Queene* (II.vii. 23):

> *And after him the owles and night ravens flew,*
> *The hateful messengers of heavy tidings,*

and referred in *Epithalamion* (i. 435) to the night raven's "deadly yells." Lyly alluded in *Sappho and Phaon* to the owl's shriek and night-raven's croak being fatal, and Shakespeare (3 *King Henry VI*, V.vi.47) wrote:

> *The night-crow cried, aboding luckless time;*
> *Dogs howl'd, and hideous tempests shook down trees;*
> *The raven rook'd her on the chimney-top.*

In *Much Ado* (II.iii.81) he makes Benedick say of Balthazar and his song: "An he had been a dog that should have howled thus, they would have hanged him: and pray God his bad voice bode no mischief. I had as lief have heard the night-raven, come what plague could have come after it." There is more here than meets the eye. In Shakespeare's thought the "nightly owl" and "fatal raven" were associated (*Titus*, II.iii.97) and also owls and howling dogs. Thus he wrote of the ominous time "when screech-owls cry and ban-dogs howl" (2 *Henry VI*, I.iv.21) and also of "owls" and "wolves' death-boding cries" (*Lucrece* 165; Cf. *K. Lear*, II. iv.213). Undoubtedly owls, ravens, night ravens, night crows and howling dogs were all closely connected in the dramatist's mind as portents of evil. As I have shown elsewhere such "image-clusters" are a constant feature of his thought. For many centuries, and up to the present time the nocturnal howling of dogs was believed to presage catastrophe. In an old volume quoted by Brand a number of superstitions are mentioned:

When Ball, his dog, at twelve o'clocke did howle,
He jogg'd his wife, and ill lucke Madge did say,
And Fox by morning stole a Goose away.

Marston wrote in *Antonio and Meltild* (1633)

No spirit moves upon the breast of earth,
Save howling Dogs, Night Crowes and screeching Owles,
Some meager Ghosts, Piero and blacke Thoughts.

The association between the night raven and howling dogs is so close and constant that we may infer with some confidence that it is ultimately derived from the myth of the Wild Hunt. In the twelfth century Anglo-Saxon Chronicle it is localised in the Peterborough district. Of course howling dogs and nocturnal birds may have been regarded as ominous before the myth was formulated, but we may justifiably suppose that it brought them into association. Since then, even where the Wild Hunt has been forgotten howling dogs and mythical nocturnal birds retain their sinister character. In this instance we can infer how dogs and ravens became linked in thought, but occasionally, as with the association between the devil and small birds mentioned in the previous chapter, the original folklore connexion has been obscured or lost. Considering how precariously folklore lives from generation to generation on the lips of simple people, who often do not understand its significance, the marvel is that continuities with the past can so often be traced.

CHAPTER 14

BIRD FISH

A BELIEF in bird-fish has been current in western Europe for more than a thousand years—in particular, a tradition that shell-fish turn into birds. (Here "fish" is used in the widest sense). Writer after writer repeated the story and according to his predilections asseverated, queried, denied or elaborated it. This protracted discussion is of interest because it provides insight into the vagaries of pre-scientific thought and also, incidentally, for the light it throws on the credulity or mendacity of scholars. So well documented is the legend that its history, which has been reviewed in detail by Heron-Allen, provides interesting side-lights on the historical and psychological factors involved in the maintenance of literary myths. The fable apparently began as oral tradition, became literary, and then, to a minor extent, became oral again. Here no attempt will be made to retrace its curious history. It will suffice to put forward an explanation of how it arose and to present a little new material.

The bird-fish is not quite extinct. My friend Professor J. H. Delargy, Director of the Irish Folklore Commission, writes (*in litt.*): "I met a teacher once in Kerry who told me he had often shot barnacle geese and had them for Friday's dinner; this type of fish being popular locally on that day. He was quite serious." Dinneen's *Irish Dictionary* states that the tradition was still believed in Donegal less than fifty years ago. At present, according to Mr. Seán Ford, those who retail such stories in the west of Ireland usually add—"if it be true." A generation ago Sir John Nelligan, sometime Recorder of Cork, reported that goose was considered legitimate Lenten fare by folk all along the Kerry coast, "not because they had any belief in the mythical story of its origin, but because they knew it lived more on the sea than on land and so acquired its fishy character." Heron-Allen quotes a letter written shortly before 1914 from an Ulster parish priest to the librarian of the Zoological Society stating that "his people were in the habit of eating the Barnacle-goose during Lent, under the impression that it was more fish than fowl."[1]

The persistence of the tradition in Ireland should be taken into consideration when attempting to discover how and when it arose. Giraldus Cambrensis, in his *Topographia Hiberniae*, read before the masters and scholars of Oxford in 1186 after his return from a journey in Ireland with Prince John, related the story and claimed to have seen birds being generated from marine organisms: "There are in this place many birds which are called Bernacae: Nature produces them against Nature in the most extraordinary way. They are like marsh geese but somewhat smaller. They are produced from fir timber tossed along the sea and are at first like gum. Afterwards they hang down by their beaks as if they were seaweed attached to the timber, and are surrounded by shells in order to grow more freely. Having thus in process of time been clothed with a strong coat of feathers, they either fall into the water or fly freely away into the air. They derive their food and growth from the sap of the wood or from the sea, by a secret and most wonderful process of alimentation. I have frequently seen, with my own eyes, more than a thousand of these small birds, hanging down on the sea-shore from one piece of timber, enclosed in their shells and already formed. They do not breed and lay eggs like other birds, nor do they ever hatch any eggs, nor do they seem to build nests in any corner of the earth. Hence Bishops and religious men in some parts of Ireland do not scruple to dine off these birds at the time of fasting, because they are not flesh nor born of flesh."

As it has been suggested that Neckam's account may be earlier than Gerald's it is quoted for comparison: "The bird which is commonly called bernekke takes its origin from fir-wood which has been steeped for a long time in the sea. From the surface of the wood there exudes a certain viscous humour, which in time assumes the form of a litte bird clothed in feathers, and it is seen to hang by its beak from the wood. This bird is eaten by the less discreet in times of fasting

---

[1]There has been confusion between the barnacle and the brent goose. Gesner's quotation from Caius' letter, quoted later (p. 234) shows that Caius regarded the brent as the young of the barnacle but as Raven points out this is omitted from a later version of his letter. The barnacle goose probably used to have a more southerly range in Ireland. Even today the barnacle (*Branta leucopsis*) and brent (*B. bernicla*) are given confusing scientific names and the two species are frequently confounded in Ireland. As the barnacle goose is uncommon in Kerry the brent must be the species most frequently eaten there on fast days.

because it is not produced by maternal incubation from an egg. But what is this? It is certain that birds existed before eggs, wherefore birds which do not emerge from eggs follow the laws relating to fishes as regards food, rather than those relating to birds which have evolved by the transmission of seminal matter. Have not the birds derived their origin from the waters according to the irrefutable pages of heavenly doctrine? How can it be said that the bernekke are not born excepting from wood treated by the sea, or from trees situated on the edges of shores?" Neckam returned to the discussion later, saying, "Rumour has it that by a process of Nature firwood steeped in the sea gives forth young birds. This is done by a viscous humour: what public opinion asserts, philosophy indignantly denies."

These versions are so similar that one must be derived from the other or both from a common source. Both mention that the creatures were produced *ex lignis abiegnis*. Critical scrutiny suggests that Neckam depended on Giraldus for the latter's version is more circumstantial. Giraldus specifies with precision the birds concerned. These accounts make it clear that, whatever rumours about bird-fish may have been current elsewhere, the belief was localised in Ireland. If it had not already been accepted there for a considerable time, the Irish bishops and clergy would not have come under Gerald's condemnation for regarding geese as fish-fare. As he disapproved of their doing so he would have argued, if he had felt able to do so, against the practice on the grounds that geese are obviously not fish. But with his credulous eyes he had seen the birds in process of gestation and he could not deny what he had seen. We may plausibly suppose that his acquaintances in Ireland, possibly some of the clergy, took Gerald to the shore and pointed out certain organisms, hoping to convince him of their scrupulousness in keeping the Lenten fast. It has long been an Irish pastime to pull the legs of visitors from across the channel. However, as will appear, his informants inherited an earlier tradition. Not surprisingly some later ecclesiastical authorities agreed with Gerald in regarding the eating of goose flesh during Lent as an abuse. Vincent of Beauvais (*Spec. anim.* xvii, 40) records that at the General Lateran Council in 1215 Pope Innocent III forbade this practice, but news of this does not seem to have yet reached the west of Ireland!

William Turner wrote that when the planks of a ship rotted in the sea "there break out what seem like fungi (*Lepas anatifera*); in these,

FIG. 85. Illustration from *An Herball* by Gerard, 1597, depicting tree-geese hatching from barnacles.

after a time, the obvious shapes of birds become visible, then these are clad in feathers, then they come to life and fly." He quotes Giraldus, mentions that the belief is held by "all the coastal people of England, Ireland and Scotland"—a statement which must be an exaggeration —and remarks that he asked an Irishman named Octavian whether he considered Giraldus reliable. This man replied that "he had himself seen with his own eyes and handled with his own hands birds still half-formed," so Turner wrote to Gesner that he was convinced of the truth of the story. The latter discussed it in detail in the Frankfort edition of his *Historiae Animalium*. Aldrovandus, deferring to the judgment of many authorities, also accepted the tale as authentic.

These writers were children of their age, setting forth their sources, assessing their value as best they might, but bowing to tradition. If we are inclined to smile at their simplicity let us remember the incredulity of anthropologists in regard to the paintings at Altamira and how long they were hoaxed by the Piltdown skull. Downright mendacity enters the barnacle goose tradition with John Gerard's assurance in his *Herball* (1597): "What our eies have seene and hands have touched, we shall declare." Between Dover and Romney he had found shells which, when he opened them in London, were found to contain "birds covered with soft downe, the shell half open and the birds ready to fall out." Plagiarist as he was, he appropriated an illustration from Mathias de Lobel's *Stirpium Historia,* adding to it realistic birds nestling within the shells (Fig. 85, p. 228). Many other writers embellished their pages with pictures of "tree-geese" which, as depicted by successive artists, tended to become increasingly life-like. Nor did occasional poets neglect to adorn their verse with references to these prodigies. Joshua Sylvester, in his translation (1584) of *La Semaine* by Guillaume de Saluste (1578) described the metamorphosis, concluding thus:

> *So rotten sides of broken Shipps doo change*
> *To barnacles; O, Transformation strange!*
> *'Twas first a greene Tree; then a gallant Hull;*
> *Lately a mushrum, now a flying Gull;*

and on Prospero's magic isle Caliban, whom Trinculo took for "a strange fish" feared that they should "all be turned to barnacles" (*Tempest,* IV.i.249).

There is copious material available for those who wish to trace the barnacle goose myth until it was at last discarded by scientific men in the eighteenth century. Instead of re-ploughing such well-tilled ground we may enquire further into the origin and early history of the barnacle bird.

As early authorities point back to Ireland the suspicion arises that the myth might occur in the vernacular literature, but Professor Gerard Murphy, an authority on Old and Middle Irish, tells me that he knows of no reference to it there. We must seek information elsewhere; indeed, in a very different quarter—Jewish Rabbinic literature.

The problem of whether wild geese were fish or fowl exercised Jews as well as Christians. Max Müller summed up some of the data: "Mordechai (Riva, 1559, leaf 142a) asks whether these birds are fruits, fish or flesh, i.e. whether they must be killed in the Jewish way, as they would if they were flesh. He describes them as birds which grow on trees, and he says that Rabbi Jehudah, of Worms (died 1216) used to say that he had heard from his father, Rabbi Samuel of Speyer (about 1150) that Rabbi Jacob Tham of Ramerü (died 1171, the grandson of the great Rabbi Rashi, about 1140) had decided that they must be killed as flesh."[1]

The earliest authority, quoting Rabbi Tam (or Tham) on birds generated from trees, is Isaac ben Moses of Vienna, who flourished in the first half of the thirteenth century. In his work on ritual *Or Zaru'a* he mentions the tradition that Rabbi Tam sent his decision regarding these birds to the "sons of Angleterre." He refers to "birds"; geese are not mentioned in the early Rabbinic sources except by Simeon ben Zemah Duran (1361-1444). This reference is in a MS collection of *Responsa* cited by S. J. Halberstam in his *Catalogue* (p. 66). Strictly speaking Rabbi Tam's decision does not imply that the original enquirers were Englishmen. Irish inquirers might have applied to Rabbinic authorities in England who, in their turn, asked Rabbi Tam's opinion on the matter.

Among other allusions in Jewish sources is a passage in the *Zohar* (Exodus. ed. Amsterdam, 1805, II, 15b) (mistranslated in the English edition edited by Soncino): "Rabbi Abba saw a tree whose fruit (shoot) produced a fowl that flew away." This work cannot be dated more exactly than about the end of the thirteenth century. These references, indicate that the nature of barnacle geese was a problem of importance for Jews in the British Isles during the twelfth century. It is significant as an indication of where the tradition arose that all the early Rabbinic writers who mention it were West-Europeans. Dr. J. Teicher, to whom I am indebted for some of them, has called my attention to an important allusion which seems to have escaped the notice of all those who have discussed this subject. It carries our knowledge of the barnacle goose legend into about the tenth century. Ibrahim ibn Ahmad at-Tortushi (from Tortosa) was a member of a diplomatic mission from Moslem Spain to the court of the Emperor Otto, and in

[1]The Rabbinic sources are mentioned by Heron-Allen but they are more comprehensively reviewed by J. Diamant (1905) and H. J. Zimmels (1926).

his description of "Shashin," which, judging by the context, is most probably Ireland, he says: "There is something marvellous there, such as is nowhere else in the world. On the sea-shore grow trees, and from time to time the bank gives way and a tree falls into the sea. The waves toss it up and down so much that a white jelly is formed on it. This goes on until the jelly increases in size and assumes the shape of an egg. Then the egg is moulded in the form of a bird with nothing but both feet and the bill attached to the wood. When Allah wills the wind that blows on it produces feathers and it detaches the feet and bill from the wood. So it becomes a bird which scuttles in the sea about the surface of the water. It is never found alive, but when the sea rises it is thrown by the water on the shore, where it is found dead. It is a black bird similar to the bird which is called The Diver. Ahmed ibn 'Omar al-'Udhri relates: A man brought to a king a piece of wood with the beginnings of the eggs already formed. The king ordered that a cupola-shaped structure similar to a cage be built over it and that it should be left in the water and not removed from the shore until the birds freed themselves from the wood inside the structure."

This account shows that in the British Isles, and most probably in Ireland, a story was current concerning birds generated from timber floating in the sea. Geese are not mentioned, but the birds are described with some exactitude—a crucial point because apart from Giraldus' description most early accounts are vague as to the species concerned. They were black, diving birds whose bodies were found on the shores of Ireland after storms and they were never seen alive. In other words, they were not known to nest in the British Islands or, indeed, elsewhere in the world. This description could apply to one species, and one species only—the little auk—a bird whose breeding range is in the arctic. Every now and then great numbers are blown ashore during inclement weather, and numerous corpses are found along the foam-fringed coast. "Wrecks" of these birds were recorded in 1895, 1900, 1910 and 1912. In the tenth century little auks may have been commoner around our coasts than at present. The recent amelioration of climate has almost driven the species from its most southerly breeding station in Iceland. To explain the origin of the myth, we have only to suppose that people, noticing barnacles on the flotsam in the foam where the birds' carcasses were drifting assumed that the shell-fish were the early stages of these birds. The transference of the legend to the barnacle goose can also be readily explained. Its nesting grounds were also unknown and, being a regular visitor and available during Lent, it could be considered a happy dispensation that its strange mode of generation brought it within the category of Lenten fare.

We have seen that Giraldus brought back the barnacle goose story from Ireland where he had seen the objects in question and that the Arab envoy's account, with its rather vague geographical reference is not inconsistent with this. The first Jewish author to locate the myth in Ireland was the anonymous translator of the cosmography *l'Ymage du Monde* which was compiled in 1245. Friar Odoric, who set out on his journey to India and China about the year 1318, remarks in his *Journal* concerning a tree reputed to bear melons holding within "a little beast like a young lamb." "I myself have heard reported that there stand certain trees upon the shore of the Irish Sea, bearing fruit like a melon, which, at a certain time of the year do fall into the water, and become birds." He may have heard this garbled version of the story from his Irish travelling companion Friar James. It was an Irishman who assured William Turner that he had seen the birds in process of generation. Thus the story was located in Ireland for some centuries of its early history and it still survives there. From the ornithological point of view this is consistent with the story having originated with the little auk and being transferred to the barnacle goose, for little auks have been "wrecked" in numbers on the Irish coast and the barnacle goose winters around the north coast of Ireland and the north and west coasts of Scotland.

Max Müller argued that "Barnacle" is a corruption of *Hibernicae* or *Hiberniculae*—indicating objects from Ireland—*Hibernia*. There is this further fact in support of his view, that in Ireland the bird is still often called "bernicle goose" and wildfowlers elsewhere commonly give it this name. Müller believed that the confusion of the names *Bernaculae* for the cirrhopods and *Berniculae* for the birds contributed to the growth of the legend. Mr. Seán Ford tells me that in Irish as early as the tenth century the barnacle goose was called *giurann*, though it is now usually *cadhan*.[1] The cirrhopod is also *giurann* in Irish and Scottish Gaelic. In Welsh the goose and the barnacle are *gwyrain*.

The Arab envoy's account is the earliest direct record of the tradition but we have, in a riddle contained in the *Book of Exeter*, evidence

[1] In a lyric of that period the clamour of the birds is mentioned as one of the signs that summer is over.

of a version perhaps two centuries older. It may have been current orally earlier than the eighth century:

> *In a narrow was my neb, and beneath the wave I lived;*
> *Underflowen by the flood; in the mountain-billows*
> *Low was I besunken; in the sea I waxed*
> *Over-covered with the waves, clinging with my body*
> *To a wandering wood ———.*
> *Quick the life I had, when I from the clasping came*
> *Of the billows, of the beam-wood, in my black array;*
> *White in part were then my pranked garments fair,*
> *When the Lift upheaved me, me a living creature,*
> *Wind from wave upblowing; and as wide as far*
> *Bore me o'er the bath of seals—Say what is my name?*

It has been claimed, with some exaggeration, that Gerald's description "reads like a close paraphrase" of the Anglo-Saxon text. However this may be the riddle describes something on the sea attached to wood which emerges as a creature with black and white coloration and is then borne over the sea. The view that the barnacle goose is indicated has been generally accepted. But the riddle may best be interpreted as referring to the myth rather than to the particular species. If we compare it, not with Gerald's twelfth century account, but with the Arab's report, we find in each the description of an organism clinging to a log of wood in the sea and then emerging as a winged creature. In neither account is there any definite indication that the creature is a goose, but in both we are told that it is black. The riddle also mentions that it is partly white. The description would apply more aptly to the little auk than to the barnacle goose. Thus the Anglo-Saxon riddle confirms the view that the origin of the myth is to be found in the discovery of "wrecked" little auks' corpses washed up around the coast. The Arab version takes the story further in mentioning the trees growing on the shore and then falling into the sea. Later writers describe and depict the organisms growing on the trees. So the fable grew by accretion. The occurrence of the riddle version of the fable does not preclude its having had an Irish origin. This is as near as we can get to locating its birth-place though it remains possible that the tradition might have arisen elsewhere on our northern shores. Certainly it struck its roots most deeply in Ireland.

Possibly the puffin became the bird-fish of England and Wales, not merely through its feeding on fish, but as an offshoot of the original version of the tradition, for the puffin is an auk and in general appearance resembles a large little auk. There were, however, strong gastronomic reasons for this development. Gesner (*De Avibus*, 99, 110) wrote of *Puffinus anglorum:* "It is eaten in Lent because in a measure it seems related to the fishes, in that it is cold-blooded ... The English make the puffin a bird and no bird, or a bird-fish." His informant was John Caius who said in a letter to him: "It is used as fish among us during the solemn fast of Lent: being in substance and looke not unlike a seal." The most plausible argument for regarding puffin as fish would have been that it feeds on fish.[1] That this argument is not used is additional reason to believe that Caius' explanation is merely a rationalisation to explain, in terms of natural history, what can only be accounted for by interpreting mythology according to its own laws. Thomas Mouffet, in his *Health's Improvement* (1655), follows Gesner in referring to puffins as "birds and no birds, that is to say birds in shew and fish in substance ... permitted by Popes to be eaten in Lent." His references to the "Branta" show that he accepted the barnacle goose legend and also the equally erroneous legend (born, perhaps, of the "sour grapes" mentality of rigorists) that the bird was unpalatable: "Barnacles both breed unnaturally by corruption and taste very un-savoury. Poor men eat them, rich men hate them, and wise men reject them when they have other meat." As he places these paragraphs in close association he apparently regards these bird-fish as in one category. Drayton wrote in *Polyolbion* (xxiv, 81-2):

> *The Puffin we compare, which coming to the dish,*
> *Nice palates hardly judge, if it be flesh or fish;*

and Nashe in *Lenten Stuffe* spoke of it as "half fish, half flesh, a John Indifferent, and an ambodexter between either." Richard Carew in his *Survey of Cornwall* (1602) said mistakenly that it is "reputed for fish as coming nearest thereto in taste." Its flesh is excellent eating and not fishy. George Owen, whose *Description of Pembrokeshire* was published a year later, commented: "The Puffin ... is reputed to be fishe, the reason I cannot learne." As Giraldus Cambrensis was born in

[1] Aran islanders used to give as excuse for eating guillemots on Friday that these birds never flew over land and lived on sea food.

Pembrokeshire, and showed his knowledge of Wales in his *Itinerarium Cambriae* he would probably have heard the puffin-fish story if it had been current in his day, and if he had known it, could hardly have avoided mentioning it when writing of the barnacle goose. This negative evidence, for what it is worth, might be regarded as indicating that the puffin became a bird-fish as an outcome of the influence of the barnacle goose fable rather than directly from the original elaboration of the little auk story.

The absence of barnacle geese and puffins from most of southern England did not prevent those who wished to do so from discovering bird-fish suitable for eating in Lent. As early as 1211 Gervase of Tilbury remarked, that a bird called "Barneta" was eaten in Lent as fish. Great numbers grew on willow trees near the Abbey of Faversham in Kent! It is anybody's guess as to what these creatures were. In 1577 William Harrison testified that there bred annually "in the Thames mouth" "a kinde of Fowle" which "hath hys beginning upon a short tender shrubbe standing upon the shore from whence when theyr time commeth they fall down either into the salt water and live or upon the dry land and perish."

Further south, in France where the barnacle goose does not winter, and the puffin is found breeding only on the Breton coast, French resourcefulness discovered another bird-fish for Lenten eating—the *macreuse*. The vagueness of some writers indicates that they were uncertain as to which bird they were discussing. Probably the brent goose and the common and velvet scoters were confused. However, Salerne, writing in 1767, mentions scoters specifically. Hecquet, who published a book on Lenten dispensations in 1709, placed the *macreuse* among the amphibia—"ambiguous creatures of doubtful origin and uncertain genus"—and classes them with beavers and turtles. He remarks that Jews considered it "unclean" and he condemns the flesh as "unsavoury and unhealthy." This did not prevent people from eating the bird. Guettard, 74 years later, remarked that as the custom was useful and "satisfies both taste and sensuality" it would probably continue for ever. Belon (1555), writing under the heading of "De l'Oye Nonnette autrement nommée un Cravant" apparently referred to the barnacle goose. He controverts the legend, as indeed Albertus Magnus (*De Animalibus*, XXIII, p. 186) and Frederick II (*De Arte Venandi cum Avibus*. Paris Bibl. Maz. MS. 3716, p. 63) had done long before, declaring that he had known these birds to lay eggs and hatch their young. As the Emperor Frederick figures the barnacle goose in his book, this suggests that the bird ranged further south than at present, due perhaps, to a more severe winter climate than now prevails.

In 1651 Cattier in a *Discours de la Macreuse* expressed the opinion that the coot answered to the description of the bird-fish, but he admitted that nobody in Languedoc ate it as fish. Somewhat more than 200 years later we find Alphonse Karr mentioning the eating of water-hen, teal and scoter during Lent. Swainson remarks of the common scoter: "The flesh of this bird is so rank and fishy, from its feeding on shell-fish that it is allowed to Roman Catholics on fast days and in Lent. This has originated a belief which prevails in Normandy that like the bernicle, it is produced from a bivalve, which is found adhering to the keels of ships. For the same reason is the proverb applied to a man on whom no reliance can be placed—Il ressemble à une macreuse; il n'est ni chair ni poisson." Swainson may be incorrect in supposing that the scoter is permitted Lenten fare as he is in error in referring to the ship's barnacle as a bivalve. He puts the cart before the horse in assuming that its being eaten as fish in Lent gave rise to the notion that it was an ambiguous creature. The scoter conveniently inherited the reputation of the barnacle goose on a coast outside the latter's normal range, and as it has considerable similarity to the goose we can be confident that the entail was direct and not with the puffin as intermediary.

While the evidence is strong that the barnacle goose myth germinated and evolved on our coasts, its growth may have been aided by other, mainly eastern, stories of incongruous generation. Ibrahim ibn Ahmad at-Tortushi may the more readily have reported his strange story because somewhat similar tales were familiar to him. Alberuni (fl. *c*. A.D. 1000) described a tree growing on the coasts of the Indian ocean with a curled leaf which flew away as a king bee. In the *History of Hagy ibn Yaqzan* by Abu Bakr ibn Tufail we are told that he was generated from a bubble. Judah Hadasi (*c*. 1148) wrote of oriental trees bearing maidens on a mythical island, and in the *Arabian Nights* we find Sindbad saying: "I saw a bird that cometh out of a sea-shell, and layeth her eggs and hatcheth her chicks on the surface of the water." It is not known whether this detail appeared in either of the Persian versions of the Sindbad story which existed in the tenth century. The tree with lamb-like fruits reported by Friar Odoric has already been mentioned.

Immediately after Giraldus Cambrensis refers to the barnacle goose he launches into a vigorous diatribe against the Jews. Did the story call up some reminiscence of Jewish or other oriental tales of a somewhat similar character and so, bringing Jews to mind, evoke invective against them?

Our use of "canard" to describe a tall story is derived from the French "l'histoire d'un canard" which became proverbial after the bird-fish story was discredited. Like many another false belief the fable persisted largely because positive evidence was not available. With the finding of the breeding grounds of the barnacle goose in the seventeenth century truth began to triumph. Mediaeval deference to authority, ecclesiastical casuistry, unscientific modes of thought, delight in the sensational and the wishful thinking of those who found fasting irksome contributed to the success of the myth in surviving to our own times.

Impressed by the history of this and other myths, the reader may feel disposed to marvel at the extent of human folly and the pertinacity of error, but he should reflect that but for the conservatism to which we owe the preservation of such traditions, our knowledge of the past would be much more incomplete than it is. Those who try to assess the significance of what folklore has preserved are chary of assuming that previous generations were more foolish than their own. The continuity of tradition which we have found exemplified in this survey has provided a foundation enabling the bolder minds of successive generations to pioneer new ways of thought, and new modes of life without undermining the foundations of society. Conservatism is society's safeguard against revolution and disintegration. Many a neglected fable teaches that we despise the past at our peril. Wisdom is justified of all her children.

BIBLIOGRAPHICAL INDEX
AND CHAPTER REFERENCES

Bracketed references in the text refer to the folktale motif-indices of Aarne and Stith Thompson.

The abbreviation E.R.E. stands for the Encyclopaedia of Religion and Ethics, and H.D.A. for Handwörterbuch des Deutschen Aberglaubens.

Where an author's name appears in the Bibliography in connexion with two works but no date is appended here, both are relevant to the context.

A reference is not repeated if it has already been cited in connexion with date on the previous page.

The Shakespeare line references are taken from Bartlett's Concordance.

ACKNOWLEDGMENTS

I REGRET the impossibility of expressing adequate appreciation of the help which so many have given, directly or indirectly, during the years this book has been in preparation. The folklorist is often indebted to simple folk as well as scholars and my life as well as this study has been greatly enriched by friends and acquaintances belonging to both categories in the Far East as well as in Europe. I would mention particularly the kindness of Professor Gahs in Yugo-Slavia, the assistance of Mr. P. B. Platts in visiting prehistoric sites in France and the help of Professor J. H. Delargy and his colleagues of The Irish Folklore Commission in Ireland.

Professor Delargy and Mr. T. C. Lethbridge read much of the book in manuscript. Professors E. O. James and J. Skemp, and Miss J. Larter read the proofs. The criticisms and comments of these scholars, each considering the subject from the point of view of a specialist in one of the themes with which the book deals have been most valuable. Dr. J. Teicher translated an Arabic document and Miss S. A. Skilliter called my attention to some Persian references. Professor T. Harrison contributed suggestions concerning the mediaeval period and English literature. Without the facilities provided by Cambridge libraries this work would have been very incomplete. The staffs of the University Library, the Haddon and Newton libraries have been very helpful. Authorities in the British Museum advised me on matters concerning Semitic and Greek antiquities.

Among those who have contributed photographs or put me into touch with sources for them I would mention particularly Mr. George Buday, Colonel Norman Colville, Mr. Kevin Danaher, Dr. J. Kunst, Mr. M. J. O'Kelly, Dr. E. J. Lindgren-Utsi, and Mademoiselle L. Mantoy. The staff of the Warburg and Courtauld Institutes were very helpful and I am much indebted to the authorities of the Museums and Institutes mentioned in connexion with the Plates and text figures and to all those who have so kindly allowed figures or photographs to be reproduced. I am especially grateful to Mr. James Walton for allowing me to use a copy of a Bushman rock painting made by him.

Miss I. Hallward made a number of the line drawings and Mr. H. H. Morley was responsible for photo-copying black and white figures.

Answers to the questionnaire circulated in connexion with the English Folklore Survey were forwarded to me by Mr. McN. Dodgson of University College, London. The data confirmed the survival of a number of beliefs about birds mentioned in the foregoing pages.

I am deeply grateful to these and others for their help

EDWARD A. ARMSTRONG.

SELECT BIBLIOGRAPHY

In order to keep the bibliography within reasonable bounds the principle followed has been to cite compilations in which sources may be easily traced, and works of special relevance, rather than to attempt exhaustive documentation of the beliefs and customs mentioned.

AARNE, A. 1928. The Types of the Folk-Tale. Helsinki.

ABBOTT, C. F. 1903. Macedonian Folklore. Cambridge.

ABGRALL, J. 1887. Berçeuses Bretonnes. *Rev des trad. pop.* 2: 310-311.

ALBIN, E. 1738-40. A Natural History of Birds. London.

ALCALDE DEL RIO, H., BREUIL, H. and SIERRA, L. 1911. Les cavernes de la région Cantabrique. Monaco.

ALFORD, V. 1953. Why do we study folklore? *Folklore, 64:* 473-483.

ALLEN, J. R. 1887. Early Christian Symbolism. London.

—— 1903. The Early Christian Monuments of Scotland. Edinburgh.

AMEISENOWA, Z. 1949. Animal-headed gods. *Journ. Warburg and Courtauld Insts., 12:*21-45.

ANDERSSON, J. G. 1934. Children of the Yellow Earth. London.

ANDREE, R. 1891. Die Flutsagen. Braunschweig.

ARMSTRONG, E. A. 1935. The Thunderbird in East and West. Thesis submitted in part fulfilment of the requirements for the degree of M.A. Leeds University.

—— 1943a. The triple-furrowed field. *Class. Rev.* 57: 3-5.

—— 1943b. The ritual of the plough. *Folklore, 54:* 250-257.

—— 1943c. The crane dance in east and west. *Antiquity, 17:* 71-76.

—— 1944a. The symbolism of the swan and goose. *Folk-Lore, 55:* 54-58.

—— 1944b. Mugwort lore. *Folk-Lore, 55:* 22-27.

—— 1944-45. Chinese bull ritual and its affinities. *Folk-Lore, 56:* 200-207.

—— 1946. Shakespeare's Imagination. London.

—— 1947a. Birds of the Grey Wind. London.

—— 1947b. Bird Display and Behaviour. London.

—— 1955. The Wren. London.

AUBREY, J. 1686-87. Remaines of Gentilism and Judaism. London.

—— 1721. Miscellanies. London.

BABINGTON, C. 1884-86. Birds of Suffolk. London.

BANCROFT, H. H. 1875-76. The Native Races of the Pacific States of North America. London.

BANKS, M. M. 1937, '39, '41. British Calendar Customs. Scotland.

BARANDIARAN, J. M. de, 1941. Die prähistorischen Höhlen in der Baskischen Mythologie. *Paideuma,* 2: 66-83.

BARING-GOULD, S. 1869. Curious Myths of the Middle Ages. London. new edn.

BARTHOLOMEW, Friar, 1485. *Liber de proprietatibus rerum* . . . Engl. tr. Berthelet, 1535, and version by Batman, 1582.

BATCHELOR, J. 1892. The Ainu of Japan. London.

—— 1901. The Ainu and their Folklore. London.

—— 1908. Ainus. *E.R.E. 1:* 239-252.

BATES, H. W. 1864. The Naturalist on the River Amazon. London. 2nd. edn.

BATTISCOMBE, C. F. (ed.) 1956. The Relics of Saint Cuthbert. Oxford. pp 505-513.

BAUDIS, J. 1914. Curoi and Cuchulainn. *Eriu, 7:* 200-209.

—— 1916. On the antiquity of the kingship in Tara. *Eriu, 8:* 102-107.

BAYET, J. 1954. Le symbolisme du cerf et du centaure à la porte rouge de Notre-Dame de Paris. *Rev. Arch. 44:* 21-68.

BAYNES, H. G. 1936. On the psychological origins of divine kingship. *Folk-Lore 47:* 74-104.

BÉGOUEN, Comte, 1912. Les statues d'argile de la caverne de Tuc d'Audoubert (Ariège). *L'anthrop, 18:* 657-665.

—— and KUHN, H. 1930. Nouvelles découvertes. *Ipek.* 116-117.

BENDANN, E. 1930. Death Customs, London.

BERGIN, O. and BEST, R. I. 1938. Tochmarc Étaine. *Eriu, 12:* 137-194.

BEST, R. I. 1916. Prognostications from the raven and the wren. *Eriu, 8:* 120-126.

BILLSON, C. J. 1895. County Folk-lore, Leics. and Rutland. F. -L. Socy. London.

BIRKET-SMITH, K. 1936. The Eskimos. London.

—— 1937. Eskimo cultures and their bearing upon the prehistoric cultures of North America and Eurasia. In *Early Man. Int. Symp. Acad. Nat. Sci. Philadelphia.* New York.

BISHOP, I. 1898. Korea and her Neighbours. London.

BLACK, G. F. 1903. Examples of Printed Folk-lore concerning the Orkney and Shetlands Islands. London.

—— W. G. 1883. Folk-medicine. London.

BLACKWOOD, B. 1929. Tales of the Chippewa Indians. *Folk-Lore, 40:* 315-344.

BLANC, A. C. 1955. Il sacrificio umano del'Addaura. *Quaternaria, 2:* 213-225.

BLOOM, J. H. 1932. *In* Gill, 1932.

BOAS, F. 1891-95. Indianische Sagen von der Nord-Pacifischen Küste Amerikas. Berlin.

BOGORAS, W. 1902. The folklore of north-eastern Asia as compared with north-western America. *Amer. Anthrop. 4:* 577-683.

BOLTE, J. and POLIVKA, G. 1913. Anmerkungen zu den Kinder und Hausmärchen der Brüder Grimm. Leipzig.

BONSER, W. 1929. The magic of the Finns in relation to that of other arctic peoples. *Folk-Lore, 35:* 57-63.

BONWICK, J. 1894. Irish Druids and Old Irish Religions. London.

BORRER, W. 1891. Birds of Sussex. London.

BOSSOM, Sir A. 1954. Guide to Exhibition. Victoria Institute.

BOULE, M., BREUIL, H., LICENT, E. and TEILHARD, P. 1928. La paléolithique de la Chine. *Arch. Inst. Pal. Hum.* Paris.

BRAND, J. 1842. Observations on Popular Antiquities. Ed. H. Ellis, London.

BREUIL, H. 1906. Le passage de la figure à l'ornement dans la céramique peinte des couches archaiques de Moussian et de Susa. *Int. Congr. Anthrop. Arch.* 1906.

BREUIL, H. 1925. Oiseaux peints à l'époque néolithique sur des roches de la province de Cadiz. *Ipek*, 1: 47-50.

—— 1936. Oeuvres d'art Magdaléniennes de Laugerie Basse, Dordogne. *Actualités scientifiques et industrielles, 382:* 1-13.

—— 1952. Quatre cents siècles d'art parietal. Montignac.

—— and BÉGOUEN, H. 1936. Quelques oiseaux inédits ou méconnus de l'art préhistorique. *Congr. préhistorique de France.* p. 478.

—— and BURKITT, M. C. 1929. Rock Paintings of Southern Andalusia. Oxford.

—— and OBERMAIER, H. 1935. La Cueva de Altamira en Santillana del Mar. Madrid.

BRITISH MUSEUM. Guides to Collections. London.

BROWN, W. J. 1936. The Gods had Wings. London.

BUCKLAND, F. T. 1866. Curiosities of Natural History. 3rd. series, London.

BULLOCK, H. A. 1816. History of the Isle of Man. London.

BURKITT, M. C. 1925. Prehistory. 2nd edn. Cambridge.

CAGNAT, R. and CHAPOT, V. 1920. Manuel d'archéologie romaine. Paris.

CAMBRENSIS, G. 1585. *Itinerarium Cambriae*, etc. London.

—— 1603. *Topographiae Hiberniae*. Frankfort.

CAMPBELL, J. F. 1860-62. Popular Tales of the West Highlands. Edinburgh.

CAMPBELL, J. F. 1940. More West Highland Tales. Edinburgh.

CAMPBELL, J. G. 1900. Superstitions of the Highlands and Islands of Scotland. Glasgow.

CAREW, R. 1602. Survey of Cornwall. London.

CARMICHAEL, A. 1928-54. Carmina Gadelica. London.

CARNEY, J. 1955. Studies in Irish Literature and History. Dublin.

CARTAILHAC, E. and BREUIL, H. 1906. La caverne d'Altamira à Santillane près Santander. Monaco.

CHADWICK, H. M. 1910. Calendar (Celtic). *E.R.E.* 3: 78-83.

CHAMBERS, R. 1863-64. Book of Days. London.

—— 1870. Popular Rhymes of Scotland. London and Edinburgh.

CHANDLER, A. R. 1934. The nightingale in Greek and Latin poetry. *Class, Journ. 30:* 78-84.

—— 1937. Larks, Nightingales and Poets. Columbus.

CHARPENTIER, J. H. R. T. 1920. Die Suparnasage. Uppsala.

CHILDE, V. G. 1931. Skara Brae. London.

CLAGUE, J. 1911. Cooinaghtyn Manninagh. Manx Reminiscences. Castletown. I. of Man.

CLARK, M. J. 1954. How the Kazakhs fled to freedom. *Nat. Geogr. Mag. 106:* 621-644.

CLARK, G. 1948. Fowling in prehistoric Europe. *Antiquity, 22:* 116-130.

COLLINGWOOD, W. G. 1912-14. The early crosses of Leeds. *Thoresby Soc. Misc. 22:* 268-338.

COLE, S. 1954. The Prehistory of East Africa. Harmondsworth.

CONTENAU, G. 1914. La déesse nue Babylonienne. Paris.

—— 1952. Le déluge Babylonien. Paris.

COOK, A. B. 1914-40. Zeus: a Study in Ancient Religion. Cambridge.

COUNT, E. W. 1952. The earth-diver and the rival twins. *In* Indian Tribes of Aboriginal America. *Proc. 29th. Int. Congr. Americanists.* Univ. of Chicago.

COURTNEY, M. A. 1890. Cornish Feasts and Folklore. Penzance.

COX, Sir G. W. 1870. The Mythology of the Aryan Nations. London.

COXWELL, C. F. 1925. Siberian and other Folk-tales. London.

CROOKE, W. 1896. Popular Religions and Folklore of Northern India, Oxford.

CROSS, T. P. and SLOVER, C. H. (n.d.) Ancient Irish Tales. London.

CROSSING, W. 1911. Folk Rhymes of Devon. Exeter.

CUMONT, F. 1899. Textes et monuments figurés relatifs aux mystères de Mithra. Brussels.

—— 1903. The Mysteries of Mithra. London.

CURTIN, J. 1890. Myths and Folklore of Ireland. London.

CZAPLICKA, M. A. C. 1914. Aboriginal Siberia. Oxford.

—— 1917. Ostyaks. *E.R.E. 9:* 575-581.

—— 1921. Tungus. *E.R.E. 12:* 473-476.

DÄHNHARDT, O. 1907. Natursagen. Leipzig and Berlin.

DALLAWAY, J. 1797. Constantinople, Ancient and Modern. London.

DASENT, G. W. 1859. Popular Tales from the Norse. Edinburgh.

DAVIES, J. C. 1911. Folklore of West and Mid-Wales. Aberystwyth.

DAWKINS, R. M. 1906. A modern carnival in Thrace and the cult of Dionysus. *Journ. Hell. Studies, 26:* 191–206.

DE GUBERNATIS, A. 1872. Zoological Mythology. London.

DELARGY, J. H. 1945. The Gaelic story-teller. *Proc. Brit. Acad. 33.*

DE LA SALLE, D. 1875. Croyances et légendes de la centre de la France. Paris.

DIAMANT, J. 1905. Jubilee volume for M. Bloch. Cit. in *Trans. Jewish Hist. Soc. England, 12:*110.

DILLON, M. 1947. The Hindu act of truth in Celtic tradition. *Mod. Phil. 44:* 137.

—— 1948. Early Irish Literature. Chicago.

DOUGHTY, C. M. 1888. Arabia Deserta. Cambridge.

DOUGLAS, N. 1928. Birds and Beasts of the Greek Anthology. London.

DRIOUR, G. 1934. Cultes indigènes des Lingons. Paris.

DUHAMEL, M. n.d. Les richesses modales de la musique Bretonne. Paris.

DUMÉZIL, G. 1924. Le festin d'immortalité. Paris.

DYER, T. F. T. 1876. British Popular Customs. London.

—— 1880, English Folk-lore. London.

ECKENSTEIN, L. 1906. Comparative Studies in Nursery Rhymes. London.

ELWORTHY, F. T. 1895. The Evil Eye. London.

EMERSON, P. H. 1889. English Idyls. London.

ENCYCLOPAEDIA OF RELIGION AND ETHICS, E.R.E.

ENTHOVEN, R. E. 1924. The Folklore of Bombay. Oxford.

EVANS, Sir A. J. 1908. *In* Anthropology and the Classics. Ed. R. R. Marett, Oxford.

—— 1929-35. The Palace of Knossos. London.

FAIRLESS, M. 1915. The Roadmender. 37th imp. London.

FAHLMANN, F.-R. 1885. Dorpater Verhandlungen.

FARNELL, L. R. 1896. The Cults of the Greek States. Oxford.

FIELD, J. E. 1913. The Myth of the Pent Cuckoo. London.

FISH, T. 1948. The Zu bird. *Bull. J. Rylands Liby.* 31: 1-10.

FRANKFORT, H. 1924-27. Studies in Early Pottery of the Near East. *Royal Anthrop. Inst. Occas. Papers, 6, 8.*

—— 1939. Cylinder Seals. London.

FRAZER, Sir J. G. 1918. Folk-lore in the Old Testament. London.

—— 1921. The origin of fire. *In* Apollodorus, 2: 326-50. London.

—— 1930. Myths of the Origin of Fire. London.

—— 1932-35. The Golden Bough. London. 3rd. edn.

—— 1936. Aftermath. London.

FRIEND, H. 1884. Flowers and Flower Lore. London.

FROBENIUS, L. 1909. The Childhood of Man, London.

—— and OBERMAIER, H. 1925. Hadschra Maktuba. Urzeitliche Felsbilder Kleinafrikas. Munich.

GADD, E. J. 1929. History and Monuments of Ur. London.

GALLOP, R. 1936. Portugal: a Book of Folkways. Cambridge.

GASTER, M. 1915. Rumanian Bird and Beast Stories. F.-L. Socy. London.

GERARD, J. 1597. The Herball or General Historie of Plantes. London.

GIDDINGS, J. L. 1951. The Denbigh flint-complex. *Amer. Antiq. 16:* 193-203.

GILES, H. A. 1926. Strange Tales from a Chinese Studio. Hong Kong.

GILL, W. W. 1932. A Second Manx Scrapbook. London.

GJERDMAN, G. 1945. Nattskärran och några andra spöksfåglar. *Arv. Tidskrift för Nordisk Folksminnesbokning. 28.*

GJESSING, G. 1932. Arktiske Helleristninger i Nord-Norge. Oslo.

—— 1944. The Circumpolar Stone Age. *Acta Arctica, 2.*

GOODCHILD, R. G. 1938. A priest's sceptre from the Romano-British temple of Farley Heath, Surrey. *Antiq. Journ. 18:* 391-396.

GOODRICH-FREER, A. 1902. The Outer Isles. Westminster.

GOODYEAR, W. H. 1891. The Grammar of the Lotus. London.

GOURY, G. 1948. Origine et évolution de l'homme. Paris.

GRANET, M. 1926. Danses et légendes de la Chine ancienne. Paris.

—— 1930. Chinese Civilization. London.

GRAVES, R. 1955. The Greek Myths. Harmondsworth.

GRAZIOSI, P. 1956. L'arte dell'antica éta della pietra. Florence.

GREEN, E. R. R. 1946. Christmas rhymers and mummers. *Ulster Journ. Arch. 9:* 3-21.

GREGOR, W. 1881. Notes on the Folk-lore of the North-east of Scotland. *F.-L. Socy. Publ. 7.*

GREGORY, Lady, 1904. Gods and Fighting Men. London.

GRIMM, J. 1875-78. Deutsche Mythologie. 4th. edn. Berlin. Cf. also Bolte and Polivka.

GROHMANN, J. V. 1864. Aberglauben und Gebräuche aus Böhmen und Mähren. Leipzig.

GURDON, C. 1895. County Folk-lore. Suffolk. F.-L. Socy.

GURNEY, O. R. 1952. The Hittites. Harmondsworth.

GUTCH, E. 1901. Examples of printed Folk-lore concerning the North Riding of Yorkshire, York and the Ainsty. F.-L. Socy.

—— 1912. Examples of printed Folk-lore concerning the East Riding of Yorkshire. F. -L. Socy. London.

HACKIN, J. *et al.* 1932. Asiatic Mythology. London.

HACKIN, J. 1939. Recherches archéologiques à Begram. Paris.

HAHN, H. 1896a. Die Haustiere und ihre Beziehungen zur Wirtschaft der Menschen. Leipzig.

—— 1896b. Demeter und Baubo. Lübeck.

—— 1909. Die Enstehung der Pflugkultur. Heidelberg.

HALL, J. 1948. Characters of Vertues and Vices. Ed. R. Kent. London.

HALLIDAY, W. R. 1922. Picus-who-is-also-Zeus. *Class. Rev.* 36: 110.

—— 1933. Indo-European Folk-tales and Greek Legends. Cambridge.

HALLSTRÖM, G. 1938. Monumental Art of Northern Europe from the Stone Age. Stockholm.

HAMEL, F. 1915. Human Animals. London.

HAMMERICH, L. L. Munken og Fuglen. Copenhagen.

HANDWÖRTERBUCH DES DEUTSCHEN ABERGLAUBENS. H.D.A. Cf. Hoffmann-Krayer.

HARDWICK, C. 1872. Traditions, Superstitions and Folklore. Manchester.

HARDY, J. 1878. Popular history of the cuckoo. *Folk-lore Rec.* 2: 47-92.

HARE, C. E. 1952. Bird Lore. London.

HARRIS, J. R. 1913. Boanerges. Cambridge.

—— 1916. Picus who is also Zeus. Cambridge.

—— 1917. The Ascent of Olympus. Manchester.

—— 1920. The woodpecker in human form. *Bull. J. Rylands Liby.* 5.

HARRISON, J. E. 1922. Prolegomena to the Study of Greek Religion. Cambridge.

—— 1927. Themis. Cambridge.

HARRISON, T. P. 1949. Night-raven lore. *Mod. Lang. Rev.* 44: 232-235.

—— 1950. The whistler, bird of omen. *Mod. Lang. Notes. Dec.*

—— 1956. They Tell of Birds. Texas Univ. Press.

HARRISON, W. 1577. Historicall Description of the Iland of Britaine. London.

HARRISON, W. 1869, 1873. Mona Miscellany. Nos. 1 and 2. *Manx Socy. Publs. 16, 21.* Douglas.

HARTLAND, E. S. 1891. The Science of Fairy Tales. London.

HARVA, U. 1938. Die religiösen Vorstellungen der Altäischen Völker. Helsinki.

HEINE-GELDERN, R. von, 1950. China, die ostkaspische Kultur und die Herkunft der Schrift. *Paideuma, 4:* 51-92.

—— 1954. Die asiatische Herkunft der Sudamerikanischen Metalltechnik. *Paideuma, 5:* 345-423.

HENDERSON, W. 1879. Notes on the Folk-lore of the Northern Counties of England and the Border. F.-L. Socy. London.

HENRI-MARTIN, F. 1929. Un oiseau sculpté trouvé dans le Solutréen du Roc (Charente). *L'anthrop. 39:* 126-128.

HENRY, F. 1940. Irish Art in the Early Christian Period. London.

HENTZE, C. 1941. Die Sakralbronzen und ihre Bedeutung in den fruechinesischen Kulturen. Antwerp.

HERD, D. 1776. Ancient and Modern Scottish Songs. Ed. H. Hecht. Edinburgh.

HERON-ALLEN, E. 1928. Barnacles in Nature and Myth. Oxford.

HOFFMANN-KRAYER, E. 1927-42. Handwörterbuch des Deutschen Aberglaubens. Berlin and Leipzig.

HOLMBERG, U. 1927. Mythology of All Races. IV. Finno-Ugric-Siberian. Boston. Cf. also Harva.

HOLMSTRÖM, H. 1919. Studier over Svanjungfrumotivet I volundarkvida och annorstädes. Lund.

HOOKE, S. H. 1937. Time and custom. *Folk-Lore*, 48: 11-27.

HOPKINS, E. W. 1915. Epic Mythology. London.

HORNELL, J. 1946. The role of birds in early navigation. *Antiquity, 20:* 142-148.

HULL, E. 1928. Folklore of the British Isles. London.

—— 1932. The hawk of Achill or the legend of the oldest animals. *Folk-Lore*, 43: 376-409.

INGERSOLL, E. 1923. Birds in Legend, Fable and Folklore. New York.

INWARDS, R. 1950. Weather Lore. Rev. edn. London.

JACKSON, K. 1951. A Celtic Miscellany. London.

JACOB, G. 1927. Arabische Berichte von Gesandten an germanische Fürstenhöfe aus dem 9 u. 10 Jhdt. *Quellen zur Deutschen Volkskunde.* I. Berlin and Leipzig.

JACOBSTHAL, P. 1944. Early Celtic Art. Oxford.

JAGO, F. W. P. 1882. The Ancient Language, and the Dialect of Cornwall, etc. Truro.

JASTROW, M. 1898. The Religion of Babylonia and Assyria. Boston.

JOCHELSON, W. 1904. The mythology of the Koryak. *Amer. Anthrop. 6:* 413-425.

JOYCE, P. W. 1907. Old Celtic Romances. London.

KARR, A. 1845. Voyage autour de mon jardin. Paris.

KARSTEN, R. 1935. The Origins of Religion. London.

KELLER, O. 1887. Thiere des classischen Altertums. Innsbruck.

KELLY, J. 1866. English and Manx Dictionary. Douglas.

KELLY, W. K. 1863. Curiosities of Indo-European Tradition and Folklore. London.

KENDRICK, T. D. 1941. Late Saxon sculpture in northern England. *Journ. Brit. Arch. Assn.* (3) 6: 1-19.

KING, L. W. 1896. Babylonian Magic and Sorcery. London.

KIRBY, W. F. 1895. The Hero of Esthonia. London.

KLEMENTZ, D. 1910. Buriats. *E.R.E. 3:* 1-17.

—— 1913. Gilyaks. *E.R.E. 6:* 221-226.

KNORTZ, K. 1913. Die Vögel in Geschichte, Sage, Brauch und Literatur. Munich.

KOMROFF, M. 1928. Contemporaries of Marco Polo. New York.

KRAPPE, A. H. 1936. Les dieux au corbeau chez les Celtes. *Rev. de l'hist. des religions, 114:* 236-246.

— 1940. Old Celtic taboos. *Folk-Lore, 8:* 196-208.

KRUGER, E. 1953. Das Tierfries-Beschlagstück aus dem Moorfund von Thorsberg. *Praehist. Zeitschr. 24-25,* 112-124.

KUNST, J. 1954. Cultural relations between the Balkans and Indonesia. *Royal Trop. Inst. Amsterdam, 107.*

LACK, D. 1950. Robin Redbreast. Oxford.

LANDT, G. 1810. A Description of the Feroe Islands. London.

LANGDON, S. 1925. *In* Cook, 2: 696.

LARSEN, H. 1950. De Dansk-Amerikanske Alaska-ekspeditioner 1949-50. *Geografisk Tidskrift, 50:* 103-193.

LARSEN, H. 1952. The Ipiutak culture; its origin and relationships. *In* Indian Tribes of Aboriginal America. *Proc. 29th. Int. Congr. Amer. Univ. of Chicago.*

LARSEN, H. and RAINEY, F. 1948. Ipiutak and the arctic whale-hunting culture. *Anthrop. Papers. Amer. Mus. Nat. Hist. N.Y. 42.*

LARTET, E. and CHRISTY, H. 1875. Reliquiae Aquitanicae, London.

LATHAM, R. G. 1854. Native Races of the Russian Empire. London.

LAUFER, B. 1914. Bird Divination amongst the Thibetans. London.

LAWSON, J. C. 1910. Modern Greek Folklore and Ancient Greek Religion. Cambridge.

LEACH, M. (Ed.) 1949. Standard Dictionary of Folklore, Mythology and Legend. New York.

LEAN, V. S. 1903. Collectanea. London.

LEATHER, E. A. 1942. Weather-wise birds. *Spectator*, 20 March.

LEGGE, J. 1891. Texts of Taoism. S.B.E. Oxford.

LELAND, C. G. 1902. Kuloskap, the Master. New York.

—— The Algonquin Indians.

LEMOZI, A. 1929. La grotte-temple du Pech-Merle. Paris.

LEVY, G. 1948. The Gate of Horn. London.

LHUYD, E. 1910. Parochialia. Archaeologia Cambrensis.

LIBJEBLAD, S. 1935. Argonauterne och sagån om flykten från trollet. *In* Saga och Sed.

LINDGREN-UTSI, E. J. Personal communications.

LITTLEDALE, M. 1955. The tower of London zoo. *Country Life, 117:* 130.

LOORITS, O. 1932. Zur Estnischen Kulturgeschichte. Tartu.

LOTH, J. 1914. Le dieu Lug, la Terre-Mère et les Lugoves. *Rev. Arch. 2:* 205-230.

LUPTON, T. 1595. A Thousand Notable Things, etc. London.

LUQUET, G. H. 1930. The Art and Religion of Fossil Man. London.

LUZEL, F. M. 1890. Soniou Breiz-izel: Chansons populaires de la basse Bretagne. Paris.

MACALISTER, R. A. S. 1935. Ancient Ireland. London.

—— 1949. The Archaeology of Ireland. 2nd edn. London.

MACAULAY, K. 1715. A voyage to, and history of, St. Kilda. Dublin.

McCOWN, D. E. 1952. A discovery which has immensely enriched the world's oldest literature. *Ill. Lond. News,* 28 June, 1084-86.

McCULLOCH, Sir E. 1903. Guernsey Folklore. London.

MacCULLOCH, J. A. 1910. Calendar. (Celtic). *E.R.E. 3:* 78-83.

—— J. A. 1911. Religion of the Ancient Celts. London.

McCURDY, G. G. 1924. Human Origins. New York.

MacDONELL, A. A. 1897. Vedic Mythology. Strassburg.

MacDOUGALL, J. 1891. Folk and Hero Tales. Argyllshire. London.

McGREGOR, —. Folklore of the West of Scotland.

MACKENZIE, D. 1913. Egyptian Myth and Legend. London.

MACLEOD, K. 1927. The Road to the Isles. London.

MacNEILL, J. (n.d.) *In* Celtic and Teutonic Religions. London.

MAHR, A. 1937. New aspects and problems in Irish prehistory. *Proc. Prehist. Soc. 3:* 261-436.

MANNHARDT, W. 1904-05. Antike Wald und Feldkulte. 2nd. edn. Berlin.

MAP, W. 1923. *De nugis curialium.* Ed. E. S. Hartland. London.

MARINGER, J. and BANDI, H.-G. 1953. Art in the Ice Age. London.

MARSHALL, J. H. Sir, 1931. Mohenjo-Daro and the Indus civilization. London.

MARTIN, M. 1716. A Description of the Western Islands. London.

MASON, M. H. 1877. Nursery Rhymes and Courting Songs.

—— 1911. Tales and Traditions of Tenby. Cf. Gill, 1932.

MÉROC, L. and MAZET, J. 1953. Les peintures de la grotte de Cougnac (Lot). *L'anthrop. 57:* 490-494.

MEYER, K. 1895. The Voyage of Bran. London.

MICHELET, M. 1837. Origines du droit français. Paris.

MILNE-EDWARDS, M. A. 1875. *In* Lartet and Christy, 1865-75, pp.226-247.

MIRANDA, A. A. de, 1954. Magia y religion del toro Norte Africano. *Archivo Espanol de Arquelogia, 27:* 3-44.

MONTELIUS, O. 1906. Kulturgeschichte Schwedens. Leipzig.

MOONEY, J. 1900. Myths of the Cherokee. *Ann. Rep. Bureau Amer. Eth. 19.*

MÜLLER, F. M. 1871. Lectures on the Science of Language. London.

MURRAY, G. 1925. Five Stages of Greek Religion. Oxford.

MURRAY, M. A. 1933. The God of the Witches. London.

NEWTON, A. 1896. Dictionary of Birds. London.

NILSSON, N. M. P. 1950. The Minoan and Mycenaean Religion. 2nd. edn. Lund.

—— 1950-55. Geschichte der griechischen Religion. Munich.

NIORADZE, G. K. 1925. Der Schamanismus bei den Sibirischen Völkern. Stuttgart.

NUTT, A. 1895-97. The Happy Otherworld. London.

OBERMAIER, H. 1916. El Hombre Fosil. Madrid.

O'BRIEN, P. 1892. Siamsa an gheimridh. Dublin.

O'DANACHAIR, C. 1955. The Bodhrán—a percussion instrument. *Journ. Cork. Hist. Arch. Socy. 60,* 129-130.

O'GRADY, S. H. 1892. Silva Gadelica. London.

O'KELLY, M. J. 1946. Excavation of a ring-fort at Garryduff, Co. Cork. *Antiquity, 20:* 122-126.

OPIE, I. and P. 1951. The Oxford Dictionary of Nursery Rhymes. Oxford.

—— 1955. The Oxford Nursery Rhyme Book. Oxford.

O'RIORDÁIN, S. P. 1953. Antiquities of the Irish Countryside. London 3rd. edn.

O'RUADHAIN, M. 1955. Birds in Irish folklore. *Proc. XI Int. Orn. Congr.* Basel.

O'SULLIVAN, D. J. 1932. The Bunting Collection of Irish Folk Music and Songs. *Journ. Irish Folksong Socy. 26.*

OWEN, E. 1897. Welsh Folklore. Oswestry.

PALLOTTINO, M. 1955. The Etruscans. Harmondsworth.

PANSA, G. 1924-27. Miti, Leggendi e Superstizioni dell'Abruzzo. Sulmona.

—— 1931-32. *Picus martius,* studio di esegesi mitica. *Folklore Italiano, 6.*

PARKYN, E. A. 1915. An Introduction to the Study of Prehistoric Art. London.

PASSEMARD, E. 1922. La caverne d'Isturitz. *Rev. arch. 15:* 1-45.

—— 1944. La caverne d'Isturitz au pays Basque. *Préhistoire, 9:* 7-83.

PATON, C. I. 1909. Manx Calendar Customs. London.

PEATE, I. C. 1936. The wren in Welsh folklore. *Man. 36:* 1-3.

PENZER, N. M. 1924-28. The Ocean of Story. London.

PÉQUART, M. and ST. J. 1942. Récente découverte de deux oeuvres d'art magdaléniennes au Mas d'Azil. *Rev. scient.* p. 91.

PIETTE, E. 1907. L'art pendant l'age du renne. Paris.

PIGGOTT, S. 1949. British Prehistory. London.
—— 1950. Prehistoric India. Harmondsworth.
—— 1955. *In* Wainwright, 1955.
PITTARD, E. 1936. Figurations d'oiseaux de la période magdalénienne. *Arch. suisses d'anthrop.* p. 185.
POLLARD, J. R. T. 1948. The Birds of Aristophanes—a source book for old beliefs. *Amer. Journ. Philol. 69:* 353-376.
PRITCHARD, J. B. 1950. Ancient Near-Eastern Texts relating to the Old Testament. 2nd. edn. Princeton.
RADFORD E. and RADFORD, M. 1942. Encyclopaedia of Superstitions. London.
RADLOV, V. V. 1884. Aus Sibirien. Leipzig.
RAFTERY, J. 1951. Prehistoric Ireland. London.
RALSTON, W. R. S. 1873. Russian Folk-tales. London.
—— 1882. Tibetan Tales. London.
RASMUSSEN, K. 1926. Grönländska Myter och Sagor. Stockholm.
RAUDONIKAS, W. J. 1936-38. Les gravures rupestres des bords du Lac Onega et de la Mer Blanche. Moscow.
RAVEN, C. E. 1947. English Naturalists from Neckam to Ray. Cambridge.
ROBIN, P. A. 1932. Animal Lore in English Literature. London.
ROES, A. 1933. Greek Geometric Art, its Symbolism and its Origin. Haarlem.
—— 1939-40. Der Hallstattvogel. *Jahrb. Prähist. Ethnographische Kunst.*
RICHARDS, A. 1956. Chisungu. London.
RIDDELL, W. H. 1943. The domestic goose. *Antiquity 17:* 148-155.
ROLLAND, E. 1883. Faune populaire de la France. Paris.
ROSS, J. 1880. Missionary History of Corea, Ancient and Modern. Paisley.
RUST, A. 1937. Das altsteinliche Renntierjägerlager Meiendorf. Neumunster.
SALMONY, A. 1928. Asiatische Kunst. Munich.
SCHMIDT, R. R. 1936. The Dawn of the Human Mind. London.
SCHOTTI, P. G. 1662. *Physica curiosa.* Nuremberg.
SCHRADER, O. 1909. Aryan religion. *E.R.E. 2:* 11-57.
SCHUSTER, C. 1952. A survival of the Eurasiatic animal style in modern Alaskan animal art. *In* Indian Tribes, etc. *Proc. 29th. Int. Congr. Amer.* Univ. of Chicago.
SÉBILLOT, P. 1904. Le folk-lore de France. Paris.
SIKES, W. W. 1880. British Goblins. London.
SIMPKINS, J. E. 1914. Examples of Printed Folk-Lore concerning Fife, etc. F.-L.Socy. London.
SIMROCK, K. 1878. Handbuch der deutschen Mythologie. 5th edn. Bonn.
SJOESTEDT, M.-L. 1949. Gods and Heroes of the Celts. London.
SKEAT, W. W. 1900. Malay Magic. London.
SMITH, A. C. 1887. Birds of Wiltshire. London.
—— B. 1956. Coleridge's *Ancient Mariner* and Cook's second voyage. *Journ. Warburg and Courtauld Insts. 19:* 117-154.
—— G. E. 1919. The Origin of the Dragon. Manchester.
—— M. 1951. British Amphibia and Reptiles. London.
SONNINI, C. S. 1800. Travels in Upper Egypt. London.
SPENCE, J. 1899. Shetland Folk-lore. Lerwick.
—— 1911. Cosmogony and cosmology. (North America). *E.R.E. 4:* 126-128.

SPENCE, L. 1947. Myth and Ritual in Dance, Game and Rhyme. London.

SPENCER, R. F. and CARTER, W. K. 1954. The blind man and the loon. Barrow Eskimo variants. *Journ. Amer. Folklore, 67:* 65-72.

SPROCKHOFF, E. 1955. European urnfield culture and Celtic La Tène. *Proc. Prehist. Soc. 21:* 257-281.

STANDARD DICTIONARY OF FOLKLORE, MYTHOLOGY AND LEGEND. 1949. Cf. Leach, M.

STOKES, W. and WINDISCH, E. 1880-1909. Irische Texte. Leipzig.

STORAKER, J. T. 1928. Naturrigerne i den Norske Folketro. Oslo.

STORMS, G. 1948. Anglo-Saxon Magic. The Hague.

STOW, G. W. and BLEEK, D. F. 1930. Rock-paintings in South Africa. London.

STUKELY, W. 1724. *Itinerarium Curiosum.* London.

SWAINSON, C. 1885. Provincial Names and Folk Lore of British Birds. London.

SWANN, H. K. 1913. Dictionary of English and Folk-names of British Birds. London.

SYDOW, C. W. von, 1948. Selected Papers on Folklore. Copenhagen.

TALBOT, P. A. 1927. Some Nigerian Fertility Cults. London.

TEGID, LL. 1911. Hunting the wren. *Journ. Welsh Folksong Soc. 1:* 90-113.

TEIT, J. 1900. The Thompson Indians of British Columbia. *Mem. Amer. Nat. Hist. Mus.; Jesup N. Pacific Exped. 1.*

—— 1906. The Lillooet Indians. *Mem. Amer. Mus. Nat. Hist. Jesup N. Pacific Exped. 2.*

THOMAS, E. J. 1923. Vedic Hymns. London.

—— N. W. 1898. La survivance du culte totémique des animaux et les rites agraires dans le pays du Galles. *Rev. l'hist. Rel. 38:* 1-53.

—— N. W. 1908. Animals. E.R.E. 1: 483-535.

THOMPSON, D'A. W. 1936. Glossary of Greek Birds. Oxford.

—— S. 1955. Motif-Index of Folk-literature. Copenhagen, Rev. edn.

THOMSON, G. 1949. Studies in Ancient Greek Society. London.

THORPE, B. 1851. Northern Mythology. London.

TILLE, A. 1889. Yule and Christmas. London.

TICEHURST, C. B. 1932. A History of the Birds of Suffolk. London.

TRAIN, J. 1845. An Historical and Statistical Account of the Isle of Man. Douglas.

TRAVER, E. 1933. Les bachelleries (Fêtes populaires) du Poitou, du Berry et de l'Angoumois. Melle.

TREVELYAN, M. 1909. Folk-lore and Folk-stories of Wales. London.

TRISTRAM, H. B. 1877. The Natural History of the Bible. London.

TUPPER, F. 1910. The Riddles of the Exeter Book. Boston and London.

TURNER, W. 1544. *Avium praecipuarium* etc. London.

VALLANCEY, C. 1786-1894. *Collectanea de rebus Hibernicis.* Dublin.

VENTRIS, M. and CHADWICK, J. 1956. Documents in Mycenaean Greek. Cambridge.

VOLKOW, T. 1912. Nouvelles découvertes dans la station paléolithique de Mézine, Ukraine. *Congr. internat. préh. 1.* Geneva.

WACE, A. J. B. 1909-10. North Greek festivals. *Ann. Brit. School Athens, 16.*

WADDELL, H. 1934. Beasts and Saints. London.

WAINWRIGHT, F. T. (ed.) 1955. The Problem of the Picts. Edinburgh.

WALDRON, G. 1731. A Description of the Isle of Man. Douglas.

WALK, L. 1933. Die Verbreitung des Tauchmotivs in den Urmeerschopfungs (und Sindflut) Sage. *Mitteil. Anthrop. Gesellschaft, Wien, 73:* 60-76.

WALN, N. 1939. Reaching for the Stars. London.

WALTON, J. 1955. The soapstone birds of Zimbabwe. *Journ. S. African Arch. Bull. 10:* 78-84.

WARD, W. H. 1910. The Seal Cylinders of Western Asia. Washington.

WEISWEILER, J. 1950. Die Kultur der Irischen Heldensage. *Paideuma, 2:* 149-170.

WERNER, E. T. C. 1910. Descriptive Sociology of the Chinese. London.

WESTERMARCK, E. 1926. Ritual and Belief in Morocco. London.

WIEGER, L. 1927. A History of the Religious Beliefs and Philosophical Opinions in China. Hsien-hsien.

WILDE, Lady, 1887. Ancient Legends, Mystic Charms and Superstitions of Ancient Ireland. London.

WILLIAMS, A. 1923. Folk-songs of the Upper Thames. London.

——— C. A. S. 1932. Outlines of Chinese Symbolism. Shanghai.

WILLIAMSON, H. 1941. Genius of Friendship: 'T. E. Lawrence'. London.

——— K. 1946. Birds in Faeroe Folk-lore. *North-west Nat. 21:* 7-19, 155-166.

——— 1948. The Atlantic Islands. London.

WILLOUGHBY-MEADE, G. 1928. Chinese Ghouls and Goblins. London.

WILMAN-GRABOWSKA, H. de, 1932. *In* Asiatic Mythology. Ed. J. Hackin. London.

WITTKOWER, R. 1939. Eagle and serpent. *Journ. Warburg Inst. 2:* 293-325.

WOODFORDE, C. 1944. Some medieval English quarries painted with birds. *Brit. Arch. Assn. Journ.* (3) *8:* 1-11.

WOOD-MARTIN, W. G. 1902. Traces of the Elder Faiths of Ireland. London.

WOODS, F. H. 1911. Deluge. *E.R.E. 4:* 545-547.

WRIGHT, A. R. and LONES, T. E. 1936, '38, '39, '40. British Calendar Customs. England. F.-L. Socy. London.

WRIGHT, J. 1904. English Dialect Dictionary. London.

ZIMMELS, H. J. 1926. Fowls growing on trees (In Hebrew). Minhat Bikurım. Festschift Schwartz. Vienna.

INDEX

Part I

PROPER NAMES

Part II

BIRDS

Part III

SUBJECTS